CW01429514

Risk, Participation, and Performance Practice

Alice O'Grady
Editor

Risk, Participation, and Performance Practice

Critical Vulnerabilities in a Precarious World

Editor
Alice O'Grady
University of Leeds
Leeds, UK

ISBN 978-3-319-63241-4 ISBN 978-3-319-63242-1 (eBook)
DOI 10.1007/978-3-319-63242-1

Library of Congress Control Number: 2017950684

© The Editor(s) (if applicable) and The Author(s) 2017
This work is subject to copyright. All rights are solely and exclusively licensed by the Publisher, whether the whole or part of the material is concerned, specifically the rights of translation, reprinting, reuse of illustrations, recitation, broadcasting, reproduction on microfilms or in any other physical way, and transmission or information storage and retrieval, electronic adaptation, computer software, or by similar or dissimilar methodology now known or hereafter developed.
The use of general descriptive names, registered names, trademarks, service marks, etc. in this publication does not imply, even in the absence of a specific statement, that such names are exempt from the relevant protective laws and regulations and therefore free for general use.
The publisher, the authors and the editors are safe to assume that the advice and information in this book are believed to be true and accurate at the date of publication. Neither the publisher nor the authors or the editors give a warranty, express or implied, with respect to the material contained herein or for any errors or omissions that may have been made. The publisher remains neutral with regard to jurisdictional claims in published maps and institutional affiliations.

Cover illustration: Your Meal/EyeEm/Getty Images

Printed on acid-free paper

This Palgrave Macmillan imprint is published by Springer Nature
The registered company is Springer International Publishing AG
The registered company address is: Gewerbestrasse 11, 6330 Cham, Switzerland

For Maisie

Preface

Performance/risk research and the focus on participation

Risk continues to be a preoccupation both within and beyond the art world and discourse around risk commands attention across the full range of disciplinary fields, not least in response to new levels of threat and terror currently experienced in numerous countries across the globe. Since the influential issue of *Performance Research: On Risk* was published in 1996 it has become well recognised that risk is a key term in performance theory and, arguably, a standard feature of all live performance regardless of any particular claim of being "risky". Nonetheless, risk in performance has become very "on trend" of late and has garnered much interest in the popular press, the professional sector, and within scholarly debate. Performance/risk is an emerging field that is starting to develop a critical mass. *Risk, Participation, and Performance Practice* gathers up the threads of this discourse, weaving them together to present a comprehensive and critically formulated perspective focusing on participatory performance practices where risk, vulnerability, and degrees of unknowing play an integral role in multiple and complex ways.

In recent times risk in performance has been variously celebrated and exaggerated, magnified and manipulated, fetishised and criticised. This collection takes *Performance Research: On Risk* (1996) as a starting point from which to consider how, some twenty years later, risk has been reconfigured, re-presented, and in some instances repackaged for new audiences with a thirst for performances that promote, encourage, and embrace risky encounters in various forms. The chapters bring together established voices on performance/risk research and draw them into conversation with next-generation academic-practitioners in a dynamic reappraisal of what it means to risk oneself through the act of making and participating in performance practice where both process and outcome might be shared, co-created, and negotiated. The collection focuses its attention on performance practice where spectators are involved, implicated, and integrated into the aesthetic via embodied participation. The collection is intentionally promiscuous and spans a range of practices that might seem otherwise to belong to very different traditions but are nonetheless tied together by their preoccupation with spectator involvement and open forms of engagement. It casts its net wide and, in so doing, offers an eclectic mix of exemplars. It moves from provocative live art in politically charged South Africa to community-based dance with recovering addicts in the UK, and from intimately autobiographical expressions of vulnerability to provocative, physical interventions in urban space. It does not seek to give a definitive answer to what it means to risk oneself in performance as this changes from instance to instance and from person to person. Instead it sheds light on a number of works that exemplify an emergent field of practice that is defined by its mobilisation of risky participation rather than by a singular disciplinary focus. It takes into account the work of performance scholars with diverse intentions, motivations, and experiences for whom risk and precarity are central concerns and seeks to move the debate forward in response to a rapidly changing world where risk is higher on the political, economic, and cultural agenda than ever before. How does risk in performance speak to that agenda and how might it offer a way of understanding and challenging the politics of vulnerability that permeates contemporary life?

Orientation and perspective

I come at this project on risk from the perspective of an educator and performance maker who has always seen openness, chance, and possibility as the necessary characteristics of human encounter and meaning making. Standing in opposition to all that appears fixed, predetermined, and finished, I embrace the risks associated with leaving gaps, spaces, cracks, and crevices for people to explore. In both my dramatic and pedagogic practice I intentionally create chasms and rifts for people to excavate and interrogate but not without helping them develop the tools required for such an undertaking. For me, navigating the unknown is an essential part of the creative process, indeed any process where development, progression, illumination, enlightenment, understanding is seen as a joint mission, a journey undertaken alongside others and where either the destination, the outcome, the precise route, or even the reasons for the journey are not yet fully realised in the minds of the travellers. To embrace risk in this way is not only a question of aesthetic choice, a playing with form, and a structuring of technique, it is also a political stance that indicates commitment to openness as meaningful encounter and exchange between humans.

Of course, risk is relative and not all risk taking leads to positive outcomes. One person's unthinkable risk is another person's day job. Sometimes we take risks because we want to, sometimes because there is no other choice. Sometimes we are placed at risk by other people or by sets of circumstances beyond our control. This is also true in the field of performance. We can choose risk as a strategy and embrace it, or we can walk away from it. We can attempt to pin down the theatrical moment as tightly as we can to avoid the unexpected, rehearsing and repeating until each showing is as similar as possible to the next, or we can build in uncertainty as part of the aesthetic encounter. The spectators, participants, performers, and theatre makers in this book have all turned towards risk and, in various ways, harnessed the vulnerabilities it produces. Why? Perhaps the simple answer is because there is, potentially, something to be gained from risk taking in this context. To embrace risk is to be open to uncertainty, to weigh up the odds, and to welcome the possible. The zone of proximal development is widened with each new moment where surrendering oneself, albeit momentarily, teaches us something about living, about humanity, about the here and now of existence.

Within the frame of performance, risks may not always be as profoundly life changing as, say, a banker gambling with a country's economy or a family boarding a flimsy boat that has a 50/50 chance of reaching land. Nonetheless, an analysis of the potential gains to be had in voluntary risk-taking practices provides potential insight into systems of cultural value currently at play. As ever, it remains important to ask the following questions: What is currently at risk and what is worth risking? What are the returns on the risks we choose to take and how have those risks altered since the turn of the millennium? Writing in 1999, Tim Etchells reminds us of the performer's commitment to risk and investment as being linked to "passion, politics and rage" (1999, 49). Since that time the world and its understanding of risk have changed. The participatory turn shines the spotlight on audience investment and the world is now full of co-creators, co-collaborators, and co-producers of meaning within the performance frame. The sharp rise in performances that claim to be aesthetically, psychologically, emotionally, structurally, socially, politically risky through their willingness to implicate audiences in the action perhaps signals a yearning for feeling, for rawness, edginess, livid and vivid experience that is missing from other spheres of daily life. This book does not blindly celebrate risk. Rather it tries to better understand its dimensions, its intentions, and its applications within the frame of performance and against the backdrop of a world that has, by necessity, been forced to adopt a different stance in relation to risk.

Key terms

A key term explored in the book is the concept of "**risky aesthetics**". Under this umbrella contributors examine an array of performance practices in which participants and performers are involved with practice where the outcome is not fully known and where there is some degree of surrender, or relinquishing of control in the presence of others. This might involve the sharing of personal stories in front of other audience members, interacting with performers in one-to-one, intimate situations, or being interrupted by performance as it unfolds on the street. In the openness, in the gaps, in the margins of uncertainty, spaces and moments of potentiality are made possible. Depending on the context, the framing of the work, and, ultimately, the participant perspective, "risky aesthetics" might be perceived variously as unpredictable, exposing, daring, thrilling, sensorial, erotic, challenging, experiential, embodied, visceral, threatening, unnerving, uncertain, organic, processual, co-authored, relational, dialogic, sensitive, intimate, exploratory, experimental, chaotic, personal, collective, individualised, social. The collection touches upon all of these potential lines of flight and draws attention to a global shift wherein artists, performers, and spectators utilise risk in performance as a way of commenting on, grappling with, and critiquing how risk is experienced in the day to day.

Risk, Participation, and Performance Practice explores risk across the spectrum of participatory performance and gives special attention to the concept of "**critical vulnerability**". It examines how the core characteristics of openness, uncertainty, and varying degrees of exposure contribute to an aesthetic paradigm where risk is deployed as an intentional tactic, a strategy of engagement, or a critical tool for the shared making of meaning. It investigates the ways in which practitioners embed risk into their work and foregrounds the challenges, implications, and consequences of working with real feelings of vulnerability within the frame of the imagination. In work that asks us to share personal anecdotes or to make use of past experiences, possibly painful ones, to create new material, we risk exposure. By crossing the threshold and moving from our position as spectator to that of participant we take a leap of faith and put our trust in someone else—the artist, the facilitator, our fellow participants. Participatory performance courts vulnerability in multiple ways and, in applied theatre practice for example, is often targeted at participants who might already be classified as "vulnerable" or as being "at risk". The idea that vulnerability can be mobilised as a critical tool offers a challenge to this perspective. At a time when "being vulnerable" has taken on new meaning in the context of global events, particularly the European migrant crisis, financial instability, and the increased terror threat from extremist groups, this collection offers a different take on vulnerability and reclaims it as productive exposure. Creating spaces in which participants might experience vulnerability *critically* becomes a deliberate aesthetic choice that foregrounds notions of openness, accountability, and trust (however precarious, contentious, and slippery those terms might be).

The underlying purpose of this book is to interrogate the ways in which the experience of risk in performance offers a means by which we may scrutinise the tensions between vulnerability and agency. It explores how and why performance practitioners create work that is intentionally risky and asks why audiences are increasingly drawn to this form. What are the personal, professional, and creative benefits of working within a risky aesthetic? What is at risk in these practices and to what extent is the risk real, perceived, or imagined? What are the gains of working within a paradigm of performance that prioritises embodied experience and risk? What are the challenges and how are they overcome? What strategies do performance practitioners and/or programmers deploy in order to facilitate, manage, and respond to participation with a variety of audiences where open engagement, embodied experience, and risk are core principles? What are the ethical considerations arising from such approaches?

The desire to harness new insights through the immediacy of participation draws on the two distinct legacies of performance art and applied theatre. The participatory impulse runs through the veins of both traditions and yet rarely are they considered alongside each other. The book moves intentionally between these two histories, weaving together practices, theories, and debates about the nature of participation across a broad spectrum of practice in order to consider what this might expose and reveal about our attitude to risk in the world at large.

Volume outline

The collection is made up of ten separate chapters that are grouped into three sections and cover the broad themes of ethics, intimacies, and identities. These themes are pertinent to all performance that works through the paradigm of participation and, therefore, run as seams throughout all the chapters. There is much overlap between them and, in many ways, the chapters can be considered as portable across sections. Certainly the question of ***ethics*** is pertinent to any work that uses risk as a participative tool and so this is where the collection begins. Readers may take those ideas forward into the next section that deals with ***intimacy*** and the experience of closeness and shared understanding which, in turn, leads to a potential reconsideration of ***identity***, both individual and collective. The intention behind these groupings is to shine a spotlight on a particular aspect of participative practice but also to see the themes as an accumulative way of interpreting the implications of risk taking in this context.

My introductory chapter surveys a range of sociological perspectives on risk and connects them to the growing literature on risk and precarity in performance studies. It positions participatory performance as a form of strategic openness and considers the interplay between agency and vulnerability in practice that plays with conventional distinctions between performer and spectator. I propose a new category of voluntary risk taking, namely "edgeplay", and consider how this offers a way of thinking imaginatively through risk in other domains.

In the first Part, "The ethics of risky aesthetics: moral codes, being decent, and doing it right", the authors consider the ethical dimension of performance practice where risk is a key feature of the work. Lourdes

Orozco offers an analysis of two contemporary productions by Simon McBurney and Robert Lepage that deploy a confessional performance mode. She argues that the narrative strategies used in both productions articulate alternative ideologies to that of the so-called risk society as formulated by Ulrich Beck and Anthony Giddens. Bree Hadley explores the ethical challenges presented in the work of politically motivated artists who utilise public participation as a way of putting the prejudices of unwitting spectators on the spot and in the spotlight. She examines how activist artists attempt to expose the participants' own role in constructing an exclusionary version of the world by placing them at risk in order for growth and change to occur. Coming from a very different perspective, psychotherapist Clark Baim examines the risks, responsibilities, and ethics associated with applied theatre practice when personal stories are used, and proposes a model for safe practice, the "Drama Spiral". This model functions as a practical tool for facilitators working with the real-life experiences of participants, many of whom may be vulnerable and working in a therapeutic context.

In the second Part, "Performing intimacies: flirting, whispering, and sharing stories in the dark", Matt Hargrave investigates the shifting dynamic between performance as vulnerability and vulnerability as performance, using Torque Show's production *Intimacy* to illustrate the discussion. Drawing on critical disability studies, he proposes a poetics of vulnerability and argues for the interruptive value of vulnerability across the social and aesthetic domains. Bruce Barton picks up on the contemporary trend for risk taking in participatory performance and proposes that audiences are perhaps more willing to accept the risk of failure and, in fact, see this as the location of intimacy. He considers how the "intimate equilibrium" between participant and performer can be maintained in work that accepts the "poetics of failure". Barton uses two of his own projects of Vertical City to work through this idea and incorporates Pil Hansen's dramaturgical perspective to illuminate the self-organising patterns of interaction prevalent in the work. From an interdisciplinary perspective that combines human–computer interaction (HCI), interaction design, and performance, Jocelyn Spence, Stuart Andrews, and David Frohlich examine the role that risk, intimacy, and dissonance play in the transition from everyday conversation to a performance that is intentionally and consciously aesthetic. In their chapter they argue that risk taking and vulnerability can offer potential points of entry into intimate, transformational performance experiences that are digitally mediated.

And finally in the last Part, “Risking the self: identities, playing with risk, and encountering the edge”, Rat Western examines the aesthetics of resistance by South African artists Brett Bailey, Gavin Krastin, and Igshaan Adams, who all include delegated performers or participatory audiences in their work as a way of complicating the political power dynamics of racial classification. She examines what John Taylor calls the “zone of contact” between the viewer and the viewed and explores the notions of authenticity and sincerity in three contrasting performances that all problematise the construction of identity. With a similar interest in authenticity, Zoe Zontou addresses the complex relationship between addiction, performance, and aesthetics and argues there is a connection to be made between risk taking in drug addiction and risk taking in performance making. Echoing Clark Baim’s chapter, she asks what happens when drug addicts dance their personal stories on stage and what political ground can be gained by challenging the juxtapositions that exist between the stigmatised and the artistic body. Brazilian scholar André Carreira completes the collection by offering insights into practice that uses the city as a type of dramaturgy and considers the risks involved for both performers and passers-by who participate in performance that unfolds within the seams of contemporary urban space.

A Final Word

The contributors to this book come from a range of cultural and disciplinary perspectives. Risk in each context is understood, undertaken, and experienced differently. The collection embraces that difference and does not attempt to find common ground but rather exposes and reveals the multiple and varied perspectives on risk and risk in performance that are part of the developing global discourse on this topic. The book draws attention to participation across a similarly diverse set of practices. It is the opening up of performance making to the possibility of chance, uncertainty, and potential, activated by the involvement of others, which underpins the intention of this book. We hope you find within its pages new tools, strategies, and ideas about risk taking and participation that shed light on what it means to be open, engaged, and involved in a world that seems preoccupied with borders, boundaries, and exclusions.

Leeds, UK,
August 2016

Alice O’Grady

Acknowledgements

My heartfelt thanks to everyone who has contributed to the development of this volume, including my colleagues at the School of Performance and Cultural Industries, University of Leeds, for their encouragement, support, and advice throughout the process. Thank you to Prof. Sita Popat for her continued support as my mentor. Thanks to Prof. Jonathan Pitches, Dr. Scott Palmer, and other members of the Place and Performance research group for reading drafts of my chapter as it developed and for providing such useful feedback. Gratitude to the Cultural and Creative Industries Exchange at the University of Leeds for funding the *Safe as Houses?* project and for being willing to take a risk. A huge vote of thanks to all the students who were involved in the project as performers and to Dr. Bonnie Meekums and PC Matt Guy for their input. Thanks to Dr. Helen Iball who was there at the start and got the ball rolling. Thanks to Anna Turzynski and Rebecca Thomason for producing the show, and to Scott Bradley and Leeds Beckett Northern Film School for their contribution. Deep thanks to the …floorSpace… family who have worked with me over the years on risky performances in risky places—you know who you are. Thanks to all the contributors to this volume for their time, effort, and generosity throughout the writing process. It has been a privilege to work with you and to see the book grow. I am indebted to the wonderful Kelli Zezulka for her administrative assistance and professional support. And finally, many thanks to JT and Maisie for putting up with me being chained to the laptop when I could have been out playing.

Contents

Editor and Contributors

About the Editor

Alice O'Grady is Professor in Applied Performance and Head of the School of Performance and Cultural Industries at the University of Leeds. With a background in drama education her research examines the ways in which performance, participation and play activate social agency and engagement across a range of diverse contexts.

Contributors

Stuart Andrews is Lecturer in Theatre Studies at the University of Surrey (UK). He researches performance and place, particularly in homes and at points of transition. He is currently developing two monographs, one on performing home and one with Matthew Wagner, on the door in performance.

Clark Baim established Geese Theatre Company UK, an ensemble working primarily in criminal justice settings, in 1987. He is now a senior trainer in psychodrama and has facilitated workshops in seventeen countries. Clark has published widely on topics including applied theatre, psychodrama, offender rehabilitation and attachment-informed practice.

Bruce Barton is a creator/scholar whose creative practice, practice-based research, and teaching focuses on physical dramaturgies in devised and intermedial performance. He is the Artistic Director of Vertical City, an interdisciplinary performance hub, and the Director of the School of Creative and Performing Arts at the University of Calgary.

André Carreira born in Brazil, has a degree in visual arts (UnB) and a PhD in theatre from the Universidad de Buenos Aires. He is Senior Researcher at CNPq and Professor at UDESC. He is also Director of Experiência Subterrânea Theatre Group and author of *Street Theatre: A Passion in the Asphalt.*

David Frohlich is Director of Digital World Research Centre at the University of Surrey and Professor of Interaction Design. Prior to joining Digital World in 2005, David worked for 14 years as a senior research scientist at HP Labs on the design of mobile, domestic, and photographic technology.

Bree Hadley is Associate Director of the Creative Lab at Queensland University of Technology. Her research on representations of identity in contemporary, pop cultural, and public space performance, and spectators' responses to these representations, has appeared in *Theatre, Social Media and Meaning Making* (2017) and *Disability, Spectatorship and Public Space Performance: Unconscious Performers* (2014).

Pil Hansen is Assistant Professor at the University of Calgary, founding member of Vertical City Performance, and a dance/devising dramaturg. Her research examines cognition in creative processes through empirical and PaR experiments. Her latest books are on *Dance Dramaturgy* (2015) and the *Cognition of Memory in Dance, Theatre and Music* (2017).

Matt Hargrave is Senior Lecturer in Performing Arts at University of Northumbria. He is the author of *Theatres of Learning Disability: Good, bad or plain ugly?* (2015) which won the 2016 Theatre and Performance Research Association's Early Career Research Award.

Lourdes Orozco is a Lecturer in Theatre Studies at the University of Leeds. Her research focuses on contemporary theatre and performance in Europe and the UK with particular focus on animals, risk and cultural policy. Recent publications are *Theatre & Animals* (2013) and *Performing Animality: Animals in Performance Practices* (2015).

Jocelyn Spence is a human–computer interaction and performance researcher. Her book *Performative Experience Design* was published in 2016 as part of Springer's Cultural Computer series. She combines theatre and performance theory, practice and design-oriented HCI research with the aim of creating unusual, thought-provoking, meaningful and even transformational experiences with technology.

Rat Western is an artist and Senior Lecturer at Rhodes University, South Africa, specialising in digital and performance art. Her site-specific work includes *Discharge* (2012), a post-apocalyptic participative performance at Grahamstown military base, and *MACHINE FOR LIVING* (2014), which won a *Silver Ovation Award* for artistic innovation and excellence in the exploration of new performance styles.

Zoe Zontou is a Senior Lecturer in Drama at Liverpool Hope University. Her research covers a wide range of topics, including autobiography in performance, addiction studies and cultural policy, which are examined through their relationship with applied theatre. She has worked as a practitioner and researcher in a number of organisations.

List of Figures

Introduction: Risky Aesthetics, Critical Vulnerabilities, and Edgeplay: Tactical Performances of the Unknown

Alice O'Grady

Introduction

The topic of risk is a preoccupation of the contemporary world and has infiltrated scholarly discourse in a range of disciplines, including that of performance studies. In taking risks, individuals and groups put their lives and livelihoods on the line either through choice, necessity, or compulsion. They weigh up the odds between the potential losses and gains to be had by engaging in risk-taking behaviours and practices before embarking on a particular course of action. Clearly not all risk taking is life threatening but, nonetheless, may incur substantive cost. Risk taking is rarely straightforward and, in many contexts, may be experienced not only as physical risk but also as social, emotional, cultural, or cognitive phenomena that bring people to experience what we might call an encounter with the edge. This introductory chapter lays the groundwork for the various perspectives on aesthetic risk taking within a broad

A. O'Grady (✉)
University of Leeds, Leeds, UK
e-mail: A.OGrady@leeds.ac.uk

© The Author(s) 2017

A. O'Grady (ed.), *Risk, Participation, and Performance Practice*,
DOI 10.1007/978-3-319-63242-1_1

spectrum of participatory performance practices that are further explored within the other chapters of this book. It brings into conversation sociological perspectives on risk taking with scholarship on participatory performance to examine the critical vulnerabilities at play in performance work which has risk embedded in its aesthetic.

By its very nature, participatory performance invites spectators into its frame of play. In doing so it has to be sufficiently open to provide points of entry in order for participation to occur. There are inherent risks involved in loosening up aesthetic form so that others can contribute, influence, and alter the course, content, and shape of a performance. There is risk to the performers, who relinquish a certain amount of control of the artwork. There is risk to the participants, who enter an unfamiliar dramatic frame based largely on trust. There is also risk to the artwork or performance structure itself which, through the process of becoming open, may lose its form completely and collapse. And yet, despite these risks, or because of them, participatory performance of varying kinds continues to flourish internationally, finding an outlet in community-based and educational settings as well as in large-scale, commercial contexts. Although audience participation is not new, in recent years the participatory performance "event" has gathered pace, with shows such as *You, Me, Bum Bum Train* (2004) setting the agenda for new forms of spectatorship that are framed as risky by virtue of the participatory demands made on audience members. The success of companies such as Punchdrunk, Secret Cinema, and Ontroerend Goed and the proliferation of one-to-one performance characterised by artists such as Franko B, Kira O'Reilly, and the late Adrian Howells indicates an intensified interest in work that is predicated on the promise of edgy, experiential, bespoke encounters that come under the umbrella of participatory performance. Much of this contemporary performance practice draws on the well-established methodologies of applied theatre practice where structured participation in the form of fictional role taking, improvisation, simulation, and other types of activated spectatorship is the norm. In these instances participation is utilised as part of a learning process which is experienced collectively. Whilst methodologies may be shared across practices, paying attention to the context in which participatory risk taking occurs is of paramount importance and guides our reading of the risks being undertaken and the possible outcomes that arise as a result. Identifying the rewards, gains, and challenges of working in ways that deliberately court risk underpins this chapter and threads through the discussion from other contributors who bring into view diverse examples of contemporary practice from across the globe where risk taking in performance has varying connotations and consequences. Putting seemingly distinct practices into dialogue with one another provides an opportunity to consider how risk has become a central concern for performance makers both within and beyond the applied theatre context and illuminates a fundamental shift in contemporary performance as a field of practice preoccupied by the ethical, aesthetic, and political challenges associated with the invitation to participate. The chapter mobilises the theoretical concept of edgework and reframes it in relation to participatory practice where playing on the edge is carried out as a tactic. Scholarship on edgework is extensive (Lyng 1990, 2005, 2008) and there is no attempt here to provide a comprehensive survey of how this concept has been developed and reworked over time. However, what it does do is take the premise that occupying the edge offers a particular type of experience that can be transcendent, resistant, and revelatory and foregrounds the playful dimension of that experience. It is now widely acknowledged that edgework no longer sits on the margins of social order but rather is integrated into many mainstream activities of institutional and recreational life. The same could be said of performance. Edgy participation has become a recurring theme in contemporary performance practice and represents a pull for audiences that want to engage with notions of vulnerability, self-actualisation, and agency by experiencing them through playful participation. The increased interest in confessional work such as *The Oh Fuck Moment* (2011) by Hannah Jane Walker and Chris Thorpe demonstrates a willingness, or desire, on the part of the audience to expose their human frailties by revealing something of themselves in the presence of others. The success of the quietly participative performance *The Artist is Present* (2010) by Marina Abramović suggests a thirst for intimacy and presence that is perhaps missing from other aspects of our daily life. However it is framed or deployed by performance makers, occupying the edge in and through play offers artists, practitioners, and participants a critical space for practising and refining their skills as players—collaborating, negotiating, and creating as they move through the play together. It should be acknowledged, however, that play can be slippery, equivocal, contingent, and, in some instances, harmful. It can lead to misunderstandings and misinterpretations as well as being a productive tool for development and growth. This chapter considers the dynamics of using the participatory play mode as a way of blurring boundaries and unsettling fixed distinctions and considers the risks for those involved. By way of exemplar, it analyses a piece of practice-led research which reveals the paradoxical effects of openness in relation to agency and vulnerability. Finally it develops the notion of "edgeplay" as a way of thinking through risky aesthetics as an ethical form of openness and exposure that the dominant risk-averse society is often keen to close down.

Interdisciplinary interest in risk research shows no sign of abating. It is a topic that has wide-ranging implications for ordinary people living through extraordinary times. Whilst risks undertaken in the name of performance do not equate to the risks faced by those living with, say, the consequences of catastrophic natural disasters, there is nonetheless virtue in revealing how and why artists increasingly choose to work through risk as a core aesthetic and why audiences continue to be drawn to it. It offers a different perspective on risk taking that runs contrary to the dominant discourse of harm reduction and prevention. It reveals the deliberate and constructed nature of risk and, applicable to all disciplines, opens up critical debate on prevalent risk behaviours in a risk-saturated world.

Shifting Perspectives on Risk

Research on risk is extensive and crosses disciplinary boundaries. It has become a key concept in Western society and the literature on it has proliferated since the early 1990s (see Zinn 2008 for an overview of risk theorisation). Risk is a topic of concern for a variety of disciplines including health, finance, and ecology, for example, and is particularly pertinent in areas where risk taking is likely to have significant repercussions for individuals or for society at large. In many respects it is a contested term that can be associated with danger, threat, and loss as well as with adventure, creativity, and profit. Risk analysis, risk assessment, and risk management are major fields of research and professional practice (for example, see McNeil et al. 2015; Suter 2007; Vose 2008). The West in particular operates within the framework of the "audit society" (Power 1997) and is preoccupied with minimising risk in a world that seems increasingly beyond our control. Extensive tools have been developed as ways of measuring and controlling risk and, in turn, its people. As Massumi (1993) argues, the population is kept in a state of low-level fear by the increased discourse around risk that pervades contemporary life.

In recent times and in response to a new wave of global terror attacks, the dial has been turned up on public fear, and the rhetoric around the threat to public safety has become ubiquitous. We have entered a new era of risk, and how we respond to it demands urgent attention across disciplinary borders.

Sociological studies on risk provide insight into the way society's relationship with risk changes over time and how meanings around it are formulated (Giddens 1990; Beck 1992; Lupton 1999). Theorists are concerned with examining the reason why the Western world has become obsessed with risk and attempt to determine how risk is constructed at both the local level and on a global scale (Douglas 1992; Johnson and Covello 1987; Lupton 1999). Clearly the symbolic and cultural meanings we attach to risk arise from the specific sociocultural and historical contexts in which we are rooted. According to sociologist Deborah Lupton, there are six major categories of risk that preoccupy the concerns of individuals and institutions in the Western world. The categories she suggests are environmental, lifestyle, medical, interpersonal, economic, and criminal (Lupton 1999, 13). Here Lupton is writing in a pre-millennium context where the risk of terror attacks, for example, was felt less acutely in the West than it is now. To Lupton's risk schema we could add the political, the radical, and the technological which, despite being core concerns during the late 1990s, have since accrued greater emphasis in today's landscape. What characterises this new era of risk so profoundly is the way in which catastrophic global events are recorded and reproduced in almost real time (Kearnes et al. 2012, 3). Shared across media platforms instantaneously, the fragility of social infrastructures is brought to the fore and penetrates our collective understanding of world order. How we perceive risk and how we attend to it in any of these categories depends on our individual context. In relation to risk, context is everything. It shapes our perspective and determines our response. As Zinn points out, "discourse into social risk behaviour is as much a discourse on defining a problem, about different values and lifestyles, power relations, and emotions as it is about 'real' risks and their rational management" (2008, 2). Clearly in the categories above, the risks to life, livelihood, and well-being are "real" and may be far removed from the sorts of risks discussed within the pages of this book. Nonetheless, placing these wider discourses on risk against a backdrop of aesthetic risk taking and performance provides us with an alternative means of investigating the values and power relations Zinn identifies. In participatory performance, in particular, where individuals are asked to risk something of themselves through the act of involvement, situated or contextual power relations take on added significance. When an audience member is asked to participate in a piece of forum theatre, to bring their personal experience of, for example, homelessness to bear on the fiction, they take a personal risk. They reveal something of themselves and in so doing enter into a new power dynamic with those who witness it. In an act of performance there may not be actual risk to life but there are other risks at play that provide insight into the constructed, and dichotomous, nature of human interaction. Participatory performance provides an arena for examining the very real interplay between risk and safety, power and vulnerability, albeit within a fictional, imaginary, or playful frame. Understanding how risk operates in this context illuminates how risk is constructed, mobilised, and experienced elsewhere.

The meaning of risk has changed over time. In the modernist period of the nineteenth century, risk and uncertainty had different connotations. Risk was where the probability of an event happening was known. Uncertainty was related to the unknown (Lupton 1999, 7). Risk and uncertainty are now regularly conflated in common discourse. In the contemporary world risk means danger; high risk means a lot of danger (Douglas 1992, 24). Risk is largely something to be avoided or, at least, carefully calculated to minimise damage. In general, people avoid exposing themselves to unnecessary risks. However, in the world of art and, more specifically, performance, risk has a different inflection. In this domain risk is seen as a necessary and integral part of the creative process. As performance maker and critic Claire MacDonald suggests, "all artists take risks: it comes with the territory" (1996, vi). Risk is viewed positively as a way of innovating practice and challenging old models. We need only to look towards the avant-garde experiments of the 1960s to see how artists took risks in an attempt to push boundaries and to find new modes of expression. Work by artists such as Grotowski, Richard Schechner, Alan Kaprow, Marina Abramović, and Chris Burden demonstrates how taking risks with space, theatrical convention, spectatorship, and the body became a key concern of performance for practitioners intent on gaining new ground. For an artist, not taking risks is a risk in itself and signals stasis. Clearly this position is not limited to the art world. In the domains of business, high finance, and entrepreneurship, for example, risk taking, innovation, and creative experimentation are often considered prerequisites for success and forward movement despite the profoundly negative impact such an approach can produce, as evidenced by the financial crash of 2007–2008.

Over the past twenty years there has been renewed interest in the field of risk/performance scholarship with a number of key publications on the topic that mirror the growth in risk research across other disciplines (Dwyer et al. 2014; MacDonald 1996; Ridout and Schneider 2012; Welchman 2008).[1] It could be argued that growth in research around risk has emerged in response to the world being constructed and perceived as riskier than ever. Certainly in the late 1990s there existed a heightened awareness of endings, a growing feeling of potential disruption, and inevitable calamity. The *fin de millennium* created a certain "mood of disorientation" (Lupton 1999, 12) that artists began to address through their work, using risk as a way of tackling a growing sense of looming catastrophe. Although the so-called "Y2K problem"[2] did not disrupt the world in the ways that were being predicted at the time, the sense of disorientation was perhaps more subtle but no less impactful in defining the world as a place of instability. As Claire MacDonald sets out in the introduction to *On Risk*, a special issue of *Performance Research Journal*:

> We live in a risk society. Risk assessment, risk management, the time bomb of environmental risk and the volatility of political systems combine to create a climate of extreme uncertainty, and a sense that the metaphors we have used to describe the world are no longer adequate to account for a situation of such inconstancy. (MacDonald 1996, vi)

Here she suggests there is a direct correlation between the world as we experience it and the art forms that must be developed to better understand it. In a risk-laden and volatile world, old metaphors are no longer useful. New forms need to be found. The artist is positioned as the risk taker, "facing that which is feared" (MacDonald 1996, vii). In many cases the artist's body becomes the site of performance and the place where physical risk is explored (Warr 1996). In turn, the theatre is conceived as a metaphorical space where risks can be taken and subversive ideas played out. It is worth remembering MacDonald was writing some five years before the 2001 attack on the World Trade Center in New York. That single event has produced what Malinda Smith calls a "vexed epochal chasm" (2014, 382) whereby the world is seemingly split into pre-9/11 and post-9/11 imaginaries. This culturally constructed and arbitrary watershed has produced a further shift in the rhetoric on risk, foregrounding danger, threat, and fear in unprecedented ways. Discourse around global threat and national vulnerability now permeates contemporary life. Drawing on Beck's original notion of the "risk society" (1992), scholarly attention now turns towards a consideration of the "risk industry" and closer analysis of how risk is "put to work" by institutions to further particular sociopolitical ideologies (Kearnes et al. 2012, 224). Working out of the Institute of Hazard, Risk and Resilience at Durham University, Kearnes et al. (2012) suggest risk research has undergone two important shifts in recent years. Firstly, the complexity of contemporary risk issues is now understood as requiring interdisciplinary and participatory research practices, and yet divisions between disciplines continue to be entrenched. Secondly, risk research, and the increasingly institutionalised role it plays in responding to disasters, renders it part of the "risk industry" it seeks to interrogate. They call for a turn towards self-reflexive, "critical" risk research where the assumptions currently made about risk calculation and its analysis and management can be interrogated more rigorously (2012, 1). As a response to the challenges they call for new forms of participatory risk research by engaging with those who encounter it. As they argue, "risk … is produced through the way it is lived, and risk itself is a lived experience" (2012, 232). With this in mind, the field of performance may offer a contribution insofar as it provides a fertile ground for interdisciplinary, reflexive research but also serves as a test bed for risk research that emphasises the participative experience of encountering risk within the frame of play. The discourse and conceptual vocabulary around risk for artists, practitioners, and scholars working through performance is distinct from that of other disciplines. In a world obsessed with risk calculation, prediction, and prevention, it is vital that other perspectives on risk are considered so that stasis does not become inevitable.

Voluntary/Tactical Risk Taking

A strand of risk research that offers a counter discourse to that of risk aversion is voluntary risk taking and pleasure (Lupton and Tulloch 2002; Lyng 1990, 2005). From this perspective risk taking is seen as having potential benefits for the individuals and groups drawn to it. In the social sciences much work has been done to investigate the symbolism of voluntary risk-taking practices and the motivations for participating in such activities (Breakwell 2007). In this modelling risk taking is conceived as an act of resistance or an "escape attempt" (Cohen and Taylor 1976/1992). It might involve participating in extreme sports and leisure pursuits, going on adventure holidays, taking drugs, or engaging in other criminal activity or behaviour considered to be deviant or transgressive. Whatever form it takes, the cultivation of risk can be understood as a means of undermining ontological security. As Giddens argues, people create situations where they take risks deliberately as a way of creating "an edge which routine circumstances lack" (Giddens 1991, 132).

Although the term "edgework" was first coined by Hunter S. Thompson, sociologist Stephen Lyng (1990) has developed the concept as a way of explaining the explosive growth in extreme sports over the past forty years as well as the rise of the "entrepreneurial spirit" that finds an outlet in the world of finance (Smith 2005), criminality (Katz 1988), and certain forms of "immersive theatre" (Machon 2013) that advocate "entrepreneurial participation" which, as Adam Alston argues, can be mapped onto neo-liberal values of self-interest (2013, 130). The edgework model functions as a general theory of voluntary risk-taking behaviour (Lyng 2008, 109) and is therefore useful as a tool to analyse forms of performance that deal with risk from the perspectives of both practitioners creating the work and participants invited into it.

Edgework takes place on the threshold between cultural boundaries that separate life and death, consciousness and unconsciousness, sanity and insanity. It is the edge between these boundaries that is attractive and alluring. Confronting and responding to uncertainties is what edgeworkers value most (Lyng 2008, 109). Risk taking is seen not as foolhardy but as evidence of having superior qualities. Edgeworkers possess the skills and attributes that mean they can take significant risks without harming themselves. They see themselves as adventurers, explorers, entrepreneurs, rule breakers, daredevils. Artists who "play on the margins of meaning" (Neelands and Goode 2008) may also perceive the edge as offering potential for growth rather than limitation. As Claire MacDonald argues:

> Risk implies a sense of possibility, not just of tragedy. It is perhaps seen most clearly in relation to "venture", a word that implies process, proceeding journey and that includes luck and uncertainty as well as commercial enterprise, daring and courage among its qualities. (MacDonald 1996, viii)

Discourses that privilege risk taking focus on the quest for self-authenticity, spontaneity, and agency (Lupton 1999). The rhetoric around this quest for self-actualisation is often steeped in the language of neo-liberalist ideals. However, the edgework model is nonetheless useful as it locates the motives for risk taking within a social context. The motivation to take risks reveals something about the society in which those risks are taken. Edgework activities provide the gateway to "an 'other world' experience that transcends the mundane reality of everyday life" (Lyng 2008, 117). The growth in these activities suggests growing dissatisfaction with the stultifying effects of contemporary Western life. Through sensual, embodied, intense experience, edgework produces a heightened sense of self that *feels* more authentic than the daily version of self. The edgeworker has taken control, become an "actor" in their own existence, and revealed something new. With this as a framework, we might begin to see the appeal of being immersed in the hallucinatory realm of Punchdrunk's *The Drowned Man* (2013) or entering the shady world of Blast Theory's *Operation Black Antler* (2016) where participants confront the ethics and implications of being undercover from a first-hand perspective. The special appeal of these edgy activities can be understood as a tension between spontaneity and constraint in human action, "a form of indeterminacy that expands the creative possibilities for human agents" (Lyng 2008, 110). This promise of agency and willingness to expand possibility by placing oneself at the edge is at the core of risky aesthetics explored in this collection.[3] In this model of practice, indeterminacy is deployed as a strategy that allows expansion through the virtue of being open, albeit to varying degrees.

One of the key aspects of voluntary risk taking is permeability:

> Against the ideal of the highly controlled "civilised" body/self is the discourse which valorizes escape from the bonds of control and regulation, expressing a hankering after the pleasures of the "grotesque" body, the body that is more permeable and open to the world. (Lupton 1999, 149)

Here the body is conceptualised as the site of permeability and as being innately open. Physical, embodied participation is then a central component of the escape mission. It is perhaps most evident in body-based works such as Franko B's *Aktion 893: Why Are you Here?* (2005), a piece that invites participants to have a naked one-to-one encounter with the fully clothed artist, but can also be found within the socially engaged work of companies such as Geese Theatre, Chol, or Cardboard Citizens, where the very act of participating physically expands participants' role repertoire for use beyond the parameters of the drama. The body and its permeability is not only the site of sensation, but also a player in what might be considered tactical or strategic risk taking.

To push this idea further, we might begin by determining the variety of reasons individuals or groups, and, in this context, artists, might deploy permeability or openness as a strategy. It is possible to view permeability or "porosity" (O'Grady 2013) as an indication of inclusivity, generosity, dialogue, and transparency. We might consider how these values and intentions resonate when applied to different realms such as politics, education, social interaction, and culture. The notion of being "open to the world" is a concept that lies at the heart of much art practice that seeks to promote and provoke interaction, mutual understanding, and learning. It has been a core principle of theatre in education practice, for example, since its emergence in the mid-1960s. It lies at the centre of the concept of risky aesthetics as explored in this volume and points towards permeability as an ethical tactic. It sits within a political framework and seeks to move communication and interaction beyond the strictures of control and regulation towards what bell hooks describes as a space of radical openness:

> For me this space of radical openness is a margin—a profound edge. Locating oneself there is difficult yet necessary. It is not a "safe" place. One is always at risk. One needs a community of resistance. (1990, 206)

This viewpoint brings into sharp relief the relationship between an occupation of the edge and the politics of openness.

Radical openness is a term that is now used across different domains including governance, politics, business, design, and software applications. It is used to describe transparency in business (Tapscott 2013), spiritual philosophy (Breed 2009), and hacktivism (Jordan 2002). It corresponds to the rise in open-source culture in what has become commonly known as the "era of the network". Returning to Doreen Massey's use of the phrase, we are reminded of the sense of movement implied within its meaning. Radical openness reworks space as the sphere of possibility and multiplicity (Massey 2005). For Massey, space is relational. It is the product of interrelations, always under construction and in a permanent state of process. In her words, "It is never finished; never closed" (2005, 9). Its very openness allows for forward travel. It affords the "openness of the future" (Massey 2005, 11) and, in so doing, allows access to the genuine notion of politics and radical democracy (Laclau 1990). It is not surprising then that artists and practitioners choose to work with open forms that are permeable, relational, and processual in order to move things forward. It is this imperative that drives much participatory practice and underpins work that stems from the two distinct but complementary traditions of applied theatre and avant-garde performance. The next section deals in more detail with the spaces created by such practices and the particular forms of risk taking they afford.

Risk, "Safe Space", and Participatory Performance

How we perceive the world has always been a key concern for artists. The theatre provides a space for an exploration of perception of the world but is set slightly to one side of it. The fictive frame offers a certain degree of protection from the realities of existence, "one step removed" (Baim et al. 2002), that keeps audience and performers safe. However, increasingly that assumed notion of "safety" is being called into question. What and who is at risk within the space of performance is of critical importance, particularly if we are to conceive of the realm of theatre as public space with the potential to operate as "creative crucibles for the democratic sphere" (Massey 2005, 153), a place where key concerns of the people can be explored and addressed collectively. Hans-Thies Lehmann argues that the politics of perception in theatre must include the "transgression of taboos" (2006, 186) if it is to succeed in its mission to address the emotional extremes of existence.

> It falls to the theatre to deal with extremes of affect by means of *an aesthetics of risk*, extremes which always also contain the possibility of offending by breaking taboos. (2006, 186–187)

For Lehmann, the theatre provides the space to take risks, to go to extremes, to confront, to challenge, to provoke reaction, and, ultimately, to remind spectators of their own presence. When spectators and performers are brought closer together, when the aesthetic distance between stage and auditorium has collapsed, borders are brought down, conventions transgressed, and "safe distance" (Lehmann 2006, 187) abolished. When the physical barriers between performers and spectators are dismantled, relationships have to be reconstituted and renegotiated collectively. In participatory practice, there is no darkened auditorium to offer a protective cloak of invisibility for silent spectators. Spectators are invited to occupy space alongside performers, to take action, and to share responsibility for the process and its outcome. Participatory performance achieves its political, ethical reality by drawing spectators' attention to their own physical and emotional presence. They are confronted with themselves as much as with others. The sensations that arise from such confrontation are not always comfortable, cosy, or "safe" but they are moments of critical vulnerability that put us in touch with the present and the presence of others.

The so-called "safe space" of performance has been described as a "truism of the applied theatre field" (Dwyer et al. 2014, 1) and is a term which demands further interrogation. As Dwyer et al. argue, the fragility of such spaces is rarely acknowledged or problematised. Rather than being confined to the field of applied theatre, the safe space/risk dynamic is a tension that lies at the heart of all performance (Dwyer et al. 2014). This paradox remains a core feature of performance whether the practice in question is situated within discourses of pedagogy or the avant-garde. Risk is a constitutive part of all performance (Dwyer et al. 2014, 2) and not confined to practices that herald themselves as being explicitly "risky" in nature. In a similar vein, all spaces have a "permeable membrane" (Cohen et al. 2011). No work of performance is hermetically sealed whether it claims to be participatory or not. Nonetheless, the manner in which that permeability is constructed, managed, and deployed is of critical importance. The intentions that underpin a move towards greater permeability will, ultimately, determine the experience and effect of the work in question. The motivating philosophy for greater porosity in performance might be artistic, pedagogic, political, or a combination of all three. Who and what is at risk and what is considered safe or unsafe can only fully be understood once these different motivations are taken into account.

Embedding risk in performance raises significant ethical issues which are brought into sharp relief when that performance involves participation (Thompson 2003). Gareth White (2013) addresses risk and participation by focusing on risk perception from the perspective of the audience/participant. He suggests risk can serve as an inhibiting force which may prevent people from wanting to participate in a performance at all. He talks of the potential risk of social embarrassment, of "losing face", of humiliation and of the potential abuses of power that can occur between audience members and the participatory practitioner who is seen to be in control of the space and the action it contains. These practitioners, or "procedural authors" (2013, 73), have ultimate responsibility for the participatory experience and for managing the risks involved in any given interaction. In many ways they are the "caretakers" of the participatory process and need to be mindful of the thresholds they construct for others to cross.

Safety and safeguarding will always be central concerns in the field of applied theatre practice and research. Levels of potential risk to participants must be considered at all times together with an understanding of the dynamics of vulnerability within the context of the drama. Applied theatre practitioners regularly work with individuals and groups considered to be "at risk" and the term has become a catch-all for those who do not appear to fit within or conform to the prevalent logic of contemporary economics. The very notion of the label of "at risk", particularly in relation to young people or NEETs (not in education, employment, or training), has been challenged by those working in the field of drama education. Diane Conrad (2005) begins to address the ways in which the behaviours of so-called "at-risk" youth might be considered as a form of voluntary risk taking as resistance. In other words, dropping out of school and rejecting authority is a risk they choose, a solution rather than a problem (Conrad 2005, 31). Although Conrad draws on the sociological concept of edgework that has already been discussed, she focuses on a particular type of socially engaged drama practice with young people. To date there has been little enquiry that brings risk research from the social sciences together with investigations into the broad spectrum of participatory performance, a gap this volume intends to address.

Participatory practice has garnered much attention in the broad field of performance and spans the spectrum of work from traditional applied theatre practice (Nicholson 2005; Neelands 1992; O'Toole 1992; Boal 1979) to the avant-garde (Schechner 1994; Goldberg 2011; Heathfield 2004), contemporary art practice (Bishop 2006, 2012; Bourriaud 1998), and socially engaged performance (Jackson 2011; Shaughnessy 2012). As Bishop argues, the issue of participation is inextricable from the question of political commitment (2006, 11). For her the "participatory impulse" has a common set of concerns, namely activation, collaborative authorship, and community. Through participation it is hoped an active subject will emerge who has been empowered by the experience. Production will be shared and will be "seen to entail the aesthetic benefits of greater risk and unpredictability". The social bond will be restored through "collective elaboration of meaning" (Bishop 2006, 12). These concerns are found in Debord's critique of spectacle (1983) and thread through literature in education (Freire 1970), theatre (Boal 1979), visual art (Bourriaud 1998), and, more recently, architecture (Hansen 2005). Whilst Rancière (2009) offers a counter-perspective that questions the theories that equate spectacle with passivity, it is the unfinished nature, the openness, and the permeability of participatory performance that is of concern here. The artwork which is unfinished invites us to think why the artist has chosen to work in this way and draws attention to its openness (Eco 1989). Here, openness and indeterminacy can be developed both as aesthetic paradigms and as instruments, ontological tools that can be put to work in different domains including education, politics, culture, and art. As Freire reminds us, "refusal of risk prevents us from becoming actors in the world" (1998, 23). In other words, avoidance of risk stunts our development and leads to inactivity, inertia, and apathy in the world at large. It is therefore fitting that the theatre be a place that allows us to rehearse action, in the Boalian sense, and a place where risk is deployed as a tactic by which we learn to act and take action in our own lives.

However, against this rather idealised backdrop of agency and empowerment, it is essential to interrogate where risk is located within participatory performance. Within the frame of play, what is at stake is not always clearly defined or made explicit. Where does the risk lie in opening up form and structure? Who is at risk and to what extent are they aware of those risks? Participatory practice can be understood as interplay between artists/performers taking risks and making themselves vulnerable and audience members/participants being encouraged to take risks through varying degrees of physical involvement. This interplay generates paradoxical feelings of vulnerability and agency on both sides. Whilst these effects could be seen in opposition as two contrasting states of experience, it could also be argued that one produces the other. In other words, the journey towards agency begins with an experience of vulnerability and an awareness of its productivity as a generative tool.

Safe as Houses?: Embedding Risk into Practice

With Kearnes et al.'s (2012) call for greater participative approaches to risk research in mind, I now turn to an analysis of my own practice-led research project that took place in November 2014. It exemplifies the complex relationship between agency and vulnerability as experienced by performers and participants within the context of a project that troubled the "safe space" paradigm. Working with student performers, I devised and directed a participatory, multi-site performance project in collaboration with West Yorkshire Police service, a commissioned piece of work aimed at raising student awareness around the issue of burglary and the emotional impact of crime. The research imperative underpinning the project focused on examining the ways in which participatory, intimate theatre could be used as a form of experiential learning. In many ways it followed a traditional applied theatre format insofar as it was designed to be instrumental and to provoke "behavioural and attitudinal change" (Jackson 2007, 128) in the participants in relation to crime prevention. The performance, entitled *Safe as Houses?*, is a useful example because it offers two seemingly contrasting experiences of risk taking within performance, one from the point of view of the performers and the other from that of the participants. It problematises the concept of openness, illuminates the challenges associated with framing creative risk taking, and draws attention to the significance of context when working within a risky aesthetic.

Safe as Houses? consisted of nine site-specific performances which took place simultaneously in nine different living rooms across the Hyde Park area of Leeds, a suburb with a notoriously high rate of burglary. The police were keen to explore new strategies for engaging young people with crime prevention and supported the work from the outset despite its "risky" approach. Uncertainty, vulnerability, exposure, and tolerance were critical parts of the performance design and permeated its realisation and reception (Figs. 1 and 2).

Riskiness of the Aesthetic: Contrasting Perspectives

Throughout the process of producing this work, the company considered themselves to be the primary risk takers (rather than the audience) and the performance aesthetic to be the biggest risk in terms of its unconventional structure and choice of location. The performers were

Fig. 1 Participants pinpoint crime-related incidents on interactive maps at Left Bank, Leeds. *Photo* Giles Smith (www.gilosco.pe)

working through a non-traditional, largely improvised, and open form, delivering performance in an unfamiliar space with an intimate and, at times, unwitting audience. For them, taking work into strangers' houses presented the greatest risk and the greatest thrill. The act of crossing the threshold constituted one of the key elements of edgework practice for the performers, codified here by Sibley as transgression:

> Crossing boundaries, from a familiar space to an alien one which is under the control of someone else, can provide anxious moments; in some circumstances it could be fatal, or it might be an exhilarating experience—the thrill of transgression. (Sibley 1992, 32)

In this environment traditional theatrical conventions associated with bifurcation of space were no longer available as a way of establishing the fiction. Establishing the rules of the playing space had to be achieved through other means. At a practical level, performers had no sense of the physical layout of the space in which they would be working. There

Fig. 2 Participants, performers, and police officers come together to discuss the project and its outcomes over food, drink, and music. *Photo* Giles Smith (www.gilosco.pe)

could be no guarantees about how many audience members would be present and they would have little control over the space once inside. Performing in the private space of someone else's home lay beyond their immediate experience so it was impossible to gauge in advance how the work would be received. Due to the improvised nature of the performance, certain elements were impossible to rehearse and would prove to be a test of the performers' ability to respond flexibly and in the moment. The possibility of failure was ever present and provided the very edge that was so alluring for the performers. To risk failure is an integral part of any creative process but, in the context of participatory performance that is shared, collaborative, and co-authored, the potential for disaster and collapse is what drives the work both aesthetically and ideologically. Closing down the possibility of failure in favour of reproducible, knowable outcomes is anathema for artists working in this vein and runs contrary to many other practices in which predictability holds currency.[4]

The project set out to use an open and permeable approach that invited the audience to participate playfully (through improvisation, gaming, and role play) in order to address the real risks associated with crime. As Gareth White points out, the management of real and perceived risk in participatory practice has ethical implications (2013, 89). Theatre makers have an obligation to participants to ensure their physical, mental, and social well-being is considered without losing the "edge" of the event itself. This was certainly the case in *Safe as Houses?* The project had undergone comprehensive ethical review. Written consent had been obtained from the participants and each household had been visited by a police officer who explained the purpose of the project. Performers ensured the level of emotional risk to participants was minimal and were fully aware of the need to maintain fictive distance from the material throughout each performance. In other words, the fictional story was the focus of the performance rather than the participants' own experience of crime. Care was taken in the devising process to ensure audience members were not coerced into participation nor encouraged to disclose information relating to their own lives.[5] Instead, they were encouraged to engage in a form of playful participation that nonetheless had an edge by virtue of the performance aesthetic. A carefully constructed conflation of time and space within the piece brought the fiction into the present and served to confront the participants with their own context and circumstances whilst maintaining a "one step removed" approach. Adopting a "risky aesthetic" and establishing "safe distance" for participants is an inherent paradox of all participatory work. "Do no harm" is generally accepted as the first guiding principle of applied theatre practice (Prendergast and Saxton 2009, 25) and yet, where embodied participation and open strategies of engagement are concerned, particularly those framed as risk, this principle cannot always be assumed.

Although using fiction to draw attention to reality was mostly effective in *Safe as Houses?*, this was not always the case and highlights the precarious nature of working through a risky aesthetic that blurs established boundaries. In many ways the project failed entirely in its mission to deliver a clear message. For some audience members the performance was entirely baffling. Some had little or no knowledge of what was happening and had no prior warning that anyone was even about to knock at their door. They were unable to distinguish between what was real and what was fiction. They were confused, bemused, and unable to "read" what was unfolding in their living rooms. In our attempt to deliver an experimental, open performance that blurred boundaries between time, space, and presence, the risks we took with theatrical convention proved to be a step too far in some instances and produced feelings of dis-ease and unsettlement for some of the participants. Nevertheless, in the words of Cesar A. Cruz (1997), if art should comfort the disturbed and disturb the comfortable, then perhaps this result would be better reframed as a positive. Interestingly, during the post-show interviews with participants, one spectator who had been particularly wary of the performers and their intentions stated, "If I'd known it was a social experiment, I'd have been totally cool with it". Even post-show this participant did not recognise that what had occurred was a theatrical encounter, framing it instead as some type of psychological experiment designed to test his response to strangers invading his home.

The way in which risks are framed is particularly pertinent to any analysis of risk, participation, and vulnerability in performance. Most practice that defines itself as "risky" deliberately disturbs, disrupts, and plays with context and framing. It is the playful reinterpretation of context that leads us to consider fresh perspectives. However, when those involved are not fully aware of the ways in which context is being realigned confusion reigns and feelings of powerlessness take over. In *Safe as Houses?*, despite best intentions, the balance of power rested with the performers. Entering the private space of someone's house was considered the biggest risk to the performers. For participants this was also true. Opening up their home for the purpose of performance meant a relinquishing of control that, for some, was overwhelming and resulted, at best, in bewilderment and, at worst, as an act of invasion.

The *Safe as Houses?* project focused on the notion of physical and emotional thresholds. Primarily it was concerned with investigating what happens when those thresholds are transgressed, when private space is occupied by performers and/or violated by criminals. It required both performers and participants to occupy the "edge" for the duration of the performance and to take some risks in agreeing to participate. However, that "agreement" was not always clearly obtained or made explicit which, in turn, led to confusion and misinterpretation. What this illuminates is the fragile and precarious nature of risk taking in performance, even when it is framed as play. The agency felt by the performers as they engaged in play was in distinct contrast to the vulnerability felt by some audience members who were unable to read what was happening as play at all. Emerging from this project, a new category of performative risk taking has developed that draws on the sociological and the performative, namely "edgeplay". This term offers a way of analysing risk-taking behaviours that are akin to that of edgework but which are undertaken within the special mode of play, particularly within the field of performance work that adopts improvisatory strategies as a point of entry for participation.

Edgeplay as a Category of Edgework

As Stephen Lyng reminds us, there are two important aspects to the word "edgework". "Edge" indicates an encounter with a threshold; "work" refers to the negotiation of that line and the implicit skills required to successfully achieve that negotiation. In line with the Marxist interpretation of free labour, Lyng argues, "under certain structural conditions work serves as a vehicle for developing human potential because it requires the combined use of multiple human capacities" (2008: 112). He goes on to say that the crucial skill for an edgeworker is the capacity for flexibility. In other words, edgeworkers need to be able to improvise. This indicates that edgework has an innate playful quality which in the realm of performance is further heightened. To make this distinction clear and to draw attention to the two component parts, let us consider this to be "edgeplay". In this context, edgeplay can be understood as voluntary risk-taking activity that occurs within the frame of play where experiences, feelings, and emotions associated with encountering the edge can be practised and rehearsed. In this modelling, it is play that is the vehicle for the development of human potential and improvisation that is the central plank of that play. As Stuart Grant argues:

> The performative moment of any given event of performance ... is always improvisation, and this improvisation entails a specific ethical responsibility. Every moment of performance, every iteration, occurs in a unique, more or less unpredictable situation to which it makes a singular, contingent, and unrepeatable response. The stakes are always changing from moment to moment. The job of every performer, as with any gambler, is to measure the stakes and hazard an irretrievable, futurally-disposed encounter with the unknown. (2014, 127)

Whilst there is no doubt that all performers must measure the stakes for themselves and respond accordingly, this becomes more problematic when audience members are reframed as performers, or at least participants in performances they might not be equipped to decode easily. Confusion stimulates mistrust and creates a barrier to participation and creative risk taking. For the non-professional participant, the stakes will undoubtedly be different to that of the trained actor. How flexible they will need to be and what risks are being undertaken may not always be apparent. Play in this context is neither benign nor trivial and, for the participant, may feel uncomfortable and troubling. Despite the association with childhood, play is not always innocent, nor is it merely an escape device. Rather, play can be adopted as a tactic by those seeking encounters with the unknown.

Within a Marxist interpretation, participation in edgework might correlate to an individual's feelings of alienation in the workplace and offers an alternative. Participation in edgework activities may offer temporary release from the highly rationalised, bureaucratic nature of the modern-day working environment. But the picture is more complex than this, and "edgeplay" provides a more nuanced way of viewing it. Max Weber argues a world purged of sacred mysteries and vibrant experiences comes to be dominated by "specialists without spirit, sensualists without heat" (Weber 1958, 152). What edgework does is to provide a particularly powerful way to re-enchant the disenchanted. It provides a moment of magic and of mystery that combines work with spirituality, the playful with the divine (O'Grady 1999). What I am proposing here is a reimagining of the concept where the playful aspect of edgework is foregrounded. That is not to say that work and play are put into opposition to form a false binary. It is clear that work and play cannot be categorised in such a way. There are many crossovers and intersections between the two modes of activity. One can play at one's work as much as one may work hard at playing. Rather, what I am arguing is that within the frame of performance, participating, risking oneself, investing, and placing oneself at the edge of experience and on the threshold between spectating and acting, play becomes a *category* of edgework. It is not concerned with the edge between life and death, between consciousness and unconsciousness, but it is concerned with the borderlands of experience. Edgeplay dabbles in the margins between the imagined and the real, between the lived and dreamed, between the fictive and the factive. Edgeplay might be considered as the smaller Russian doll sitting within a larger version of itself, edgework.

The concept of voluntary risk taking, edgework, and this new category of edgeplay are useful theoretical tools for understanding the processes at work in participatory performance that seeks to deploy openness as a tactic, whether that be for pedagogical, political, or aesthetic purposes. Playing on the edge can offer an opportunity for growth and development that places emphasis on the present, co-located nature of human interaction. Edgeplay offers a space for potential development by virtue of being located in the fictional, the imaginary, and the invented. Risk taking within the frame of play has the ability to move things forward even though it is not concerned with the same sorts of thresholds as conventional edgework. It places value on the playfulness of the exchanges themselves rather than placing value on what they might produce. Playing on the edge, as opposed to working on the edge, favours creativity over productivity and reveals the constructed nature of human interaction by placing emphasis on those interactions in play. As with all risk-taking activity, however, edgeplay is dependent on context. The slippery nature of play makes it unfixed, unstable, and precarious. This is both its allure as a medium and the risk it poses as an aesthetic tactic.

The Utility of Playing on the Edge

The concept of edgeplay offers an alternative means of considering the way risk is perceived and incorporated into performance across a spectrum of practice. It provides a way of thinking through the risks involved in participating in performance that does not result in a false binary between "real" and "perceived", or "real" and "imagined", risks. We might play within the imaginary realm, for instance, but the risks we take there may produce new insights and have profound consequences for our daily lives. In fact, we may bring some of that playful spirit to bear on our day-to-day activities as a tactic for dealing with the indeterminacy, the precarity of contemporary living as it is being currently constructed. Risk taking through play, as conceived in the world of performance, provides a way of disrupting ontological security but does so with greater flexibility compared with other edgework activities. Whilst you would not encourage six-year-olds to take up base jumping for obvious reasons, that does not mean they cannot be exposed to risk through other means. Under the umbrella of edgeplay, individuals and groups can be encouraged to engage with risk taking as a critical and strategic tool rather than as an activity to be feared for its potential harmful consequences. As a category of edgework, the model of risk taking may still contribute to the sense of personal growth and development afforded by encountering the edge but does so within a different frame. The imaginative role playing within theatre in education, for example, encourages children to cross the threshold into an open or permeable performance structure by stepping into the fiction and taking action for themselves. It enables them to take some creative risks, sharing ideas and creating new meanings. In a similar way, but at the more extreme edges of participatory experience, the work of contemporary performance companies such as Blast Theory, for example, encourages audiences to undertake more visceral risk taking and to experience adversity through participation in interactive gaming structures. Still framed as play, the experiences are nonetheless designed to test participants' agency to its limits (Blast Theory 2016). With these two examples we can see that the category of edgeplay covers an array of risk-taking activity but can be sufficiently flexible to accommodate ethical and safeguarding issues associated with diverse participant groups. Moving beyond the world of performance, it is also pertinent to consider how the concept of edgeplay influences risk taking in other areas such as finance, business, health, and so on. Although playing in these contexts is less widely acknowledged, adopting play (rather than work) as a lens through which to view the risk taking that occurs in these contexts may significantly shift how certain practices are considered or reconsidered. What if the banker's gambling with a nation's investments is read as a form of risk-saturated play (rather than a legitimised form of work) and is treated as such by the banker? Does this alter the symbolic register of its consequences? Does it alter how the world views these practices in future in order to mitigate them? Clearly there is more work to be done here and more questions to be asked, but if playing at the edge offers us a way of engaging with alternative futures and being generally more open to the world, then it can be adopted as a strategy for action and as a tool for interpreting behaviour not limited to the world of performance.

Finally

Over the course of writing this chapter, the world has seen indescribable events that have once more brought the subject of risk, terror, and threat into most people's daily vocabulary. Whilst the topic of participatory performance may seem a long way from these events, examining how individuals and groups respond to risks in situations that are framed as playful participation may illuminate how risk behaviours are understood in other contexts. As the world begins to feel riskier than ever, we run the risk of closing our doors, barricading ourselves in, and preventing open contact with the unknown and unknowable. It is in these very circumstances, however, that adopting a stance of radical openness becomes even more urgent. Performance will always respond to the sociopolitical context from which it emerges. In a new era of risk production, reception, and dissemination, performance will find a way to react. Whether performance will become riskier or safer as a result remains to be seen. What is clear is that understanding the interplay between agency and vulnerability continues to be of primary concern for artists, practitioners, and participants who value playing on the edge as a way of prioritising encounter, experience, and growth.

Notes

1. A simple search on the topic of "risk" using Web of Science results in over one million hits in the last five years alone.
2. The Y2K issue, or the Millennium Bug, was a computer problem that threatened to compromise the operations of financial organisations, government agencies, air traffic control, and so on. It was feared that computers would not be able to distinguish the year 2000 from the year 1900 and that when the time rolled over to 1 January 2000 all computers might crash, leading to devastating consequences.
3. "The Aesthetics of Risk" is the title of Mark Stranger's semiotic study of Australian surfing culture published in 1999. In this work the emphasis is on the aestheticisation of risk-taking pursuits in the quest for transcendent experience and the role of the media in constructing images of the sublime. The "aesthetics of risk" is a phrase mobilised by theatre scholar Hans-Thies Lehmann (2006) and contemporary art historian John C. Welchman (2008). The inversion of the phrase to "risky aesthetics" denotes emphasis on aesthetic practice which is intentionally risky in its construction and implementation rather than the aesthetic dimension of risk taking in other contexts.
4. Given the contemporary preoccupation with risk assessment, this project on risk posed an interesting problem insofar as the performance spaces could not be risk assessed in the usual way. Although a generic risk assessment could be carried out that was formulated on "best guess"

assumptions about each living room, performers had to undertake continuous or dynamic risk assessment whilst the performance was under way. In practical terms this meant each individual was responsible for continually assessing and reassessing the context in which they were performing *during* the performance itself, a process not dissimilar to Schön's reflection in action (1995). The risk assessment was neither fixed nor written down but in a state of constant development, in flux, and part of a negotiated process that had been discussed at length by the company during the rehearsal phase.

5. A qualified counsellor was in attendance at the social event after the performance and was available to offer guidance to anyone who needed to discuss their own experiences as necessary.

References

Alston, Adam. 2013. Audience Participation and Neoliberal Value: Risk, Agency and Responsibility in Immersive Theatre. *Performance Research: A Journal of the Performing Arts* 18 (2): 128–138.

Baim, Clark, Sally Brookes, and Alun Mountford. 2002. *The Geese Theatre Handbook: Drama with Offenders and People at Risk*. Winchester: Waterside Press.

Beck, Ulrich. 1992. *Risk Society: Towards a New Modernity*. London and Newbury Park, CA: Sage.

Bishop, Claire (ed.). 2006. *Participation*. London: Whitechapel.

Bishop, Claire. 2012. *Artificial Hells: Participatory Art and the Politics of Spectatorship*. London: Verso.

Blast Theory. 2016. Blast Theory: Art that Mixes 90s Clubbing Culture with 'escaping the boredom' of Being You. http://www.itsnicethat.com/articles/blast-theory-operation-black-antler-brighton-festival-120516. Accessed 8 Aug 2016.

Boal, Augusto. 1979. *Theatre of the Oppressed*. London: Pluto Press.

Bourriaud, Pierre. 1998. *Relational Aesthetics*. London: Les Presses du Réel.

Breakwell, Glynis M. 2007. *The Psychology of Risk*. Cambridge: Cambridge University Press.

Breed, George. 2009. *Radical Openness*. Bloomington: iUniverse.

Cohen, Cynthia E., Robert Gutierrez Varea, and Polly O. Walker. 2011. The Permeable Membrane and the Moral Imagination. In *Acting Together: Performance and the Creative Transformation of Conflict*, ed. Cynthia E. Cohen, Robert Gutierrez Varea, and Polly O. Walker, 161–189. Oakland, CA: New Village Press.

Cohen, Stanley and Lauren Taylor. 1976/1992. *Escape Attempts: The Theory and Practice of Resistance to Everyday Life*. London: Allen Lane.

Conrad, Diane. 2005. Rethinking 'at-risk' in Drama Education: Beyond Prescribed Roles. *Research in Drama Education: The Journal of Applied Theatre and Performance* 10 (1): 27–41. doi:10.1080/13569780500053114.

Cruz, Cesar A. 1997. *To Comfort the Disturbed, and to Disturb the Comfortable: Onward Children of the Sun.*

Debord, Guy. 1983. *Society of the Spectacle.* Detroit, MI: Black and Red.

Douglas, Mary. 1992. *Risk and Blame: Essays in Cultural Theory.* London: Routledge.

Dwyer, Paul, Mary Ann Hunter, and Justine Shih Pearson. 2014. High Stakes: Risk and Performance. *About Performance.* Sydney: Department of Performance Studies, University of Sydney.

Eco, Umberto. 1989. *The Open Work.* Cambridge, MA: Harvard University Press.

Freire, Paulo. 1970. *Pedagogy of the Oppressed.* New York: Continuum.

Freire, Paulo. 1998. *Pedagogy of Freedom: Ethics, Democracy and Civic Courage*, trans. Patrick Clarke. Lanham, MD and Oxford: Rowman and Littlefield Publishers.

Fuerdi, Frank. 2004. *Therapy Culture: Cultivating Vulnerability in an Uncertain Age.* London: Routledge.

Giddens, Anthony. 1990. *The Consequences of Modernity.* Cambridge: Polity Press.

Giddens, Anthony. 1991. *Modernity and Self-Identity.* Cambridge: Polity Press.

Goldberg, Rose Lee. 2011. *Performance Art: From Futurism to the Present*, 3rd ed. London and New York: Thames and Hudson.

Grant, Stuart. 2014. 'What if? Performance is risk.' *About Performance* 12: 127–144.

Hansen, Oskar. 2005. *Towards Open Form.* Frankfurt: Revolver.

Heathfield, Adrian. 2004. *Live: Art and Performance.* London: Tate.

hooks, bell. 1990. *Yearning: Race, Gender and Cultural Politics.* Boston, MA: South End Press.

Jackson, Antony. 2007. *Theatre, Education and the Making of Meanings: Art of Instrument?* Manchester: Manchester University Press.

Jackson, Shannon. 2011. *Social Works: Performing Art, Supporting Publics.* New York and London: Routledge.

Johnson, Branden B., and Vincent T. Covello (eds.). 1987. *The Social and Cultural Construction of Risk.* Dordrecht: D. Reidel.

Jordan, Tim. 2002. *Activism! Direct Action, Hacktivism and the Future of Society.* London: Reaktion.

Katz, Jack. 1988. *The Seductions of Crime: Moral and Sensual Attractions of Doing Evil.* New York: Basic Books.

Kearnes, M., Francisco Klauser, and Stuart Lane (eds.). 2012. *Critical Risk Research: Practices, Politics and Ethics.* Oxford: Wiley Blackwell.

Laclau, Ernesto. 1990. *New Reflections on the Revolution of our Time*. London: Verso.

Lehmann, Hans-Thies. 2006. *Postdramatic Theatre*. London: Routledge.

Lupton, Deborah. 1999. *Risk*. London: Routledge.

Lupton, Deborah, and John Tulloch. 2002. 'Life would be pretty dull without risk': Voluntary Risk-taking and its Pleasures. *Health, Risk and Society* 4 (2): 113–124.

Lyng, Stephen. 1990. Edgework: A Social Psychological Analysis of Voluntary Risk Taking. *American Journal of Sociology* 95: 851–886.

Lyng, Stephen. 2008. Edgework, Risk and Uncertainty. In *Social Theories of Risk and Uncertainty*, ed. Jens O. Zinn. Maiden, MA and Oxford: Blackwell.

Lyng, Stephen (ed.). 2005. *Edgework: the Sociology of Risk-taking*. London and New York: Routledge.

MacDonald, Claire, (ed.). 1996. On risk. *Performance Research: A Journal of the Performing Arts* 1(2): 1–121.

Machon, Josephine. 2013. *Immersive Theatres: Intimacy and Immediacy in Contemporary Performance*. Basingstoke: Palgrave.

McNeil, Alexander, Frey Rudiger, and Paul Embrechts. 2015. *Quantitative Risk Management: Concepts, Techniques and Tools*. Princeton, NJ: Princeton University Press.

Massey, Doreen. 2005. *For Space*. London: Sage.

Massumi, Brian. 1993. Everywhere You Want to Be: Introduction to Fear. In *The Politics of Everyday Fear*, ed. Brian Massumi, 3–38. Minneapolis, MN: University of Minnesota Press.

Neelands, Jonothan. 1992. *Learning Through Imagined Experience*. London: Hodder and Stoughton.

Neelands, Jonothan and Tony Goode. 2008. Playing in the margins of meaning: the ritual aesthetic in community performance. *NJ: Drama Australia Journal* 32 (1): 82–86.

Nicholson, Helen. 2005. *Applied Drama: The Gift of Theatre*. Basingstoke: Palgrave.

O'Grady, Alice. 1999. *Research in Drama Education*.

O'Grady, Alice. 2013. Exploring Radical Openness: A Porous Model for Relational Festival Performance. *Studies in Theatre and Performance* 33 (2): 133–151.

O'Toole, John. 1992. *The Process of Drama*. London: Routledge.

Power, Michael. 1997. From Risk Society to Audit Society. *Soziale Systeme* 3 (1): 3–21.

Prendergast, Monica, and Juliana Saxton. 2009. *Applied Theatre: International Case Studies and Challenges for Practice*. Bristol: Intellect.

Rancière, Jacques. 2009. *The Emancipated Spectator*. London: Verso.

Schechner, Richard. 1994. *Environmental Theatre*. New York: Applause.

Schön, Donald A. 1995. *The Reflective Practitioner: How Professionals Think in Action*. Aldershot: Arena.

Shaughnessy, Nicola. 2012. *Applying Performance: Live Art, Socially Engaged Theatre and Affective Practice*. Houndmills, Basingstoke and New York: Palgrave Macmillan.

Sibley, David. 1992. *Geographies of Exclusion: Society and Difference in the West*. London: Routledge.

Smith, Charles. 2005. Financial Edgework: Trading in Market Currents. In *Edgework: The Sociology of Risk-Taking*, ed. Stephen Lyng, 187–200. London and New York: Routledge.

Smith, Malinda. 2014. Africa, 9/11, and the Temporality and Spatiality of Race and Terror. In *At the Limits of Justice: Women of Colour on Terror*, ed. Suvendrini Perera and Sherene H. Razack, 380–405. Toronto: University of Toronto Press.

Suter, Glenn W. 2007. *Ecological Risk Assessment*. Boca Raton, FL: CRC Press/ Taylor Francis.

Tapscott, Don. 2013. *Radical Openness: Four Unexpected Principles for Success*. TED Conference, LLC.

Thompson, James. 2003. *Applied Theatre: Bewilderment and Beyond*. Oxford: Peter Lang.

Ridout, Nicholas and Rebecca Schneider. 2012. Precarity and performance. *TDR: The Drama Review* 56 (4): 1–177.

Vose, David. 2008. *Risk Analysis: A Quantitative Guide*. Chichester: Wiley.

Warr, Tracey. 1996. Sleeper. *Performance Research: A Journal of the Performing Arts* 1 (2): 1–19.

Weber, Max. 1958. *The Protestant Ethic and the Spirit of Capitalism*, trans. T. Parsons. New York: Charles Scribner's Sons.

Welchman, John (ed.). 2008. *The Aesthetics of Risk: SoCCAS Symposium*, vol. III. Zurich: JRP Ringier.

White, Gareth. 2013. *Audience Participation in Theatre: The Aesthetics of the Invitation*. Basingstoke: Palgrave.

Zinn, Jens O. (ed.). 2008. *Social Theories of Risk and Uncertainty: An Introduction*. Maiden, MA and Oxford: Blackwell.

PART I

The Ethics of Risky Aesthetics: Moral Codes, Being Decent, and Doing it Right

Theatre in the Age of Uncertainty: Memory, Technology, and Risk in Simon McBurney's *The Encounter* and Robert Lepage's *887*

Lourdes Orozco

The Beginning

At the 2015 Edinburgh International Festival, Simon McBurney's last piece, *The Encounter*, and Robert Lepage's European premiere of his last production, *887*, could be seen side by side and during the same week in the Edinburgh International Conference Centre (EICC). The EICC is a government-owned building in central Edinburgh welcoming the visitor with a corporate-style glass façade and into an open plan lobby in which a café, an information desk, and the temporary box office are located. This could be a hotel, an airport, a bank, a "non-place" which, in the words of Marc Augé, inspires a sense of belonging, one of those locations where contemporary life so often takes place (Augé 1995, xii). These are places designed to produce an experience of safety and comfort, recognisable spaces across the globe, which generate similar ways of

L. Orozco (✉)
University of Leeds, Leeds, UK
e-mail: L.Orozco@leeds.ac.uk

© The Author(s) 2017

A. O'Grady (ed.), *Risk, Participation, and Performance Practice*,
DOI 10.1007/978-3-319-63242-1_2

being and make easier the risky activity of decision making that characterises everyday life.

The EICC's steep escalator takes the visitor to the lower floor where two different conference auditoria are being used as theatres for this edition of the festival. In these venues, audiences can see Simon McBurney's *The Encounter* and Robert Lepage's *887* back to back on the same day. The programming is perhaps coincidental and certainly not based on the shared ideologies that the productions display and that this chapter will outline. However, it is not surprising that these two well-established theatre practitioners, who were born in the same year (1957) and are at similar stages in their careers, have produced two solo shows that can be read as a response to the impact that technological progress has had and continues to have on contemporary life, especially in relation to time (past, present, and future). It is not surprising either that, while the theatrical vocabularies are noticeably different, the ideologies behind the pieces are not, both marked by a certain bitter nostalgia for a time that, if not better, at least took longer to pass, for a time that moved at a speed more akin to human pace. The two pieces not only share some formal aspects (they are both solo shows which use direct address to the audience) but they also present a common ideological starting point: a signalling towards memory, remembering, and documenting as a response to the contemporary obsession with the future enabled by the prominent presence of technology.

Simon McBurney's *The Encounter* is a solo piece inspired by Petru Popescu's novel *Amazon Beaming* (1992) and is delivered in its entirety through headphones. While the title of the piece signals a single meeting, the one narrated in Popescu's novel between photographer Loren McIntyre and the Amazonian Mayoruna tribe, McBurney's piece stages a variety of encounters, the most interesting being the intimate one that the performer has with his audience. This encounter is mediated by binaural technology—the recording and distributing of sound three-dimensionally—as McBurney delivers his narrative through a dummy head microphone. The microphone, which is located centre stage for the entirety of the piece, produces a "binaural stereo experience [that] moves the listener into the scene of the original performance, in contrast to other space-related recording techniques, where the acoustic event is moved to the listener".[1] There is a strange moment in the piece when the performer blows softly into the right ear of the binaural head microphone, and suddenly a rush of warmth can be felt through the headphones and into the ear of each audience member. The warm feeling seems real even though there is no actual contact between McBurney and the audience. Somehow, the feeling of warmth is actually produced by the body's knowledge of the possibility of it happening. Proximity and embodiment are key to the production. Its intention is to enter the audience's consciousness through the headphones, producing the illusion for audience members that McBurney is talking directly, and exclusively, to them.

On the stage next door, director and performer Robert Lepage also proposes a close encounter with his audience, talking directly to them in a confessional manner about his childhood in Québec alongside the sociopolitical histories of the city. In *887*, he is also interested in producing an immersive experience, which encourages the audience to emotionally engage with the personal and national histories that Lepage unearths for them, and to travel with him to locations that signify critical moments in the development of his identity and that of his city and his country. He does this by talking openly about both his childhood and his current feelings about that period of his life. He talks about where he lived, his relationship with his father, his memories of his neighbours and friends. However, the production is not only preoccupied with the past; it is intermittently haunted by the future as Lepage's character expresses anxiety about his obituary, which will be published in the national press, and his fears about how he will be remembered after his death.

Both shows set out to produce a close encounter with their audiences, marked by an emotional and sensual proximity. This fits in well with recent trends in theatre and performance practice proven by the rise of shows and companies interested in work that has been defined as immersive and participatory. Correspondingly, the question of risk within the research field of theatre and performance studies has primarily concerned itself with practices that rely on the actual participation of the audience to achieve their artistic intervention. However, this chapter proposes a different engagement with the question of risk in performance. *The Encounter* and *887* cannot be considered immersive and participatory in the ways that are described above as they are not interested in producing an actual risk-taking theatrical experience in which spectators are in physical or psychological danger.

Risk understood as danger is at the core of theatre practice. It is visible in the creative and personal risks taken by practitioners, programmers, and audience members every time they engage in theatrical activity. It is also key to theatre as an art form. Risk and uncertainty are intrinsic to the liveness that makes theatre unique, and it is this uniqueness that Lyn Gardner (2015) sees as theatre's chance to be saved from extinction. Gardner suggests that if theatre wants to ensure its chances of survival it should embrace risk taking in programming but also in all aspects of this artistic practice.

Lepage's and McBurney's productions exemplify some of this tangible risk taking. Theirs are solo shows that place enormous pressure on the performer alone on stage for two hours to deliver the performance well, to remember lines and operate the complex technology that both productions utilise. They have been generated through a creative process that engages innately in risk taking, dominated by uncertainty and difficult decision making. Both practitioners hold a particular status within contemporary theatre practice, seen as heralds of experimental theatre making, their reputations are on the line each time a new creation is unveiled. The context in which both productions were presented, the 2015 Edinburgh International Festival, is one in which risk taking is expected and also closely scrutinised as theatre programmers' decisions across the country and internationally are informed by the festival's programming choices. These are all known risks that are inherently associated with theatre practice and that scholars within theatre and performance studies have already identified in previous works on these questions.[2]

In this chapter, however, I argue that *The Encounter* and *887* engage with risk in a different way. I believe that their investigation and theatrical articulation of risk happens primarily through their consideration of time and technology, which are key aspects of risk theory in the social sciences. This is perhaps a less obvious, but no less powerful, contribution to the current debates on risk originated in the social sciences in the 1990s that continue to resonate today and also one that enlarges the engagement of theatre and performance studies with these enquiries.

I believe that the two productions can be seen as examples of performance that demonstrate the ongoing preoccupations with the basic concepts of what Beck and Giddens, at the beginning of the 1990s, termed the risk society: technological dependence, an obsession with the future, and a focus on the individual. What I propose here is that both productions are able to simultaneously highlight the continuing problematics related to those questions and, through their intense blurring of the actual and the fictional, serve as a platform to destabilise the simplistic dichotomies (past/future; technological/pre-technological; individual/community) that have underscored debates around risk.

I believe that both *The Encounter* and *887* demonstrate how performance can critically participate in the debates around the risks and effects of technology. Their narratives of loss and memory are, I argue, poignant examples of the impact that technology has on the contemporary subject. As Spitzer suggests, "wherever there are effects, there are risks and side effects. This truism does not just apply to medicine but to any field of human activity. The automobile was a great invention for mobility, but causes obesity by inactivity, injury and death, as well as environmental hazards" (2014, 81). McBurney's and Lepage's productions dig deep into these effects and the great transformations that they have produced on societies, communities, and individuals while, simultaneously, their performances represent the great technological achievements of the twenty-first century, without which the shows would not exist.

Working within the social sciences, Beck and Giddens argue that contemporary societies (especially in the West) are chiefly concerned with the risks brought about by technological progress and obsessively preoccupied with the future and its management. I understand *The Encounter* and *887* as nuanced engagements with those concerns and the mechanisms of social control that they produce. This chapter takes an interdisciplinary approach to McBurney's and Lepage's productions by placing them under both a sociological and a performance analysis lens. The analysis of the productions is framed theoretically within social theory due to its influential input in the research area of risk studies. However, the chapter goes beyond an application of social theory on performance and gives attention to how performance—especially in its production of intimate settings, participatory experiences, and confessional modes of delivery—can offer important insights into the place of risk in contemporary society. In the chapter, I unpack the risk society's main mechanisms for social structure and emphasise their politicisation, their use to support particular political agendas, in order to understand how risk is not only material but also contributes to the formation of ideologies. I explore this by uncovering the way in which both productions represent the pathologies that are already engrained in the fabric of Western societies to prevent such risks, and by exploring the elusive ways in which both pieces engage with risk, not so much as a practical aspect of theatre making, but as an ideological concept that underpins the life experience of the contemporary subject. There is an ethical responsibility in these engagements, both in the making—by McBurney and Lepage—and in my writing. Risk, as it is understood in this chapter, demands an ethical approach to individual and community constructions of responsibility. It is important, I argue, to understand this concept as constructed and thus malleable. It is important also to understand how the question of responsibility is key to the technological developments that inflect understandings of memory, time, and identity. Through my analysis of these recent works I want to begin an ethical reconsideration of responsibility, and the endless loops that it is caught up in between the individual and the community, in order to challenge monolithic approaches and understandings to this key concept within contemporary life.

The Middle

The proximity that both *The Encounter* and *887* achieve and defend, through technology and an emphasis on honest and confessional deliveries, generates the mood and attention required for storytelling to take place. Storytelling is key to both productions not only as a formal structure but also as an ideological framework in which to engage with their central concerns: time, identity, and their subsequent politicisations. Storytelling produces an intimate encounter, one that suspends the running of real time and allows for an immersion into a world other than the immediate one that surrounds both the teller and the listener. More importantly, storytelling is a key aspect of identity formation. In *The Human Condition* (1958), philosopher Hannah Arendt defends the importance of storytelling as a way of understanding the human experience by relating it to identity formation. For Arendt, a way of understanding "life" is to relate it to narrative and to recognise birth and death as the beginning and the end of a/the story. However, what makes "life" specifically human is the ability to transform this narrative into a story that can be told: "the chief characteristic of the specifically human life, whose appearance and disappearance constitute worldly events, is that it is itself full of events which ultimately can be told as a story, establish a biography" (1958, 97), and a biography, I would add, is one's identity. More recently, Richard Kearney has written about the role of narrative in the realisation of identities in "our postmodern era of fragmentation and fracture" (2002, 4). For Kearney it is "only when haphazard happenings are transformed into story, and thus made memorable over time, that we become full agents of our history" (2002, 3). The telling of the story is a way of claiming back agency in history and "this becoming historical involves a transition from the flux of events into a meaningful social or political community" (2004, 3). Storytelling helps to form individuals and communities, it transforms biological life into human life, and, above all, it gives individuals and communities the power to produce their own history/ies and build their identity/ies.

I believe that McBurney and Lepage use storytelling knowingly in order to produce a close encounter with their audiences and also to signal theatre's contribution to identity formation through the sharing of stories communally. However, their narratives mirror today's era of "fragmentation and fracture", suggested by Kearney, and replicate the feelings of uncertainty that are part of the everyday experience of life in the West. McBurney's telling of Loren McIntyre's story and Lepage's stories of his childhood are fully embedded in a way of telling that cannot be linear but is necessarily disjointed. Both McBurney and Lepage go back and forth from various pasts to the present, travelling through several layers of fiction, piecing together documentary material, personal accounts, and fictionalised scenes. The constant interruptions to their stories and irruptions of other stories within them is, in McBurney's case, aided by the production's heavy reliance on technology and, in Lepage's, propelled by the inability to remember produced by technological overdependence. The shows are subtly linked, clearly proposing that technology is both the cause and the effect of how societies and individuals in the West operate, producing a life experience dominated by uncertainty and risk.

Beyond McIntyre's and the Mayoruna's stories and those of McBurney and Lepage, the story that both *The Encounter* and *887* are really keen to tell is that of the impact of technology on the contemporary subject, its role in the shaping of time, and its contribution to processes of identity formation, devolution, and individualisation. They do so through their confusion of the fictional and the actual, the live and the mediatised so characteristic of the contemporary society in which their productions happen.

In both shows, the boundaries between character and performer are blurred as McBurney and Lepage, playing "themselves", display their compulsive documentation of their day to day (McBurney) and discuss their inability to remember and memorise (Lepage). The private and the public are cleverly intertwined as both performers signal the formation of alternative and multiple identities that is enabled by technology. In this sense, both productions inhabit a space in which the virtual, the factual, the real, and the fictional coexist, mirroring the contemporary blurring of these locations and the production of "glocal" (the global and the local) sites (Beck 2002, 31) in media- and technology-focused societies.

McBurney and Lepage invite the audience to believe that their personal stories and the facts presented about Amazonian tribes and Canada are real. In the shows, McIntyre, the Mayoruna, and the many characters that populate Lepage's narrative are also real, as are the sites where their actions take place (the Amazon, London, Québec city). The audience is even encouraged to think that the performers might be holding their actual mobile phones, that the pictures shown and the voices heard are those of their true children, parents, and friends, of true scientists, artists, politicians. However, this authenticity is constantly, and very openly, undermined throughout the productions. Very early in *The Encounter*, when McBurney hammers down a VHS tape presumably containing all of his dad's Super 8 films, the audience gasp. He soon picks up an identical VHS tape and reassures them that this is actually the real one. The audience need and want to believe that all that valuable material, McBurney's documentation of his past, has not been lost. However, they are taken from the risk of the real to the instability of the unknown, and they are invited to consider the possibility that they no longer know what is real and what is not. The most important aspect of this confusion between the real and the fictional in McBurney's piece is, arguably, its undermining of the certainty produced by technology and information technology. After the initial scene, the audience are able to realise that in fact recordings might not actually be playing out of McBurney's iPhone, that the mixing of jungle sounds that he presumably produces live on stage might actually be pre-recorded, and, in various moments in which the synchronisation "fails", they realise that even the red and green microphones that alter McBurney's voice might actually be a gimmick. The audience's trust in the performance to provide a genuine account of the events that it depicts vanishes, and they are invited to embrace uncertainty as the context in which the performance and, by extension, contemporary life takes place. Lepage's performance of "himself", which exposes him personally in physical and emotional ways, also signals his intention to blur the real and the fictional. The audience are encouraged to believe that the character in Lepage's *887*, which is Lepage himself, is narrating Lepage's actual history, that the people and the events mentioned in the production are real and actually took place.

However, when the character reads his obituary, the production begins to signal to the multiplicity of identities that media-led societies can produce and the audience's sense of truth in relation to the production's materials is severely undermined. In reading his own obituary, Lepage questions how much of who he thinks he is will be remembered by his nation and how much what the nation will remember of him is part of who he thinks he is.

The blurring of the real and the fictional, the virtual and the actual is also encapsulated, and indeed enabled, by the iPhone, an object that is key to both productions. Both McBurney and Lepage open their performances by holding their respective iPhones and stating the role of smartphones in documenting humanity and in constructing life narratives and memories that will be carried into the future. McBurney speaks of how the thousands of images of his children archived in the device will help them to remember and will, irremediably, shape their memories of the past. He contrasts these digital images with the materiality of the VHS tape, which requires the force of a hammer to be destroyed rather than the inconspicuous malfunction of technology. He speaks about consciousness being split between the brain and the technologies with which we interact every day, and, in one of the production's climactic moments, he illustrates contemporary society's subordination to technology by stopping a hammer a millimetre away from his iPhone: the object that Western societies will never give up. The iPhone is also, paradoxically, presented as the object that stops humans from being able to remember, because it does all the remembering for them, and distances them from life experience itself. This reminds the audience that memories are mediated and, to an extent, fabricated by technology.

In Lepage's piece the focus on memory and remembering is also clearly established from the beginning. The production's articulation of these topics is delivered through a narrative that dips in and out of Lepage's childhood memories to remind its audience that the present is made up of the future but also the past. In *887*, risk is presented in relation to forgetting and clearly linked to the impact that technological progress has had and continues to have on human societies. Lepage offers an intimate theatrical journey through some of the most difficult episodes of Québec's twentieth-century history—the Quiet Revolution and the early years of the Front de Libération du Québec—seeking to alert the audience to the risks of forgetting. However, like McIntyre's, the struggle in Lepage's *887* is also one of survival. Not so much of literal survival, in which dangerous animals and treacherous wild environments threaten to end human life, but a metaphorical one in which an individual, who is representative of the Québecois nation, performs an act of remembrance to establish his identity and thus his existence, as well as that of his nation. *887* is an act of resistance against a society in which remembering is an obsolete practice eradicated by human reliance on technology, and against a society obsessed with the future and its relentless shaping of the present.

The productions take place in the context of cases such as the recent court case of Deric White—a London pensioner vs Apple-in November 2015 which clearly demonstrates how fragile and technology dependent memories are in the early twenty-first century. The 68-year-old Londoner sued the corporation when all his contacts and some of his photographs were wiped off his iPhone 5. In her article "Photos are memories we hand over to clouds" for the *Guardian* newspaper, Nell Frizzell accurately narrates this new way of understanding memory as something that we "hand over to clouds" (Guardian November 2015). *The Encounter* and *887* are firmly situated in this era where memories are intangible and immaterial, but increasingly important for identity formation. This, in turn, generates an obsession with documentation.

In *The Encounter*, this interest in documentation is clearly linked to knowledge, memory, and control. As McBurney explains in his opening monologue, it is inextricably associated with the contemporary Western fixation on archiving and its impact on identity formation. In the first minutes of *The Encounter*, the director addresses society's reliance on technology to document its histories by telling his audiences about his own obsessive documenting of his children's lives. More importantly, recording is presented as a response to a permanent sense of loss, to the imminence of that loss, to the risk of losing through forgetting. Here archiving is part of the process of storytelling, part of the mechanisms by which the contemporary subject builds her biography, and, as Arendt and Kearney suggest above, part of what makes humans specifically human. In this context, loss has dramatic consequences: without the technological archive, the contemporary subject cannot tell her story. Because of this, the central narrative in *The Encounter* also depicts a process of documentation: photographer Loren McIntyre's attempts to photograph the unknown-to-the-West Mayoruna tribe from the Amazon jungle. In telling that story, McBurney seeks to produce a theatrical experience in which the audience follows very closely the physical and psychological dangers and risks undertaken by McIntyre in his travels in the still-to-be-conquered-by-technology Amazon jungle, while also producing a moral fable about the sociopolitical consequences of technology's prominence and its impact on how humans produce a sense of themselves in relation to time. In McBurney's production, the Mayoruna are able to tell their story orally with no form of documentation other than that inscribed in their bodies (their scars, their memories, their rituals) and, as a result, own their histories without the aid of information technology, dispensing of all material objects.

Lepage offers a similar account of contemporary life experience when he recalls remembering his childhood address—887 Avenue Murray, Montcalm, Québec, from which the show takes its title—and phone number but confesses to not being able to memorise his current mobile phone number because technology remembers it for him. This is what science philosopher Manfred Spitzer has called "addiction to technology", a term used to explain the relationship of dependence that humans have with technology in the twenty-first century and the effects that dependency has on memory. It is an addiction that has been linked to short-term memory dysfunction and degenerative brain diseases such as dementia and Alzheimer's. In his 2013 book *Digitale Demenz*—published only in German and Spanish—Spitzer calls this phenomenon "digital dementia" and adds it to the long list of risks, real or panic generated, produced by a highly technologised society. Later in his work on the use of IT in education, Spitzer clearly explains the detrimental effects that the increased use of technologies in schools has on reading, writing, and memorising. He also identifies an added risk relating to the fact "that the internet, computers, tablets, and smart phones have a strong potential to cause *addiction*" (Spitzer 2014, 82, italics in original).

Spitzer also explains in *Digitale Demenz* that there is a clear link between current society's (high) use of technology and neurological dis/malfunction. Given that the brain is not able to "not learn"—it is in constant learning mode, and continuously adapting and evolving—high levels of exposure to information have clear effects on language development, attention span, intelligence, and, more importantly, memory (2013, 15). In today's societies the human brain is no longer the vessel for knowledge. Similarly to Frizzell's point, Spitzer explains how technology does all the archiving of memories and knowledge that was once the brain's task (2013, 16).[3] The old-fashioned methods of learning by heart names of mountains, rivers, countries, and multiplication tables is deemed outdated, but, in Spitzer's view, it is a necessary tool to educate the mind into being an archive and becoming less technology dependent (2013, 16).

Spitzer argues that current neurological diseases have to be understood as "an expression of the lack of balance between an old way of life and a modern way of life", pressing for technology and technological development as the cause of the problem in much the same way that Beck, Giddens, and other risk theorists have done (2013, 15). In this way, Spitzer aligns himself with debates around the effect that progress, especially technological, has on contemporary post-industrial societies. These debates have been generated within the social sciences by authors such as Beck and Giddens for whom the risk society is a key concept to understanding contemporary life. This is a society primarily fixated on safeguarding the future, which is perceived to be threatened by technological development. It is a society constantly catching up with itself, monitoring its progress and how to manage the consequences that that progress brings, a society that becomes "reflexive", which, as Beck, Giddens, and Lash explain, "is to say it becomes a theme and a problem for itself" (1994, 8). This is the basis on which risk is built and a paradigm that is at the core of McBurney's and Lepage's productions. Both *The Encounter* and *887* suggest that the fear of losing one's memories, one's past, is both a solution, because it allows humans to find ways to prevent that loss (e.g. technology), and the origin of the problem, since with technology humans are unable to remember. This is a key aspect of Beck and Giddens' concept of the risk society: a society in which risk management is both the solution and the problem because it makes humans aware of risks that might otherwise be imperceptible and invisible to them.

In his 1992 book *Risk Society: Towards a New Modernity*, Beck famously coined the concept of a society that is more concerned with the risks produced by progress than by progress itself. This society is, as Giddens explains in his own study of the concept, one invested in the future and chiefly preoccupied with how the future will impact (almost always negatively) on the present: "the idea of risk is bound up with the aspiration to control and particularly with the idea to control the future" (1999, 3). As such, the calculation and prevention of risks are principal concerns of this society and these preventive practices infiltrate political ideologies and social structures, affecting all aspects of contemporary life in the West. This view is also supported by cultural analyst

Kathleen Woodward, whose work *Statistical Panic* points towards this chief concern with risk, calculation, and their use to support particular political agendas. The new fear used as a control mechanism by late capitalist economies and governments is the "fear of risk itself" (1999, 178). For Woodward, "we live in a society of the statistic" and "rather than anchoring us to a stable life-world, statistics that forecast the future engender insecurity in the form of low-grade intensities that, like low-grade fevers, permit us to go about our everyday lives but in a state of statistical stress" (1999, 180). What follows is a commitment to self-regulation to fit into the statistics that promise success rather than into those that predict failure, death, disaster, and so on. These views still pertain to Western societies today, as international political agendas are chiefly concerned with the prevention and management of life threats such as pandemics, environmental disasters, and terrorism, which are presented as paradoxically preventable and inescapable. This future-focused politics engenders self-regulatory strategies, state control mechanisms, and a politics of devolution in which the individual is made to feel responsible for what the future will bring.

This is where *The Encounter* and *887* concur. This is the shared ideology behind both productions: a refusal to accept that life experience is all about what is to come. *The Encounter*'s and *887*'s journeys to the past, their representation, their re-enactment of documenting as a way of understanding the experience of the contemporary subject, and their defence of remembering as an act of resistance are all mechanisms to disturb contemporary society's fascination with this statistic- and control-obsessed future.

Anthony Giddens's article "Risk and responsibility", published in 1999, establishes an important terminological distinction between the risk society understood as a society preoccupied with danger and one that is concerned with the future. Giddens states a key difference between an understanding of risk as a threat to materiality and risk as an ideology, which is resonant in McBurney's and Lepage's pieces. As he suggests:

> The idea of "risk society" might suggest a world which has become more hazardous, but this is not necessarily so. Rather, it is a society increasingly preoccupied with the future (and also with safety), which generates the notion of risk. The idea of risk was first used by Western explorers when they ventured into new waters in their travels across the world. From

> exploring geographical space, it came to be transferred to the exploration of time. (Giddens 1999, 3)

In Giddens's view, the risk society is one "increasingly preoccupied with the future … which generates the notion of risk" (1999, 27). Understood in this way, risk is not only a material threat but a way of understanding the world: an ideology. Thinking about the future, and preventing it from taking particular paths, has become part of the contemporary Western life experience. As Beck explains in his article on the cosmopolitan society (a society to which national borders do not apply, mainly due to the presence of technology), the idea of deterritorialisation, the fragmentation of collective memories, the loss of traditional social structures (religion, family, social class) necessitates a process of "re-traditionalisation", by which new forms of tradition that enable identity formation and facilitate in turn an understanding of the human experience are generated (2002, 27). Beck suggests that in today's societies tradition means "the tradition of the future": a tradition based on a global concern for the future (2002, 27).

This has interesting repercussions. The obsession with the future produces a constant need to calculate the risks in the present that have to be managed and this management, as Giddens suggests, has become central to political decision making: "a good deal of political decision-making is now about managing risks—risks which do not originate in the political sphere, yet have to be politically managed" (1999, 5). As an example, Giddens discusses the bovine spongiform encephalopathy (BSE) crisis in the UK, when decisions about the size of the pandemic and the need to take radical action against its spread—the slaughter of over four million cattle—were, while scientifically informed, taken by politicians. If an obsession with the future brings about the management of risks as a key issue in political agendas, what follows is that, as Lupton suggests, "risk has become a mechanism for understanding social processes", and that it has to occupy a central position when apprehending the functioning of contemporary Western societies (Lupton 2006, 13). In her study on risk and sociology, Lupton summarises a trend within risk studies particularly concerned with governmentality that is useful to my exploration of risk in this chapter. In her view, a society governed by an ideology that is focused on the future issues a form of self-regulation in which individuals are expected and expect to take responsibility for their own actions (2006, 14). This is, as Lupton explains, what Foucault categorised as "disciplinary power", a form of governmentality in which "citizens are not often overtly regulated by oppressive strategies: rather, they are encouraged to adopt certain practices voluntarily as 'good citizens' and in pursuit of their own interests" (2006, 14). Examples of this might be, she explains, wearing a seat belt or eating a healthy diet: forms of self-regulation designed to prevent damage to the human body and ensure the survival of the species. Risk, as an ideology, becomes then a form of governmental control intended to produce good and appropriate behaviour, subservience, and individual versus collective responsibility. The latter is what Beck and Beck-Gernsheim have termed "individualization", an important term to understand the changes that the risk society has brought for the individual, which I will explore later in this chapter. There are two critical points to be made here. Firstly, it is clear that self-regulatory mechanisms are at work in all theatregoing experiences where audience participation is regulated by an invisible but well understood contract, which means that the audience will behave in the ways desired. McBurney and Lepage have no intention to rewrite that contract, and, in fact, their productions are very much in control of audience responses by giving the audience very limited agency, if any. *The Encounter* atomises the audience through the use of technology (the headphones, for example), by producing individual rather than collective experiences, perhaps signalling towards the individualised contemporary society that the audience inhabits in relation to the communal way of life of the Mayoruna. While not actively participatory, the performances encourage a participatory way of life in which individuals and communities regain agency from their dependence on technology: a way of life in which the West burns its material possessions and Lepage remembers his poem without technological aid.

I understand the narratives of past and memory, the foundations on which both *The Encounter* and *887* develop their stories, as responses to contemporary Western society's fixation with the future and its impositions on the individual subject. In *The Encounter*, McBurney's invitation to remember through his own re-enactment of McIntyre's travails is mirrored by the Mayoruna's voyage to the past. When McIntyre, who travels to the Amazon jungle in order to photograph the as yet unknown-to-the-West tribe, finds himself lost, the Mayoruna are his only chance of survival. He decides to follow them in their journey to "the beginning", the sacred place where they will come to an understanding of who they truly are. "The beginning" is a journey to the past in which the tribe will dispose of all material belongings, do away with permanent settlement, and establish a new social hierarchy. It is a gesture pointing to the need to remember as a journey for self-discovery and identity formation. At one of the climactic points of the performance, McBurney, stepping out of character, questions contemporary society's ability to travel to its "beginning". He points to society's dependence on the material world and its inability to control its obsession with the future. This is summarised in a highly theatrical moment in which McBurney, who has hammered down part of the set, stops millimetres away from smashing his smartphone. The Mayoruna's journey up the Amazon River is one of purge and embraces the risk of giving up material belongings in order to overcome the risk of being forgotten, while McBurney is incapable of destroying the object that does the remembering for him. This is how the production represents, in slightly problematic ways, how diametrically opposed the direction of the tribe's and the West's journeys are: as the Mayoruna (the exoticised good) travel to the past, Western societies (inherently evil) fixate their gaze on the future as a way of safeguarding the present.

Safeguarding the present also entails constant documentation. McIntyre's photographs, Popescu's book, McBurney's piece are all efforts to document an event. The link between these texts is established at the production's opening. The need to document the undocumented that drives McIntyre's journeys is also at the heart of McBurney's project. This is seen in the metatheatrical material around the making of the piece found within the production, and also in the extensive documentation of the project itself through the programme notes and McBurney's online diaries that record his own encounter with the Mayoruna tribe for the making of the piece.[4]

Travelling back and forth from London to the Amazon jungle, the production asks the audience to inhabit risk in the in-between space produced by the collision of the virtual and the actual: the virtual jungle representing a set of physical risks and the actual theatre in which the more metaphorical risk of forgetting is being proposed as a key aspect of contemporary human experience. Documenting, through different technologies, is then presented as a solution to this forgetting, and issues of responsibility arise when the production addresses directly what and who should be remembered, how this remembering should happen, and who is responsible for the remembering. The production seems to reject modern technologies and instead defend bodily ways of remembering (tattoos, storytelling, dance, and other rituals). However, in a world where the human and the machine can no longer be separated, *The Encounter* knowingly relies on the technologies and the very strategies that it appears to reject. Remembering is the responsibility of the—technological or not—human subject, McBurney seems to propose.

In Lepage's *887* forgetting is also depicted as a risk. This is represented by the narrative that frames the production. Lepage has been invited to perform a public reading of Michèle Lalonde's famous poem "Speak White", which was originally performed by the poet at the emblematic Nuit de la Poésie in Montréal in March 1970. Lepage builds *887*'s journey to the past around his incapacity to remember the poem and his own anxieties about how his nation will remember him. In various scenes in the play the audience witness Lepage's struggles to learn the poem's lines, and this exploration of memory and what it might do to identity culminates in his reading of the impersonal obituary that a journalist friend has written in anticipation of his death. What cannot be remembered (the Lalonde poem, which speaks to the dominance and oppression of the English over French-speaking Canada) is obscured with what will be remembered: a distorted and subjective vignette of Canadian history metaphorically encapsulated in Lepage's unappreciative obituary. *887* is an attempt to present an alternative to these histories and to demonstrate the role of the individual in the making of those histories and memories. The end of the production is indeed a celebration of the individual as Lepage is able to recite the poem in full and receives a grand applause which overlaps with the applause he receives for *887* when the audience realises that this is also the end of the show they have come to EICC to see.

Forgetting is also depicted as a tangible risk in the production's reflections on dementia. Describing his grandmother's developing dementia, Lepage finds a powerful way to produce a theatrical metaphor that links technology, forgetting, and processes of national identity formation when the fireworks in celebration of Québec's liberation projected on a large screen turn into the malfunctioning neurones of his grandmother's brain in one of the most visually stunning scenes in the show.

The focus on documentation, memory, and remembering that is at the core of the two productions can be understood as what Andreas Huyssen describes as a process of "self-musealization" which consists of constantly documenting and archiving human experience (2000, 24). Huyssen suggests that "we try to counteract this fear of forgetting and danger of forgetting with survival strategies of public and private memorialization" and that "the turn toward memory is subliminally energized by the desire to anchor ourselves in a world characterized by increasing instability of time and the fracturing of lived space" (2000, 28). This is precisely how I think *The Encounter* and *887* function within the context of the risk society. If this is a society focused on the future and thus characterised by uncertainty and instability, the narratives of memory contained in both productions are a gesture towards the stitching together of those fractures in order to make sense of contemporary human experience. In his article "Present pasts: Media, politics, amnesia", Huyssen describes "the emergency of memory as a key concern in Western societies, a turning towards the past" as a paradoxical phenomenon to a sociopolitical Western discourse focused on the future. He clearly describes the turn to the past as a response to what critics consider a media- and technology-aided focus on the future, but intelligently proposes the idea that, as Freud suggested, forgetting and remembering are inextricably linked, that "memory is but another form of forgetting, and forgetting a form of hidden memory" (2000, 27).

If the future is uncertain, however, the past is also unstable. Yet McBurney and Lepage are directing their criticisms at what Huyssen calls "mass-marketed memories", the obsessive media-led frenzy of contemporary societies in McBurney's *The Encounter* and the official historical discourses in Lepage's *887*. As Huyssen suggests, these "mass-marketed memories we consume are 'imagined memories' to begin with, and thus more easily forgotten than lived memories" (2000, 27). This is why both McBurney and Lepage turn precisely to the "lived memories" of individuals as a way of responding to the current prevalence of "mass-marketed" ones. In doing this, they both contain representations of the processes of devolution from the state to the individual that are at the heart of the risk society and that Giddens has signalled as a problematic shift in responsibility in which, as I have previously mentioned, the individual is expected to regulate herself.

These processes of individualisation are important to understand how Beck and Giddens's risk society exerts control. These are mechanisms by which individuals are made to take responsibility for their own actions, made accountable for their decision making, and made responsible for their impact on the wider society. These are what Beck and Beck-Gernsheim have termed the "do it yourself biograph[ies]", the "risk and tightrope biograph[ies]" that are produced by the slow privatisation of the welfare state and the relinquishing of state responsibility (2002, 2). More importantly, as Giddens suggests, this process of devolution from the state to the individual takes place in the context of rising uncertainty. Individuals are asked to make decisions and self-regulate in order to prevent risks that are known but, in many ways, impossible to prevent.

Decision making is an important aspect of the management of risk and an activity central to understanding how individuals and communities relate to and comprehend risk materially and conceptually. The process of making choices is, arguably, far from an activity that demonstrates individual agency and is instead situated at the crossroads of political, social, cultural, and economic agendas. As Alan Hunt suggests:

> Everyday risks present us with the necessity of making a seemingly never-ending set of choices. The significance of these choices is compounded by the disparate pressures of the mechanisms of responsibilization that demand that we make them in a context that requires us to treat our lives as a project over which we should exercise a deliberate and long term calculative effort. (2003, 169)

"Responsibilization" is a process of devolution from the state to the individual, which Ulrich Beck, Anthony Giddens, and Scott Lash recognised as central to their concept of "reflexive modernization". This process means that "individuals are now expected to master 'risky opportunities', without being able, owing to the complexity of modern society, to make the necessary decisions on a well-founded and responsible basis, that is to say, considering the possible consequences" (1994, 8). For the authors, the liberated individual of the late twentieth and early twenty-first centuries is thrown into a world in which "opportunities, threats, ambivalence of the biography, which it was previously possible to overcome in a family group, in the village community or by recourse to a social class or group, must increasingly be perceived, interpreted and handled by individuals themselves" (1994, 8).

Furthermore, making decisions in the context of risk implies trust in contemporary society, and trust is supported by knowledge. Individuals tend to trust what they know and make decisions based on either what they know or the expert knowledge that they trust. This explains the power of global brands, whose logos and products are easily recognisable across the world, and of the production of spaces such as the EICC, a secure location that individuals trust because they recognise it in the same way that they embrace the familiarity of a Starbucks café or a Wagamama restaurant. As Alan Scott explains, individualisation and, more generally, reflexive modernisation imply a return to uncertainty and insecurity (2000, 37). This is why the security provided by spaces such as the EICC is so important to the individual's sense of being in control. Once in the building, individuals become part of a recognised community: theatregoers, the Edinburgh International Festival's audiences who are used to going to the theatre in places like this and who find safety in the knowledge that nothing "risky" will happen in such a place.

In this way, while individualisation can be seen as a positive reclaiming of individual agency, it can also be understood as a problematic shift in responsibility, which leaves the individual vulnerable in the cases of financial and environmental crisis. It is worth thinking about how this shift in responsibility can be mapped on the recent increase in participatory practices in which audiences are made responsible for the theatrical event taking place. Avoiding direct audience participation but tackling individualisation in their narratives and, in *The Encounter*'s case, through the segregation of audience members, the productions are able to expose these questions without replicating their political mechanisms.

The End

The end of the twentieth century and the early twenty-first century were marked by a series of endings: Francis Fukuyama's end of history was a way of establishing democracy as the only possible sociopolitical system (1992); Donna Haraway's end of nature and culture was the birth of naturecultures and a way of finally dismantling the artificial distinction between the wild and the human-made world (2007). In their work, Giddens and Beck also suggest another ending. The end of tradition is that in which traditional social structures such as the family, religious beliefs, and gender roles have been challenged and deemed outdated, giving way to new ways of identity formation (individual and communal). This series of "endings" is also a source of instability and uncertainty and produces and brings a sense of risk to the experience of life in the West.

Theatre practice is not aloof to these changes. The recent increase in immersive and participatory practices, one-to-one performance, and the inclusion of "risky" subjects such as animals, children, and nonprofessional performances in productions are some of the strategies that theatre has utilised to engage critically with the permanent sense of risk that is a feature of contemporary life in the West. As I have argued in this chapter, *The Encounter* and *887* propose more subtle interventions into these enquiries by focusing on some of the features that generate that sense of risk, danger, and feeling of imminent loss. The victorious endings that close the productions depict McBurney finally being able to make his daughter fall asleep while he tells her McIntyre's story after a disruptive night, and Lepage reciting Lalonde's poem publicly in full after a difficult journey to make his memory work. They are peaceful and reflective moments that put an end to the productions' fractured narratives. They signal a shift in pace, the achievement of what seemed impossible at the start. McBurney's soothing storytelling allows him to foreground the importance of ancient ways of identity formation that do not rely on post-industrial technologies. The reading of the book, the comfort of the voice, and the touch are what is needed to finally put an end to the question of how memories are transmitted and how remembering happens. Retraining his brain and using old-fashioned memorising techniques to learn the Lalonde poem, Lepage is also rejecting certain modes of technology and redirecting the responsibility to remember towards the individual. However, these individual subjects (the characters played by McBurney and Lepage) are embedded in communities, as are their learned practices, attitudes, and ways of being. There is a distinct message being suggested in the pieces about the entanglements that are so key to identity formation and how they are facilitated and produced through modern or ancient technologies. There are also questions posed about whose responsibility it is to safeguard those entanglements and the processes by which they happen. These are all key questions that relate to the perception of risk, its management, and its conceptualisation, which both productions chiefly address.

As the audiences leave the safe space of the EICC, the process of decision making, and its attached risks, begins again: where to go, how to get there, what to do—decisions that are tightly linked to identity, culture, time, memory, and also to the learned understandings of risk that the contemporary subject is trained to manage.

Notes

1. Manufacturer's notes.
2. This includes my own work (Orozco 2010), the work included in Claire MacDonald's special issue of *Performance Research* "On Risk", Gareth

White's book on audience participation (2013), and Adam Alston's work (2013).

3. Author's translation from Spanish to English.
4. See McBurney's Amazon Diaries 1 and 2 at https://www.youtube.com/watch?v=ZioqgcYWXVQ and https://www.youtube.com/watch?v=VX2zFnPEj98.

References

Alston, Adam. 2013. Audience Participation and Neoliberal Value: Risk, Agency and Responsibility in Immersive Theatre. *Performance Research* 18 (2): 128–138.

Arendt, Hannah. 1958. *The Human Condition.* Chicago; London: The University of Chicago Press.

Augé, Marc. 1995. *Non-places: Introduction to an Anthropology of Supermodernity.* London: Verso.

Beck, Ulrich. 1992. *Risk Society. Towards a New Modernity.* London; Thousand Oaks; New Delhi: Sage.

Beck, Ulrich. 2002. The Cosmopolitan Society and Its Enemies. *Theory, Culture & Society* 19 (1–2): 17–44.

Beck, Ulrich, and Elisabeth Beck-Gernsheim. 2002. *Individualization. Institutionalized Individualism and its Social and Political Consequences.* London; Thousand Oaks; New Delhi: Sage.

Beck, Ulrich, Anthony Giddens, and Scott Lash. 1994. *Reflexive Modernization. Politics, Tradition and Aesthetics in the Modern Social Order.* Cambridge: Polity Press.

Frizzell, Nell. 2015. Photos are Memories we Hand Over to Clouds. No Wonder they Are so Fragile. (30 November 2015). *The Guardian* online. www.theguardian.com/commentisfree/2015/nov/30/photos-memories-clouds-fragile-apple-pictures-iphone. Accessed 22 Feb 2016.

Fukuyama, Francis. 1992. *The End of History and the Last Man.* London: Penguin.

Gardner, Lyn. 2015. The Greatest Risk in Theatre? Not Taking any Risks. *The Guardian* online (12 August 2015). http://www.theguardian.com/stage/theatreblog/2015/may/12/greatest-risk-in-theatre. Accessed 25 May 2016.

Giddens, Anthony. 1999. Risk and responsibility. *The Law Review* 62 (1): 1–10.

Haraway, Donna. 2007. *When Species Meet.* Minneapolis; London: University of Minnesota Press.

Hunt, Alan. 2003. Risk and moralization in everyday life. In *Risk and Morality*, ed. Richard Ericson and Aaron Doyle, 165–192. Toronto; Buffalo; London: University of Toronto Press.

Huyssen, Andreas. 2000. Present Pasts: Media, Politics, Amnesia. *Public Culture* 12 (1): 21–38.

Kearney, Richard. 2002. *On Stories (Thinking in Action)*. London; New York: Routledge.

Lupton, Deborah. 2006. Sociology and Risk. In *Beyond the Risk Society: Critical Reflections on Risk and Human Security*, eds. Gabe Mythen, and Sandra Walklate, 11–24. London: Open University Press.

Manufacturer's notes. Neumann Head Microphone. https://www.neumann.com/?lang=en&id=current_microphones&cid=ku100_description.

Orozco, Lourdes. 2010. Never Work with Children and Animals: Risk, Mistake and the Real in Performance. *Performance Research* 15 (2): 80–85.

Scott, Alan. 2000. Risk Society or Angst Society? Two Views of Risk, Consciousness and Community. In *The Risk Society and Beyon: Critical Issues for Social Theory*, ed. Barbara Adam, Ulrich Beck and Joost Van Loon, 33–46. London; Thousand Oaks; New Delhi: Sage.

Spitzer, Manfred. 2013. *Demencia Digital. El peligro de las nuevas tecnologías* (in Spanish from original in German). Barcelona: Ediciones B.

Spitzer, Manfred. 2014. Information Technology in Education: Risks and Side Effects. *Trends in Neuroscience and Education* 3 (3–4): 81–85.

White, Gareth. 2012. On Immersive Theatre. *Theatre Research International* 37 (3): 221–235.

White, Gareth. 2013. *Audience Participation in Theatre: Aesthetics of the Invitation*. Basingstoke: Palgrave Macmillan.

Woodward, Kathleen. 1999. Statistical panic. *Differences: A Journal of Feminist Cultural Studies* 11 (2): 177–203.

Putting Prejudices on the Spot and in the Spotlight: The Risks of Politically Motivated Public Space Performance Practices

Bree Hadley

Introduction

The term "participatory performance" typically refers to live art, performance art, or installation practices in public spaces in which performers and spectators both play an active role. Of course, all theatrical performance is participatory in the sense that spectators' laughter, cheers, tears, or applause can affect the way the event flows, feels, and makes meaning. What distinguishes work under the participatory performance umbrella is the emphasis on the active participation of spectators as co-creators whose attitudes, actions, and choices can actually change the way the event unfolds. This active participation is frequently favoured by artists who want to use the power of performance to transform spectators' perspectives or positions on political issues. For these politically motivated artists, participation provides unique opportunities to put spectators on the spot and in the spotlight in order to

B. Hadley (✉)
Queensland University of Technology, Brisbane, Australia
e-mail: bree.hadley@qut.edu.au

© The Author(s) 2017

A. O'Grady (ed.), *Risk, Participation, and Performance Practice*,
DOI 10.1007/978-3-319-63242-1_3

interrogate their role as co-creators of current cultural realities (Hadley 2014). Well-known works such as Aaron Williamson and Katherine Araniello's *Assisted Passage* (2007), which asks passers-by to react to a petition to send the disabled Araniello to Switzerland where assisted suicide is allowed, or Guillermo Gómez-Peña and Coco Fusco's *Two Undiscovered Amerindians Visit* (1992), which asks bystanders to react to a Latin American couple in a cage, or Yoko Ono's *Cut Piece* (1964), which asks passers-by to react to a request to cut a woman's clothing off, all use similar strategies. They unfold in public spaces and places, and use controversy as a way of provoking participation. The artist enacts an ableist, racist, or sexist scenario that typically plays out in that same public space—sometimes with exaggeration, abstraction, or artifice, and sometimes with so much subtlety it is difficult to distinguish it from daily life. They invite the passer-by to become a co-creator in a daily-cum-dramatic performance of this social situation. In doing so, the artists put the spectators' choices on display, so fellow spectators and society at large can judge their insightful, stereotyped, or prejudiced reaction to people marked by disability, race, gender, or other differences. The encounter becomes risky, not just for the artist, but also for the passer-by-cum-co-creator, who may not want to be vulnerable to the charge that they have responded to marginalised others in an inappropriate way.

In this chapter I want to investigate the ethics of participatory public space performances that ask both artist and spectator to take the risk that their attitudes, actions, and choices will be judged. In particular, I want to investigate the ethics of practices that judge spectators' attitudes towards socially, culturally, or politically sensitive topics such as disability, race, or gender without clear consent. For the purposes of this chapter I will concentrate on practices that judge spectators' attitudes towards begging, unemployment, underemployment, homelessness, disability, and appropriate behaviour towards beggars encountered in public space. I will use the ethical performance theory of Hans-Thies Lehmann, together with the risk theory of Mary Douglas, Ulrich Beck, and Jens O. Zinn, to analyse a series of performances designed to showcase spectators' attitudes towards beggars by artists as diverse as Kim Sooja, Debi Oulu, and Carina Reich and Bogdan Szyber. Though they differ in performance style, structure, and intent, what these performances share is a strategy that sees them engage passers-by in public streets as unwitting—and thus potentially unwilling—spectators in the work.

What makes these practices risky is the fact that they force artists and spectators alike to engage with an event that is both a daily reality and a dramatic representation of a reality designed to critique it at once. In cultural theories of risk, particularly those based on the anthropological theories of Mary Douglas (1985), a risk is defined as a threat to a person's well-being that comes from the crossing of a symbolic, social, safety, or legal boundary. To take a risk is to take part in an activity that could potentially cause a person to cross the boundary from safe to non-safe, sanctioned to non-sanctioned, profitable to non-profitable, or some other border. Of course, as Jens O. Zinn says, what is considered safe, sanctioned, status-improving, or profitable is determined by "socialcultural and individual values" (2008, 4) and thus also by the authorities that hold power in a given culture at a given time. The risk comes from the fact that the outcomes of these potentially transgressive or transformative activities are uncertain. Though taking a risk is often framed in negative terms in what Ulrich Beck (1986) calls today's "risk society", taking a risk is in fact often a necessary part of personal, social, or political life. To succeed in life, a person often needs to try something new in their family relations, friendships, social life, work life, or business to try to improve their status, to innovate, or to create change. The activity can be fraught, pressure-filled, or conflicted, though, because there is no way to be certain about the outcomes and consequences beforehand. What makes the performances in focus in this chapter risky is the fact that the works deliberately blur the boundaries between dramatic performances in which a spectator can engage without consequences and daily social performances in which a spectator cannot engage without consequences. This dual status creates what Hans-Thies Lehmann (2006) calls an uncertainty at the heart of the encounter. This uncertainty makes it more difficult for spectators to respond to this practice than to purely representational theatre practice. The spectators find it more challenging to try to perform the "right" response but, at the same time, feel more pressure to perform the "right" response. This creates the conditions of possibility for an ethical encounter because it makes it more likely that spectators will pause, reflect on what they see, reflect what they think of it, and reflect on what they think of their own response to it. For advocates, this is precisely what gives participatory performance the power to prompt a change of perception in the spectators who find themselves pulled into this ethical face-to-face encounter. For activist artists, spotlighting the spectators' role in co-creating the daily social dramas of ableism, racism, or sexism is risky but worthwhile because it makes spectators responsible for their own role in constructing an inclusive or non-inclusive society. No longer silent, comfortable, and safe in a darkened theatre, these spectators have to respond, and reflect on how they respond, in a more thorough way. At the same time, though, the fact that spectators are often drawn into these encounters without having consented—or, at least, without having bought a ticket and planned to come—paradoxically also raises questions about the ethics of the encounter.

Investigating a set of begging performances that use these strategies provides a useful platform for examining the potential benefits as well as the ethical paradoxes of works where spectators suddenly find their own point of view subject to public scrutiny. It thus provides a useful opportunity to discuss why performers, spectators, and society might be willing to take the risks that come with this sort of work. Analysing these practices here I will argue that, for many of the artists, there is a belief that they have to put themselves, their spectators, and society at risk in order to have real conversations, with real others, and thus genuinely take each other out of the comfort zone where growth and change is not always possible. Allowing any of the parties—themselves, their spectators, or the society in which they come together—to stay in their comfort zone would thwart the potential of the encounter in political and ethical terms.

Performing Beggars and Begging

The beggar is, as Paola Pugliatti (2003) argues, a problematic figure in depictions of public space, relationships, and power on Western stages and screens. In traditional plays, performances, and popular culture the beggar who asks strangers for food, money, or other means to survive has typically been portrayed as a figure of tragedy, pity, or fear, and thus used as a shortcut to signify the threat supposedly non-productive people can present to Western culture. This means the beggar can induce complex emotions in many people, including guilt, righteousness, and indignation, as the request for a charitable contribution to the beggar forces the passer-by to decide if this person is a victim of misfortune on whom they should take pity or a lazy malingerer who does not want to take care of themselves.

In the twenty-first century, as discourses of austerity compete with discourses of social justice, sharing, sustainability, and the need to take care of others—including others affected by capitalist economic paradigms—it is not surprising that many activist artists have taken a new interest in interrogating the figure of the beggar. There are dozens of examples of public space performances about begging being produced by artists today. The range of issues these artists explore is diverse. They include questions about attitudes towards the poor, unemployed, disabled, and other supposedly non-productive citizens. They also include questions about art and commodity in a context where some artists see themselves being stereotyped as "non-productive" in a globalised, capitalist society with little concern for individuality and individual sensation, emotion, or enjoyment. In *Begging: The Performance* (2013), Daniel Lozano begs for a sex change, in places around Paris, to make the point that this might be a matter of survival for some people more visible to mainstream cisgendered society. In an untitled action, Edgar Askelovic (2011) places a mannequin of Queen Elizabeth II in a Birmingham street with a sign that reads "Donation for Blessing of England", to draw attention to how talk of crisis in his native Lithuania differs from talk of crisis in his adoptive Britain, and how well off British beggars are compared to some people (Daily Mail Reporter 2011). In *Begging for a Chanel* (2010), Yolanda Dominquez uses begging performance to comment on consumerist, capitalist sensibilities that bring us to the beggars' plight (Dominquez 2010). In *Gimme, Gimme, Gimme* (2007), Kjetil Skøien uses begging performance, plus lecture, in festival precincts around Scandinavia to show the historical connection between art and begging (Performance Art Oslo, n.d.). In another untitled action, Erykah Badu (2014) uses begging performance to draw attention to how little people value her work as a musician (Bradford 2014; Sargeant 2014). In *BEGGING #1: Detoxification of Preconceptions About Money* (2012), Dana Fain fasts and begs people for forward-thinking solutions to integrate art into current economic models, to benefit the whole community. She then begs for money for her own art and, in doing so, tries to get spectators to make their systems of values more visible.

These, along with dozens of other journalistic (more so than artistic) "secret camera stunts" to see and show the world how passers-by will respond to beggars and begging, all show the complexity of the issue and the potential people see in public space performance to politicise around the issue.

Here, I want to look a little more closely at three performances of begging, each presenting begging as participatory performance in very different ways—an installation and street performance by Kim Sooja, a street performance by Debi Oulu, and an installation-cum-art-intervention by Carina Reich and Bogdan Szyber.

Kim Sooja—A Beggar Woman

In *A Beggar Woman* and *A Homeless Woman* (2000–2001), Korean-born New York- and Paris-based artist Kim Sooja presents a series of pieces inspired by homeless people, particularly homeless women, who sleep on the streets. Wanting to "[f]eel and understand their position" (Sooja, quoted in Smith 2013), Sooja created these pieces in which she presents herself sitting or lying in a meditative position in a public space. Originally presented as a solo piece in Times Square in New York City, this work was later presented in and around the Vancouver Art Gallery (2013), with "a group of people [sitting] in meditative yet sculptural begging positions amid the masses of partygoers" (Smith 2013) at a Friday night FUSE event. Sooja has also presented similar works around the world such as *A Homeless Woman—Delhi* (2000), where she lay down in a busy streetscape (cf. Goodman 2003), and other works in Mexico City, Cairo, and Lagos (Art21 2009).

With *A Beggar Woman*, *A Homeless Woman*, and the various iterations of these related works in various cities, Sooja blurs the boundaries between art and life, the actual beggar and the artistic representation of a beggar, to see how passers-by or partygoers will respond to someone sitting in a public space in such a vulnerable position. "I didn't know if I'd be taken as a real beggar", Sooja says, reflecting on the work presented in Vancouver (2013), until "a man quite far away stood for a while, not moving, then I immediately felt this man will give me money. Then I suddenly felt so vulnerable and realised I'd become a real beggar now" (Sooja, quoted in Smith 2013). A silent statement on need, and social responses to need, Sooja's piece focuses on the vulnerabilities of the beggar and other needy human beings. For Sooja, as for many contemporary performance artists, it was important that the piece was recorded, documented, and then disseminated to other spectators online on her own YouTube site (Sooja, n.d.) and other press and commentary websites (Smith 2013; Art21 2009). A silent, still, and meditative style of performance art, as suited to an installation as to a street, in which, as Sooja says, "[m]y body becomes like a stone on the street, it's nothing more than that, [and] everything has equal value in this situation" (Sooja, quoted in Smith 2013), *Beggar Woman: Conditions of Anonymity* is subtle in the calls it makes on spectators. As Jonathan Goodman (2003) argues, it is political, but its politics operates by means of affect, rather than by means of actual direct demand for social action about the needs, interests, or desires of marginalised citizens. "There is a tremendous strength and assertion in her apparently anonymous actions", he says, "which are not so much transgressions as they are recognitions of fate" (ibid.). These actions, for Goodman, force spectators to reflect on the universality of the situation or struggles represented. The work, he says, uses "the anonymous as a metaphor for the wish to merge with forces and circumstances usually acting against the forthright assertion of self" (ibid.).

In public space, *A Beggar Woman* invites passers-by to become players in the drama Sooja creates. In public space, the pose has a likeness to life—it could be a reality. However, it also has an aesthetic and locative flag when it is situated in or near a gallery—it could be a representation rather than a real reality, a fiction rather than a fact, that has come outside the closed doors of the art institution. This dual status encourages spectators to engage with the work more thoughtfully. In later documentation online, a secondary group of spectators can engage with the initial reactions from passers-by, as well as reflect on their own reactions had they been called on to become a player in this sort of public space encounter. In this sense, Sooja says, "[a]nother encounter occurs when audiences see the video resulting from my performance. My body functions as a barometer, as a needle connecting people from a different time and space" (Sooja, quoted in Smith 2013). Together, these strategies are what makes Sooja's work challenging to respond to, and what makes the spectators' challenges in responding visible to the public to consider too.

Debi Oulu—Begging for Youth

In *Begging for Youth*, Debi Oulu, an interdisciplinary installation and performance artist, presents a very different style of public space participatory performance to interrogate the relationship between beggars, passers-by, and society. As an artist interested in creating conversations and communications between people, often about core concerns such as sexuality, humanity, and life itself, Oulu often brings her art into contact

Fig. 1 Photos courtesy of Debi Oulu – Begging For Youth

with people in everyday settings such as bus stations, schools, nightclubs, and public streets (Oulu n.d.) Fig. (1).

Performed outside P8 Gallery in Tel Aviv in 2013, *Begging for Youth* was about the fact that, as an artist and a woman approaching 50, Oulu was becoming conscious of how those not young, and not productive, were not so visible in social and professional situations. "When women reach the 'granny' stage in their appearance", Oulu says, "they are largely ignored by society and treated as redundant if not completely invisible" (ibid.). In this piece, in public space, Oulu used slogans—"48 Years Old, Mother of 3, Needs to make art to SURVIVE" and "Will make art for money"—to draw people's attention to this phenomenon. "I was open to passers-by to talk with me, argue with me, there was no 'hiding'", she says, reflecting on the piece, and "[i]t was amazing how many people stopped to talk about the issue, all with very strong reactions" (ibid.). The work created a clear opportunity to call passers-by into conversation about these issues, and the fact, as Oulu says, that "we need to change our attitude towards things that are 'old', 'broken', 'used', whether it is electronic equipment, clothing, or people" or these ignored not-quite-citizens "will become a heavy burden financially as well as socially". For the artist, however, being in "the position of the homeless beggar" (ibid.) also made her feel uncomfortable. "I felt no matter which cardboard sign I used, it still felt like I was 'crying' poor old me", (ibid.), she says, signalling the complexities of the issue.

Oulu's attempts to draw people into her performative intervention on the issue of begging created complexity and uncertainty, for herself and her spectators. Again, Oulu's work had a likeness to life. Again, though, Oulu's work also had the locative flag of being outside a gallery, together with the "artist" references in the signs, to position it as more than merely a moment in daily life. The performance blurred the boundaries between art and life, an actual beggar and an artist's representation of a beggar, in a public space, to bring passers-by into the piece. The passers-by became co-creators of the conversations that unfolded. It was, though, far more active and interactive because it moved from an installation aesthetic to a more street or community art or even protest-style aesthetic. This community protest-style aesthetic is clearly captured in the documentation of the piece on Oulu's website, where still photos show passers-by stepping right into the piece with the signs. In Oulu's piece, as in Sooja's piece, the documentation makes the spectators visible to the public and vulnerable to public judgement, whether they are aware of this new role they have taken on or not.

Carina Reich and Bogdan Szyber—Persondesign

Persondesign (2012), by Swedish artists Carina Reich and Bogdan Szyber, together known as Reich+Szyber, is a little different from the other works discussed here in that it is part of a bigger project, called *Beggars Saturday*, "a three-year art project about trust, shame, guilt and revenge ... loosely based on Shakespeare's *Titus Andronicus*" (Reich + Szyber n.d.). A response to constraints on welfare and reactions to Romany beggars coming to Sweden, *Persondesign* asks what a person can rightfully ask for, and rightfully expect to receive, as well as what a passer-by will give, in a begging encounter in a city street or space. "Almost without exception", Reich and Szyber say, reflecting on their relation to beggars, "while being out [i]n town, we actively tried in various ways to ignore the beggars and look away (this was especially evident in meetings inside subway cars), and soon after such an encounter we felt a vague sense of discomfort" (ibid.). What they describe is, as noted earlier, a sense of discomfort not common in social reactions to beggars Fig. (2).

Fig. 2 Photos courtesy of Reich + Szyber – Persondesign

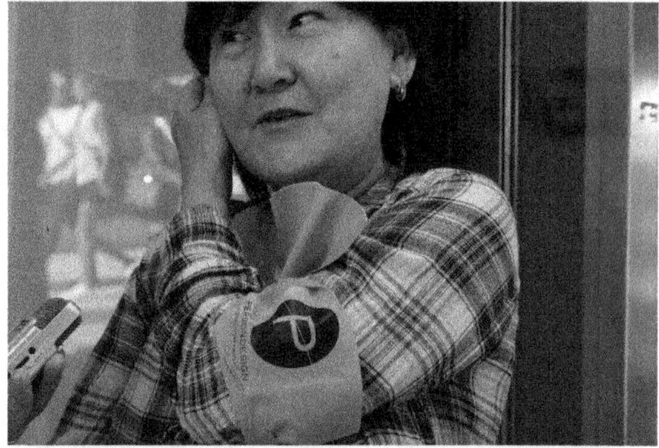

Swedish charity seeks to employ 'beggars'

Published: 9 Aug 12 15:37 CET | Double click on a word to get a translation

A Swedish charity has placed an ad in a magazine, looking to hire beggars to work the streets of Stockholm. The idea is that it will be lucrative for both the charity and the employees.

In *Persondesign*, the artists wanted to see what would be required to get people to look, give, and get beyond guilty feelings in this sort of begging encounter. They did this by means of a hoax announcing a new beggar business called Persondesign and advertising for people who might want to be employed by this business. They then got the people to beg for whatever they wanted—money, jewellery, pricey paintings, a birthday gift for grandmother, or teeth—and gave them 100 kroner an hour to do this, plus half the money they managed to beg, over four hours, on the streets. In the meantime, seven beggar hosts talked to passers-by about this business. The "art" context made the project impotent, Reich and Szyber felt, so they had to say the art was actually a business to get the public and press interest they would not otherwise get. They had to use a young entrepreneur—Per Johnson—to help change the context. In doing this, the artists were, clearly, tapping into the idea that things need to be marketable to be meaningful in the new world economy, and those producing them need to be entrepreneurs. They were, they say (ibid.), experimenting with what they saw as a marketing model applied to pain, suffering, need, and desire, to see how passers-by would respond. In the process, they were also taking this marketing of suffering outside the safe (and not so impactful) black or white box into the (impactful) online and offline public agora or square. "In a fully economized worldview a business idea that offers a street begging service, isn't any remarkable phenomenon", they say, and "[t]he thought experiment to apply a market-oriented commercial model on alms praying and need, allowing so to speak the entrepreneurial template to overflow wider areas of our relationships to each other, can possibly reveal, for us all, something about the contemporary life" (ibid.).

In the eventual piece, 35 beggars of all different ages, genders, and races allowed Reich and Szyber to gather a lot of information about people's attitudes to begging, reported in their recording and documentation of the piece on their website, for later spectators to see and judge. They found that being specific—saying teeth, rather than just survival—made a beggar more successful. Extravagances, for example jewellery, made nothing. But, surprisingly, non-essential little luxuries such as teeth got the most, more than rent, which flagged people as really poor. Swedish beggars were more successful than Romany beggars. Clearly, people wanted to help the working poor, those working hard to get by, to get those little extras the middle class take for granted, but were not willing to help those who they suspected were poor and homeless simply because they were not working to pay for food, rent, or clothing. In this way, Reich + Szyber's participatory public space performance confirmed some of their worst suspicions about society: who matters, who does not, who gets help, and who does not, and why.

The piece, with its hoax dimensions, did garner a lot of interest—for example, requests for radio interviews—with some commentators understanding, some angry, and some confused by a piece that used prankish practices that could be critiqued as unethical to raise questions about ethics. The responses to the questions about how we deal with people's needs and desires thus raised questions, dealt with at length on Reich + Szyber's website. This piece is, in many ways, much more complex than either the Sooja or Oulu public space performances. It is much more open to criticism in that it takes too many risks and thus becomes unethical. The piece relies on a complex conceit to set up everyday encounters in public space. It has a likeness to life but, clearly, ramps it up with the "entrepreneurial" frame placed around the begging to start bringing it out of day-to-day life. It invites both participants and passers-by to get involved, actively, and, in doing so, generate the information about their own and others' responses to beggars and begging that would be later be recorded, documented, and analysed in such detail on Reich + Szyber's website.

Putting Prejudices on the Spot and in the Spotlight

What these participatory public space performances share is more than just an interest in investigating Western society's attitude to people who—as a result of being underemployed, disenfranchised, disabled, or simply unable to find a market to pay for their art—have to beg. Though they differ in style, structure, and intent, these performances all highlight the productivity-orientated paradigms by which Western citizens have been taught to read beggars and begging in drama and in daily life. They all do this by presenting a beggar in public space and asking passers-by to respond to this beggar in some way. In doing so, they strategically blur the boundaries between representation and real life. The spectators are confronted with a situation they do not immediately know how to respond to, and questions they do not immediately know how to answer, factors that are, for Nicholas Ridout (2009), the very things that create the conditions of possibility for an ethical encounter. Accordingly, the spectators feel more pressure to respond but, at the same time, more confusion about how to respond. The performances all document the spectators' responses so that fellow spectators and society can judge them. The goal is to show spectators and society that these are cultural constructs, which could be changed, should the individuals involved choose to change them.

On the one hand, the artists stage begging this way to prompt spectators to reflect on the fact that they do have the power to challenge the social realities they encounter in public space. The politics of these interventions, at least in the immediate moment, is not what Elizabeth Grosz (1999, 171–173) calls a "programmed" approach to political progress in which potential futures are planned, mapped out, and pursued in logical, linear, chronological time, with transformations taking place step by step over years or decades. It is, rather, what Grosz (ibid.) calls a "non-programmed" approach to political progress in which an activist artist takes a chance that deviations, disruptions, or deterritorialisations in the flow of time will produce sudden shifts in perception, attitude, and action. The passer-by-cum-performer is put on the spot, forced to improvise their actions, reactions, and answers on the spot. If the terms of the encounter become so confusing that ready-made reactions no longer seem to apply, then new responses or reflections might have to emerge. The uncertainty, undecidability, and mixed messages in the performances thus create room for novel or unpredictable responses to emerge. This, as I have argued elsewhere (Hadley 2014), following the ethical theory of Lehmann (2006), is because this undecidability creates a deferral in meaning making, a liminal moment in which a passer-by has to work out whether to apply the responses history, memory, and habit provide, riff off those responses, or improvise a new response. In this moment, a passer-by can find themselves vulnerable. This vulnerability can show up in embarrassment, laughter, giggles, an urge to pull away, or even at times aggression (Hadley 2014), indicating the passer-by's attempts to cover an awkward moment in which they are faced with something they do not know how to respond to. Prising performers and spectators alike out of the flow of things, these performative interventions can—potentially, though not predictably—produce intensities of sensations that cause people to stop, think, and then do things differently—if not in this moment then in the future.

On the other hand, however, artists also stage begging this way to prompt the secondary spectators to judge the first spectators' insightful, stereotyped, or prejudiced response to the beggars. In doing so, they create the follow-on, the far more programmed, step-by-step approach to political action. The secondary audience, who see the documentation, lectures, or later in-theatre showings of the footage—often with artist commentary now attached, as in Sooja's, Oulu's, and Reich + Szyber's works—have much more time, space, and safety to think about what they have seen in a more conventional theatrical context. Accordingly, they have much more time, space, and safety to think about whether they want to be like those initial spectators or not. These documentations and commentaries thus become equally performative and equally important to the political potential of the work—which, as Amelia Jones and Adrian Heathfield say in *Perform, Repeat, Record: Live Art in History* (2012, 181), is why it is sometimes so difficult to distinguish the performance from the performative documentation of it in this sort of work.

For advocates, participatory performance practices work because they "emancipate" the spectator, in Jacques Rancière's (2011) terms. They enact the democratisation that Susan Bennett had already a decade earlier identified "not only as a desirable, but as a crucial, aspect of new developments in performance and theory" (1997, 10). They establish a more balanced set of power relations, in which artists and spectators are more equally responsible for the way a work unfolds in the moment, the way it makes meaning, and the way it makes an impact in the public sphere in the days, weeks, or months to follow—though, of course, that the work considered here unfolds in public space rather than in private for a paying audience complicates the power relations in this sort of participatory performance. For the artists, the pleasure and power of this style of performance comes from the fact that it enables them to "elicit perverse, disturbing, and pleasurable experiences that enlarge [the spectators'] capacity to imagine the world and our relations anew" (Bishop 2012, 284). For the spectators, the pleasure and power of this style of performance come from the fact that it enables them to play a part, think about the part they play, and, at least potentially, think about playing their part differently next time they see a situation like this in daily life. If this works well, it can lead to the change in social relations that underpins the agenda and ambitions of many practitioners of politicised participatory performance.

For detractors, however, participatory performance practices also present problems and risks for all involved—the artist, the spectator, and society. Amongst the most well recognised is the risk to the artist, in particular the risk that the artist's work will be misread as part of the problem it is trying to challenge. The ephemerality of the work, and the participatory, collaborative, co-creative emphasis of the work, means it is not finished until the moment the spectator steps into it (Bennett 1997, 20; cf. Lehmann 2006). This makes it difficult for even the most confident artist to be certain of the meaning, impact, and short-, medium-, or long-term legacy of their work. They cannot know how spectators will react, because those reactions are plural, unpredictable, and dependent on the spectators' individual positions in the social field, their personal impression management practices, and their personal idiosyncrasies. The work is open to out-of-the-ordinary responses, misreadings, and even violent opposition. The point can be missed. The point can be taken, prompting the change of perception for the single spectator that theorists such as Nicholas Bourriaud (1998) position as the most critical to the political power of participatory performance, but still fail to prompt the move from thought to action in the public sphere. Indeed, there are those, such as Claire Bishop, who doubt that individual changes in perception can ever create a political impact large enough to become more than "harmless and unthreatening to social and cultural stability" (2012, 190). At a certain point, Bishop argues, "art has to hand over to other institutions if social change is to be achieved: it is not enough to keep producing activist art" (ibid., 283).

A less recognised risk is the risk to the spectator. Putting the spectator's role as co-creator on the spot and in the spotlight, in the moment, and in the documentation of the moment shown on a website, in a lecture, in a later performance, or in a retrospective puts the spectator at risk. They can feel uncertain, vulnerable, and pressured in their responses. However, this type of work does not just invite the spectator to reflect on their response in their own private space and time. It invites a whole range of spectators—the initial spectator encountering the work in a public space, secondary spectators seeing the encounter in that public space, and still other secondary spectators seeing the encounter in the documentation the artist circulates—to reflect on that first spectator's response. Indeed, at least part of the power of the work comes from the fact that it positions that first spectator to play out their insightful, stereotyped, or prejudiced attitude towards the character or scenario staged, so they become fodder for fellow spectators and society to judge. The performer often prompts the first spectator to take on the role of the oppressor to show the second spectator how strange the oppressor's prejudices seem. The first spectator thus often becomes the representation of the problematic attitudes to the poor that the performers want to make a political point about. This creates a risk that the initial spectator will become the subject of public debate about beggars, begging, and the level of benevolence in Western society going forward. It thus raises questions about whether the collaborative, co-creative, democratic relations that characterise participatory performance are in fact as democratic as they are often touted to be, or whether the spectator is at risk of becoming an object rather than an active player with agency in the encounter.

In raising these risks as part of their effort to create an ethical face-to-face encounter, and the personal and political change that can come of it, these works are in many ways tapping into spectators' worse fears. As Gareth White (2007, 2013) says, while participatory performance carries many risks—psychological, physical, social, in relation to enjoyment in democratic states, or in relation to more extreme consequences in non-democratic states—the risk of being "embarrassed" is amongst the biggest. "To expose your thoughts or emotions in a public event like this is risky", White says, because "there is a chance of public embarrassment by revealing too much or by failing to look competent" (White 2007, 6). In these types of performances, the spectators' struggles with awkwardness, embarrassment, vulnerability, and even anger at the fact that their habitual behaviours are being highlighted and interrupted can come out all too clearly. These struggles are influenced not just by literacy, prejudices, and personal impression management practices, but also by self-consciousness, the sense of being on the spot. The spectators' struggles—insightful, ignorant, or otherwise—become the story, the thing for fellow spectators and society to think about while watching the performance.

Risky Relations

The political strategy behind performance of this sort is clear. The practices are participatory, collaborative, and co-creative, and thus potentially democratic and emancipatory, in Rancière's (2011) terms, because both performer and spectator hold power to determine the way things unfold. However, if the artists are presenting these pieces deliberately, and even deceptively if spectators do not know their choices will become fodder for public judgement, to make the artist's point about prejudice, there is a question about how democratic, emancipatory, and ethical they really are. Are the artists inviting passers-by to become co-creators of a face-to-face ethical encounter upon which a democratic political debate about sensitive topics such as begging, unemployment, homelessness, and disability can be built? Or are they turning their spectators into puppets to make their own point about people's attitudes, actions, and choices? Certainly, the political reason for highlighting the spectators' co-creative role in constructing the daily social drama of beggars and begging is clear, and in some cases effective, evocative, and/or entertaining. The question beneath, though, is whether the work really is activating the spectators' political agency. Are the artists asking spectators into a democratic public debate? Or are the artists alienating spectators within that debate?

In these works, for all their uncertainty, the artists do take control over the style, scope, and degree of agency displayed in the participation, what White calls the "horizon of participation" (2013, 60), via the forms of invitation, the offers, the counter-offer, and the relative level of likeness to life. They determine the choices called for, the gaps in which choices can be inserted, the range of potential responses, and, therefore, what White calls "a limit, and a range of potentials within that limit" (ibid., 59). There are flags to show this is an invitation to perform—the signs, the symbolic poses, the sheer volume of publicity around the new begging business, and so forth. In some cases, though, these could be missed by people who might otherwise just be on their way to work, not thinking as deeply about their response as they might if they received this invitation in a theatre or a community hall. This is positive, in the sense that these strategies mean this is not the "banal, mundane, deadly" participatory art of which commentators such as Bishop (2012) have become so critical (Henry 2012). But this is also potentially problematic in that the participants' level of control over the call to perform, choices available, and context is limited. There is, in particular, a risk that artists who favour this sort of intervention—which provokes spectators to perform particular sorts of responses to beggars, more sympathetic in Sooja's work, more social in Oulu's work, and more selective and judgemental in Reich + Szyber's work—might be dealing with spectators' identities in reductive, prankish ways in order to set them up for the later documentation: a risk, in other words, that the non-programmed politics of the acts in the real-time moment are simply servicing the more programmed political activity that comes afterwards via retrospective commentary on them in footage or a more heavily framed in-theatre show. In this later footage, lecture, or in-theatre show, of course, the subsequent spectators will at least know they are part of a performance. They will be safely protected in the knowledge that fellow spectators will not see and judge what they think while they watch. Accordingly, they will not face the same risks as the initial spectators.

There can be no definitive answers to the question of why so many artists find a practice with such paradoxes so powerful and worth pursuing as part of their political agenda. This said, a partial or provisional answer lies in the fact that for many artists who work this way, there is always already an acceptance that notions of democracy, and democratic public debate, are never all that democratic. As Chantal Mouffe (2005) notes, the dominant definition of democracy is tied to ideas of freedom, and progress, by means of community consensus. The actuality of democracy, however, is more one of fraught relationships, and conflict, in which there are always power plays, winners, losers, and moments of wounded pride, as consensus balances precariously against a binary of included/excluded, and the pace and pattern of change in who is included or excluded in a consensus model remain unpredictable. This is the actuality of democracy, in theatre as in other arenas. This means that attempts at democratic engagement in theatre, as in other arenas, are themselves always already fraught with personal, social, and political risk. To take part in democratic activity and debate is to get involved in an activity that presents a threat to status, because it brings players to the point where they are playing with the boundaries between agency and non-agency, power and non-power, and inclusion and non-inclusion, and none of these players can predict outcomes before taking part. To take part in democratic activity and debate is, therefore, inherently risky for all involved.

Working with this more nuanced notion of what it means to be involved in a public debate, artists working in this type of performance put both themselves and their spectators at risk of being upset, judged, or judged to be on the wrong side of culture, conflict, or history. Indeed, some artists put themselves and their spectators at risk of aggression, abuse, or violence if it turns out that some of the participants they pull into the encounter feel very threatened by it (Hadley 2014)—though this is not something Sooja, Oulu, or Reich+Szyber have noted in their commentary on the works considered in this chapter. For these artists, though, this is a risk worth taking because it is the only way to create the conditions of possibility for changes in perception, interpretation, and co-created cultural legacies. It is the only way to create encounters that can lead to changes in perspective, position, or cultural paradigm. As noted at the outset, risk taking is a necessary part of personal, social, and political life. "The notion of *risk taking*", as Zinn puts it, "refers to a positive and a negative side as a weighing up between gains and losses" (2008, 58, italics in original). If people are not taking risks, by choice, by compulsion, or by a combination of the two as in the sort of work considered here, they are not going to be in a position to experience positive change or growth. They will not experience anything but a stagnant status quo. As result, the value placed on participating in risky activities with the potential to bring positive gains in the form of change, growth, or profit is increasing in what Beck (1986) calls the "risk society" of the late twentieth and early twenty-first centuries. In a "risk society" negotiating risk is a critical priority for all participants in the culture. At times, though, negotiating risk means experiencing it rather than escaping it. This, according to Stephen Lyng (2008), is why so many people say that it is only when they are participating in what he calls "edgework"—practices that play at the edge, in the liminal space between safety and non-safety, sanction and non-sanction, and status and non-status—that they feel truly alive with possibility, potentiality, and the capacity to grow and change.

For artists creating performances of the sort I have considered here, this practice is a form of edgework. It creates the conditions of possibility for change, and growth, and new relationships between people, even if the outcomes necessarily remain unpredictable. For these artists, the ethical encounter, and the political change that can follow on from it, is created by coming face to face with the specific, complex, messy, difficult to deal with little "o" others, who can confirm, challenge, and change the artist's own views as readily as the artist can change theirs, not by coming face to face with the universalised, clear, clean, culturally sanctioned, capital "O" Other (cf. Hadley 2014). That is, the ethical encounter is created by coming face to face with the specific reality of a person in the street, who might become upset or unpredictable or angry (what I mean by little "o" other), rather than the universalised representation of a persona or character in the mainstage theatre, who might not be upsetting, unpredictable, or provocative enough to really push people to have to think about that character anew (what I mean by capital "O" other).

Clearly, this "edgework" does make the encounter uncertain, unpredictable, and sometimes uncomfortable and open to questions about its ethics. There is risk and vulnerability and the possibility of losses as much as gains for artists and for spectators, as Sooja, Oulu, and Reich+Szyber all noted when speaking of moments of discomfort in presenting the works considered here. There is a risk that the artist's identity will be reduced to stereotype, as much as the risk that the spectator's identity will be reduced to stereotype. Both end up taking the chance that, in the effort to encounter their other, they will fail to fully understand each other as a unique "other" worth valuing rather than as the universalised "Other" who is just a stereotype. Both take the chance that people will judge them harshly for doing this. But, if the ethical encounter is in fact characterised by what Lehmann (2006) calls a momentary deferral of meaning making, what Ridout (2009) calls questions we cannot answer, or what Helena Grehan (2009) calls ambivalence about how to answer, these risks may be an unavoidable part of pursuing the encounter and the change of perception or cultural politics the encounter can evoke.

For the creators of these types of performances, their work is based on the belief that they have to create platforms for edgework that puts them and their social interlocutors at risk to have real conversations, with real others, that really take all of the parties involved out of their comfort zones. They have to have conversations that take the artist out of their comfort zone, take the first spectator who can become fodder for judgement out of their comfort zone, and the secondary spectator who watches the footage afterward out of their comfort zone. The goal for the artists is to provoke public debate, but to provoke public debate defined in terms of dialogue, conversation, conflict, and argument in which multiple perspectives are heard, rather than in terms of consensus, in which one voice ultimately dominates. This is why documenting the work, disseminating it more widely, and drawing more and more sets of spectators into the discussion is often such an important focus. It provides the artists—who are conscious of the complexity of what they are doing here—the opportunity to engage in debate with broader groups, beyond those able to be present at live, ephemeral, participatory public space events. For these artists, this conversation, conflict, and debate that comes out of the paradoxes in play in the work is the point of participatory art. It is what makes the risks it entails, for performers and for spectators, worth taking.

References

Art21. 2009. Kimsooja: 'A Beggar Woman' & 'A Homeless Woman' | Art21 Exclusive. Art21. https://www.youtube.com/watch?v=0le-hqLVJm0. Accessed 1 Jan 2015.

Beck, Ulrich. 1986. *Risk Society: Toward a new modernity*. London: Sage.

Bennett, Susan. 1997. *Theatre Audiences: A Theory of Production and Reception*. London and New York: Routledge.

Bishop, Clare. 2012. *Artificial Hells: Participatory Art and the Politics of Spectatorship*. London and New York: Verso.

Bourriaud, Nicolas. 1998. *Relational Aesthetics*. Dijon: Les Presses du Réel.

Bradford, Sean. 2014. Art vs. Begging and the Reality of Modern-Day Manhattan (21 October 2014). http://www.huffingtonpost.com/sean-bradford/art-vs-begging_b_6019760.html. Accessed 1 Jan 2015.

Daily Mail Reporter. 2011. "Queen Goes Begging on Streets of Birmingham and Makes £12 an Hour ... not Bad for a Mannequin of Her Majesty" (8 August 2011). http://www.dailymail.co.uk/news/article-2023718/Queen-goes-begging-streets-Birmingham-makes-12-hour–bad-mannequin-Her-Majesty.html. Accessed 1 January 2015.

Domínguez, Yolanda. 2010. Begging for a Chanel. http://rebelart.net/yolanda-dominguez-begging-for-a-chanel/004187/. Accessed 1 Jan 2015.

Douglas, Mary. 1985. *Risk Acceptability According to the Social Sciences*. London: Routledge & Kegan Paul.

Fain, Daria. 2012. BEGGING #1: Detoxification of Preconceptions About Money. http://www.dariafain.net/begging. Accessed 1 Jan 2015.

Gómez-Peña, Guillermo and Coco Fusco. 1992. *Two Undiscovered Amerindians Visit*.

Goodman, Jonathan. 2003. Conditions of Anonymity: The Performance Art of Kim Sooja. *Art AsiaPacific*, Fall 2003. http://www.kimsooja.com/texts/goodman.html. Accessed 1 Jan 2015.

Grehan, Helena. 2009. *Performance Ethics and Spectatorship in a Global Age*. London: Palgrave Macmillan.

Grosz, Elizabeth. 1999. Becoming ... An Introduction. In *Becomings: Explorations in Time, Memory and Futures*, ed. Elizabeth Grosz, 1–12. Ithaca, NY, and London: Cornell University Press.

Hadley, Bree. 2014. *Disability, Public Space Performance and Spectatorship: Unconscious Performers*. London: Palgrave Macmillan.

Henry, Joseph. 2012. Straight to Hells. *The New Enquiry* (11 October 2012). http://thenewinquiry.com/essays/straight-to-hells/. Accessed 30 Aug 2014.

Jones, Amelia, and Adrian Healthfield. 2012. *Perform, Repeat, Record: Live Art in History*. London: Live Art Development Agency.

Lehmann, Hans-Thies. 2006. *Postdramatic Theatre*. London and New York: Routledge.

Lyng, Stephen. 2008. Edgework, Risk, and Uncertainty. In *Social Theories of Risk and Uncertainty: An Introduction*, ed. Jens O. Zinn, 106–137. Oxford: Blackwell Publishing.

Lozano, Daniel. 2013. *Begging: The Performance*. Caccorolozano. http://cachorrolozano.tumblr.com/post/71574945100/begging-performance-paris-2013-the. Accessed 1 Jan 2015.

Mouffe, Chantal. 2005. *On the Political*. Abington: Routledge.

Ono, Yoko. 1964. *Cut Piece*.

Oulu, Debi. n.d. Begging for Youth—Interactive Street Performance Art. P8 Gallery (2013). http://debioulu.com/begging-youth-interactive-street-performance-art. Accessed 1 Jan 2015.

Performance Art Oslo. n.date. Kjetil Skøien. http://www.performanceartoslo.no/kjetil-skoslashien.html. Accessed 1 Jan 2015.

Pugliatti, Paola. 2003. *Beggary and Theatre in Early Modern England*. Aldershot: Ashgate.

Rancière, Jacques. 2011. *The Emancipated Spectator*. New York: Verso.

Reich, Carina, and Bogdan Szyber. 2012. Beggars Saturday & Persondesign. Reich + Szyber (13 October 2014). http://reich-szyber.com/en/portfolio/beggars-saturday-persondesign. Accessed 1 Jan 2015.

Ridout, Nicholas. 2009. *Theatre & Ethics*. London: Palgrave Macmillan.

Sargeant, Jordan. 2014. Erykah Badu Made 3.60 Busking Anonymously Because New York Sucks. Gawker (15 October 2014). http://gawker.com/erykah-badu-made-3-60-busking-anonymously-because-new-1646796177Accessed 1 Jan 2015.

Smith, Janet. 2013. Beggar Woman—Conditions of Anonymity. The Georgia Straight (29 November 2013). http://www.straight.com/blogra/540141/kimsoojas-moving-performance-art-piece-begging-appear-vancouver-art-gallerys-fuse. Accessed 1 Jan 2015.

Sooja, Kim. n.date. Kim Sooja. http://www.kimsooja.com. Accessed 1 Jan 2015.

Sooja, Kim. n.date. Kim Sooja. https://www.youtube.com/playlist?list=PL518D7878C38144A3. Accessed 1 Jan 2015.

White, Gareth. 2007. Navigating the Ethics of Audience Participation. Applied Theatre Researcher 7. https://www.griffith.edu.au/__data/assets/pdf_file/0004/52915/white.pdf. Accessed 30 Aug 2014.

White, Gareth. 2013. *Audience Participation in Theatre: Aesthetics of the Invitation*. London: Palgrave Macmillan.

Williamson, Aaron and Katherine Araniello. 2007. *Assisted Passage*.

Zinn, Jens O. (ed.). 2008. *Social Theories of Risk and Uncertainty: An Introduction*. Oxford: Blackwell.

The Drama Spiral: A Decision-Making Model for Safe, Ethical, and Flexible Practice when Incorporating Personal Stories in Applied Theatre and Performance

Clark Baim

Introduction

During the past one hundred years, and more particularly in the past several decades, there has been a rapid expansion in the use of people's personal stories in the theatre, in both applied and commercial theatre contexts. This expansion has included the development of new genres of theatre including verbatim theatre, testimonial theatre, autobiographical theatre, tribunal theatre, documentary/investigatory theatre, the theatre of witness, playback theatre, reminiscence theatre, self-revelatory performance, and a range of related forms. While there are many positive reasons for incorporating personal stories in theatre and drama workshops, and indeed many examples of good practice, such work has inherent risks because it is often conducted with vulnerable groups. Even when groups are not identified as vulnerable or at risk, the nature of the stories shared,

C. Baim (✉)
Birmingham Institute for Psychodrama, Birmingham, UK
e-mail: admin@birminghampsychodrama.co.uk

© The Author(s) 2017
A. O'Grady (ed.), *Risk, Participation, and Performance Practice*,
DOI 10.1007/978-3-319-63242-1_4

the processes used, or the manner in which the story is presented to (and critiqued by) others may make participants vulnerable. As Zoe Zontou explains in Chap. 9 of this volume, working with risk and vulnerability through drama is a specialised field. Therefore, there are important issues in relation to duty of care, reflexive practice, transparency, and structure, which are important aspects of the drama process when personal stories are used.

Given the highly personal and exposing nature of much of the material that is used in such processes, it is imperative that theatre artists interrogate the ethics of this work and develop models of practice that maintain sound ethics, stay within appropriate boundaries, and avoid exploiting and harming participants, performers, and audiences (LaFrance 2013; Rifkin 2010; Barnes 2009). With this imperative in mind, in this chapter I examine the ethics, risks, and responsibilities associated with applied theatre when personal stories are used, whether this be in classes, workshops, rehearsals, or performances.

The chapter begins with a discussion of the proliferation in recent decades of theatrical forms based on personal stories and real events. This is followed by an analysis of the risks and vulnerabilities inherent in theatre that is drawn from the personal life experiences of participants. I then offer guidelines for ethical practice based on this analysis and describe a model I have developed called the Drama Spiral. This is a practical decision-making tool intended to help theatre and arts practitioners to negotiate the complex, contested, and inherently risky terrain of personal stories. As I will explain, the Drama Spiral emerges from a broad synthesis of cross-disciplinary ideas and is designed to offer a clear and coherent model for safely regulating the degree of distance and focus in drama-based processes, from the fictional to the highly personal. The Drama Spiral is comprised of six rings: in the outer rings, participants are involved in creative activities and work at the metaphorical and fictional level. As one "spirals in" towards the centre, the rings represent stories that are increasingly personal and sensitive for the participants. The Spiral includes the entire range of theatrical and drama-based forms and, perhaps controversially, includes within the scope of the theatre practitioner those forms that are ordinarily presumed to be the exclusive domain of qualified therapists, most particularly psychodramatists and dramatherapists. I offer guidance within the chapter and thoughts regarding why and how even the most vulnerable and risky topics (and people) should remain—*with necessary safeguards, including appropriate training for and supervision of the practitioner*—within the purview of applied theatre and performance.

Burgeoning Forms of Personal and Collective Narratives in the Theatre

Contemporary theatre has seen a rapid expansion in the range and hybridisation of forms and processes based on personal stories and collective narratives about real events (Foster 1996; Martin 2012, 2013; Leffler 2012). I offer here a partial list, with the caveat that the distribution into categories is largely for ease of reference and is not intended to restrict any of these forms into a single category. Cross-blending of these forms is continuous and ongoing.

Autobiographical theatre

- self-revelatory performance (Emunah 2015)
- autobiographical and auto-ethnographic theatre (Heddon 2008; Stephenson 2013; Pendzik et al. 2016)
- life story theatre (O'Connor and Diamond 2014)
- testimonial theatre (Forsyth 2013)
- playback (Salas 1993)
- lifegame (Johnstone 2015; Gardner 2010).

Documentary and investigatory theatre

- theatre of witness (Sepinuck 2013)
- documentary/investigative/journalistic theatre (Forsyth and Megson 2009; Innes 1972; Cantrell 2013; Smith 2001, 2006)
- verbatim theatre (Hammond and Steward 2008; Cantrell 2012)
- tribunal theatre (drawn from court transcripts) (Brittain et al. 2014)
- refugee performance (Balfour 2013)
- veteran drama (Balfour et al. 2014; O'Connor 2015)
- ethnotheatre (Saldana 2011) and ethnodrama (Saldana 2005)
- war, battle, and historical re-enactment, and restored village performances (Schneider 2011; Martin 2013).

Theatre and drama workshops where personal or collective stories are often used or adapted

- reminiscence theatre (Schweitzer 2007)
- community-based performance (Coult and Kershaw 1983; Haedicke and Nellhaus 2001; Govan et al. 2007)
- senior theatre (Basting 1998)
- issue-focused theatre (Cossa et al. 1996)
- forum theatre and related forms (Boal 1979; Rohd 1998; Schutzman and Cohen-Cruz 1994)
- applied theatre workshops and residencies (Baim et al. 2002; Bradley 2004; Prendergast and Saxton 2009; Prentki and Preston 2009).

Theatre and drama-based workshops aimed primarily at the education, personal growth, skills development, or psychological healing of participants

- psychodrama (Moreno and Moreno 1975; Dayton 1990)
- dramatherapy (Jennings and Minde 1993; Jones 1996; Jennings 2009)
- theatre-as-therapy (Evreinov 1927; Iljine [see Jones 1996]; Walsh 2013)
- prison drama (Thompson 1998; Baim et al. 2002; Balfour 2004; Shailor 2011; McAvinchy 2011)
- theatre with trauma survivors (van der Kolk 2014)
- issue-based drama workshops focused on individual change (Landy and Montgomery 2012; Jennings 2009)
- applied improvisation (Blatner and Blatner 1988; Blatner and Wiener 2006).

The question of *why* there has been such an expansion of forms is a fascinating one that has been explored by other authors such as Martin (2013), Zarilli et al. (2010), Nicholson (2014), and Foster (1996). Several large-scale movements within the theatre and a convergence of psychosocial forces both ancient and modern have contributed to the rapid expansion in theatrical forms that dramatise personal stories and the “real”. The following section offers an analysis of five of these broad trends and their synergistic convergence.

1. Experimentation in the theatre. In the theatre, in keeping with the modernistic trends across all of the arts, and developing on from trends including realism, naturalism, and the avant-garde from the 1850s onwards, the early twentieth century saw the rise of theatre as a site of experimentation and innovation, where the notion of the theatrical laboratory gained prominence (Zarilli et al. 2010; Croyden 1974).

Within this laboratory context, directors, actors, and playwrights sought to break free from what were seen as the outmoded praxes of traditional theatre and, in one strand of development, began to emphasise authenticity and to hold as the highest value that theatre must put us "in contact with the real" (Cull 2009, 5) and be, in the words of Kama Ginkas, "personal and confessional" (Ginkas and Freedman 2003, 7). While Artaud saw the actor signalling through the flames, baring his soul *in extremis* (Artaud 1977), and Vakhtangov encouraged his actors to bring their personal authenticity and imagination to the role (Malaev-Babel 2013), Stanislavski (1961) encouraged his actors to draw on life experience in the service of developing character and action. Likewise, Grotowski encouraged his actors to imaginatively expand life experience and recall emotion in order to bring authenticity to the character and the play (Kumiega 1987; Richards 1995; Milling and Ley 2001). With these innovations, we see that the personal experiences of the actor are being explicitly drawn upon as a key to unlocking emotional truth in performance, and in this sense the theatre becomes a place of self-revelation for the actor, a place where the personal and private world of the actor becomes public.

2. The influence of Freudian ideas. A further ingredient is the emergence of the field of psychoanalysis and, more generally, the field of psychotherapy (Freud 1953/1986; Feltham and Horton 2012). Freud's ideas about unconscious processes had an enormous influence on twentieth-century theatre. Playwrights and directors began to examine in explicit and intense ways the inner workings of the mind and the impact of personal histories and personal traumas on human relationships and human functioning (Neuringer 1992).

In this newly emergent context, where the trend towards experimentation and innovation in the theatre gained such prominence, and the focus of actor training increasingly included an exploration of the inner archaeology of the actor, we can see that it was only a small further step to entirely discard the fictional, scripted element of theatre and performance and to move the actors themselves—rather than the fictional characters they normally portray—into the protagonist role, complete with their complex psyches, inner landscapes of emotion, and individual histories. This brings us into the realm of psychodrama, perhaps the most radical theatrical experiment of all.

3. The emergence of psychodrama. Psychodrama, which dates from the 1920s, developed from the theatre experiments of Dr J.L. Moreno

(1889–1974) in Vienna and later in New York, where Moreno placed the lives of the performers themselves at the centre of the action (Moreno 1924; Moreno and Moreno 1975). Later, Moreno went one step further and developed a theatre without actors, which he termed *psychodrama*—derived from Greek root words meaning "the mind in action". The radical concept at the heart of psychodrama is that *the audience members become the protagonists* and the dramas that unfold are focused encounters that develop directly from the protagonists' perceptions, memories, and experiences (Moreno and Moreno 1969/2012). It is a theatrical form that eliminates the playwright, the actors, the producers, the designers, and the process of rehearsal, in order to provide a space for the impromptu exploration of people's lives under the guidance of a trained facilitator who is called the *director* and whose training, above all, prepares her to work collaboratively with the protagonist and the group to co-produce the enactment. The psychodramatist is trained to respond reflexively, sensitively, and with a deep understanding of her own relation to the story and the protagonist, in order to direct the action in as safe a manner as possible without getting bound up in the issues being explored. This is a style and manner of facilitation that is relevant to any facilitator of drama processes. Psychodrama is a method that has had deep and wide-ranging influences on the fields of theatre, improvisation, psychotherapy, psychology, and sociology (Moreno 2014; Scheiffele 1995; Blatner 1997; Nolte 2014).

Psychodrama is now a widely practised method with many thousands of practitioners around the world, although in most countries where it is practised it has to a large extent lost sight of its theatrical roots and is mainly confined to the mental health professions. This separation has historical roots, in that J.L. Moreno was a psychiatrist and therefore the method was associated from the start with both the theatre and with the medical and psychological professions. This has led to some countries seeing psychodrama as the exclusive territory of medicine and psychology. This is unfortunate; psychodrama needs to rediscover its theatrical roots and be reclaimed by theatre artists, as there are many insights and practical approaches that can be of mutual benefit to all three fields if they rediscover their common ancestry.

Moreno himself had a global vision for psychodrama and the related methods he created, such as sociodrama and sociometry. He saw psychodrama as being relevant to the psychiatric clinic but equally to the public sphere (Moreno 1946/1972). Indeed, for more than two decades he simultaneously operated a psychiatric hospital in upstate New York, where the psychodrama stage was a centrepiece of the treatment, and a public theatre in Manhattan. His public theatre of psychodrama was open six nights per week from the late 1940s to the early 1970s and became a well-established fixture of Manhattan life, furthering Moreno's vision of making the therapeutic theatre available to all (Moreno 2014). So, while one might be led to think that there is a clear distinction between theatre and therapy, and that the two approaches to human progress and personal healing arise from distinct ideologies, in the case of psychodrama and theatre this distinction runs counter to Moreno's intention. While it is beyond the scope of this chapter to offer a full account of the history and underlying reasons for the separation of psychodrama from its theatrical roots, readers who are interested in this topic and in the applications of psychodrama "outside of the clinic" can find useful accounts in J.D. Moreno (2014), Scheiffele (1995), and Nolte (2014). Schutzman and Cohen-Cruz (1994) also write about the connections between psychodrama and the work of Augusto Boal, and Jennings (2009) is a useful resource exploring the links between theatre, therapy, and activism.

As long as the mutual estrangement continues, applied theatre practitioners are cut off from almost one hundred years of research, writing, and theatrical experimentation that is, at last count, represented in more than 7300 publications exploring psychodrama and its effects, processes, and influences (see, for example, the online bibliography of psychodrama at www.pdbib.org). I offer this view from my perspective as a trained psychodramatist who is also a performer and director of applied theatre working with vulnerable populations. For psychodramatists, I would make the point that the research and writing within the field of theatre and performance studies, and in particular the field of applied theatre, is a fruitful area to explore.

4. Social and cultural influences. The profound shifts within the theatre, including the theatrical experiments leading to the creation of psychodrama and its offshoots, occurred in the context of wider cultural and social forces that played out in the aftermath of the two world wars. The emergence of the Cold War and the threat of nuclear annihilation saw the widespread politicisation and the rising political consciousness of younger generations determined not to repeat the pattern of blind adherence to corrupt authority or to fall victim to nationalistic propaganda or oppressive political regimes. Thus emerged, from the 1920s to the 1960s and continuing to this day, a range of politically committed theatre companies focused on social issues and social problems (Blau 1964; Innes 1972; Croyden 1974; Boal 1979; Itzin 1980; Coult and Kershaw 1983). This movement, encompassing community theatre, applied theatre, theatre in education, agitprop, and political and activist theatre of many stripes, was underpinned by extensive interrogation of the status quo and of the politics of power and oppression. Such an interrogation of the status quo necessarily includes the voice of the oppressed, that is, the individual and collective stories of people who are marginalised in complex systems or exploited by more powerful forces (Flyvbjerg et al. 2012; Butler 1997).

Added to the politically and socially engaged trends in theatre, with the increasing availability and affordability of consumer electronics and the advent of the internet, we see the ever-expanding democratisation of media, global communications, and the rise of the citizen–journalist (Rancière 2009; Zarilli et al. 2010). Social media and the rapid expansion of celebrity culture and reality television have added their influence too. Ever-increasing portions of the global population can now be curator of their own stories, cultivating a performative presence to be consumed by audiences anywhere. We have entered the post-privacy era, where the personal is not just political—it's public.

5. *The instinctive and healing impulse behind storytelling.* At the root of all theatre, and indeed all storytelling, is the human need to make meaning of the world and to communicate this meaning to other people in the form of stories. The powerful instinct to share one's story is an ancient one and is very likely bound up in the prehistoric origins of human communication and the emergence of consciousness and language. Such meaning making and storytelling is at the core of what makes us human and is intimately related to the development of our minds, our core sense of self, and our understanding of our place in the world (Schechner 1988; Wasilewska 2000; White 2007; McConachie 2013). We are *homo narrans*—the storytelling primate (Warner 2012).

Furthermore, we are shaped by the stories we tell and the stories we believe. Many strands of research and fields of study, including educational theory, psychology, philosophy, religious studies, cognitive neuroscience, computer science, and artificial intelligence, converge on the idea that the way in which human beings interpret the world and our place in it, and the way we explain the world to each other, is through deep narratives that guide our lives and our sense of self (Campbell

1949/2008; Jaynes 1976; Schank 1990; Crittenden 1994; Mattingly 1998). In the theatre, when we tell *fictional stories* to each other, we share contemplation of the human condition and we join together in shared cultural understandings. When we tell *personal stories* to each other, we are doing the same thing, but with the added possibility that the recollection and formulation of our personal story, the sharing of that story, and the feedback and support we receive after telling the story will all combine to affect the way in which we interpret the story and the effect that it has on our lives.[1] We also have the chance to *revise* the story, as we examine it in more detail and perhaps identify some of the plot inconsistencies, the previously disguised power relations, and the distorted understandings we may previously have had about the story. In doing so, we have the chance to generate a more adequate story that feels more authentic, liberating, or useful to us.[2] In other words, sharing our stories can heal our broken stories, our broken hearts, and our broken minds. Through stories we construct and reconstruct our sense of who we are.

Summary. Thus we see how experimental trends within the theatre, combined with social, political, cultural, and historical factors, have contributed to the proliferation of reality-based and autobiographical forms of theatre and performance.

Working with Vulnerability Through Drama: Why the Need for Special Attention?

The proliferation of theatre forms utilising personal narrative has been accompanied by detailed and searching critiques exploring the politics, power relations, aesthetics, and epistemologies of practice (Fischer-Lichte 2008; Diamond 1992; Salverson 1996; Thompson 2009b; Jennings 2009; Khaiat 2011; Leffler 2012; Martin 2013; Wake 2013; Holmwood 2014). As Salverson points out, a potential weakness of theatre that draws on the personal stories of vulnerable participants is that the director or facilitator may buy into the romanticised idea that staging vulnerability and pain is in itself a worthwhile or even noble goal (Salverson 1996; see also Cizmic 2012). Merely staging pain and suffering is not an answer in itself and runs the serious risk of voyeurism, collusion with oppression, and even re-abuse and retraumatisation of victims. If we are to remain ethical as theatre practitioners, personal stories of pain should never be presented as an unexamined spectacle and never with the assumption that the theatre artist is rebalancing the scales of justice simply by restaging traumatic events without examining and taking heed of the wider sociocultural forces impacting on the participants, their stories, and the context in which their stories are now being told and will be shared in future. To do otherwise is to risk working within the context of forced, narcissistic solidarity, the "violence of the 'we'" (Diamond 1992; Salverson 2001, 124).

In developing the Drama Spiral ("the Spiral"), I have taken a cue from Salverson when she suggests that theatre artists and educators using theatre for social change should:

> bring a more *deliberate attention* to the dynamics within the processes and performances we create and attempt to *build structures within which attention can be paid*, obligation traced but not required, and meanings touched but not pinned down. In this way performance and pedagogy might act as a doorway, an *instrument of encounter*, a place of public and private negotiations—where the goal is not just to empathize, but to attend, and perhaps eventually even to witness. (Salverson 2001, 125, emphasis mine)

The Spiral is just such an attempt at building a structure through which to pay "deliberate attention" to group processes and power relations, and to assist decision making during drama and theatre-making workshops that are, in deep and profound ways, "instruments of encounter" between people and between public and private domains.

Why is such "deliberate attention" necessary? Theatre practice that draws on the personal narratives of participants is most typically undertaken with and focuses on the stories of marginalised, vulnerable populations who may have been ignored, injured, excluded, or disadvantaged. When working with people who face such challenges and are vulnerable, unresolved issues are often at or near the surface, still very raw. Indeed, in many cases the trauma, abuse, or other struggle may be ongoing even as the theatre work proceeds. While on the one hand such individuals are often remarkable survivors, and in that sense "tough" and "resilient", on the other hand, facilitators have a duty of care to work with an awareness not only of the outward, often highly proficient coping exterior of the participant, but also with the person as a whole, who might have underlying vulnerabilities that may to a certain extent lie outside the person's conscious awareness because their coping roles have predominated in order to keep them alive and safe. They may also feel unable to challenge a powerful and confident facilitator, particularly if they perceive that this would go against the group norm. Facilitators therefore need to build in constant checks and balances, where participants are encouraged to ask questions, offer suggestions, and, most of all, say "no" when activities feel too risky for them.

Deliberate attention is also needed because wider forces are in play beyond the rehearsal room. We all exist within systems at many levels, for example at the family, peer, institutional, community, regional, national, and international levels. As Thompson (2005, 2009a, 2009b), Saldana (2011), Sepinuck (2013), Salverson (1996, 2001), and others have pointed out, the applied theatre practitioner is wise to be mindful of the broader cultural and sociopolitical context in which they are working and how this will influence the degree to which they encourage personal disclosure by participants. For example, in some cultural contexts, personal disclosure and the sharing of personal stories or even ideas may go against cultural norms, particularly in mixed-gender groups, groups where there are people of differing socioeconomic or cultural backgrounds, or in groups where there is or has been conflict. Furthermore, in situations of war, occupation, civil unrest, political or police oppression, dictatorship, forced migration, corruption, and other contexts in which injustice and/or inequality may predominate, the applied theatre practitioner must hold in mind these influences and how the group of participants and/or audiences may be impacted by their participation in the applied theatre experience. Moreover, the applied theatre practitioner working in such contexts must be politically and psychologically savvy enough to understand how the applied theatre workshops, rehearsals, or performance may be viewed by "outsiders"—including neighbours, other people in the institution, the wider public, and those in power with a stake in preserving the status quo. Indeed, the very fact of participation may be highly contested, for example: "Who gets the treats and who doesn't?"

The first principle must always be to "do no harm". With this principle in mind, the applied theatre practitioner may need to radically adapt the aims and expectations of a given process, project, or performance, not only in terms of how the work is undertaken but also how and with whom the work is organised, negotiated, undertaken, explained, advertised, promoted, reported, and documented. The risk of being culturally or politically naive is that the applied theatre practitioner may inadvertently set up their participants for failure or place the participants' safety, livelihood, or freedom at risk. Further, the worker may be subject to manipulation by those in power and further exacerbate an oppressive system.

Yet still, when the context is right and when the applied theatre practitioner has the informed consensus of a participant group with the capacity to make such decisions for themselves—in full awareness of the potential risks involved—there is, within the role and remit of the applied theatre practitioner, the important possibility of helping groups of people to find hope and to strive towards self-determination and political and social change. In doing so, the applied theatre enterprise can move from the tactical level to the strategic level of impact (Thompson 2009a, 121). In short, our idealistic hope to be agents for positive change in the world must be balanced by political awareness and shrewd artistic facilitation choices.

Understanding Abusive Dynamics in the Drama Process

Given the significant vulnerabilities of these populations, it follows that, if the theatre process is to use the personal stories of the participants, it is crucial to include in such processes a number of safeguards and structures in order to protect people from re-oppression and from exacerbating their struggle. The theatre of real stories certainly has the power to transform and heal, but it can also be a form of theatre that can do harm, by worsening the vulnerability of injured participants and also by passing on unresolved and uncontained (and typically unacknowledged) pain to audiences and performers (Barnes 2009).

To offer a visual representation of the potential roles that can inadvertently be played out during the process of eliciting and working with personal stories, it may be useful to refer to the work of Karpman (1968) and what has become widely accepted as a key role dynamic within contexts of conflict, violence, and abuse. Karpman's model consists of a triangle where the three corners represent the roles of *perpetrator*, *victim, and rescuer.* I add to this a fourth element, the role of *abandoning authority* (roughly synonymous with the role of *bystander)*, which is drawn from the work of Hudgins with trauma survivors (Hudgins and Toscani 2013) (see Fig. 1). In situations of conflict and abuse, the abandoning authority/bystander is the person—or the people—who could have stopped the abuse but did not. When people feel threatened, they

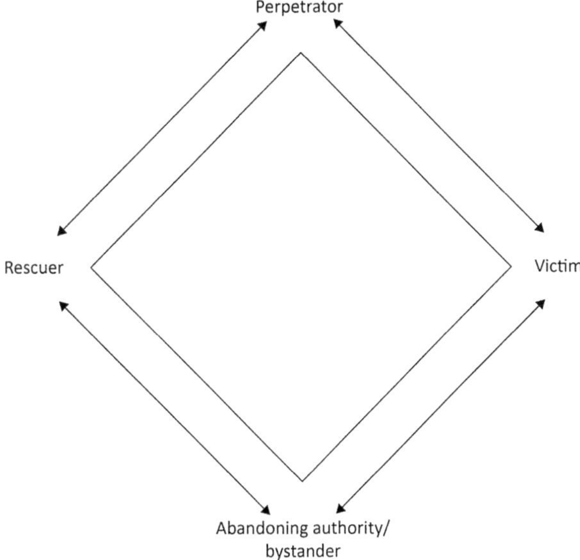

Fig. 1 Typical roles played out in conflict situations and in situations of abuse. It is important that facilitators work with conscious awareness of these role dynamics and avoid being pulled into unconscious conflictual and abusive dynamics.

often take mental and behavioural shortcuts as strategies for self-preservation, and these four roles represent the most common shortcuts.

The four roles of *perpetrator*, *victim*, *rescuer*, and *abandoning authority/bystander* can manifest in many ways during situations of conflict or abuse, and they are also likely to emerge in any context in which highly emotive material and potentially traumatic stories are revealed, such as in the context of drama processes working with personal stories of vulnerable people. The four roles can emerge spontaneously and can be played out by participants, practitioners, organisers, production and support staff, and audiences. The risk is that such dynamics are typically beyond the level of conscious awareness until it is too late and the damage has been done.

For example, facilitators can become overly encouraging of disclosure and set up participants to be overexposed and unsafe during a public performance for which they are underprepared. In this instance, the facilitator has become a perpetrator (all the while telling him or herself that they are helping) and is potentially harming the participants, who are made victims of the facilitator's ambition and disregard for their vulnerability. This is a serious lapse of the duty of care, and I have seen it happen when facilitators have unreflexively taken on the "enthusiasm of the helper" (Salverson 2001, 121) in their eagerness to alleviate oppression and "empower" their participants. I have also seen this dynamic played out when false promises were made to a group of service users who were used as the source material for a verbatim piece done by an internationally renowned theatre company. The process left them bitter, resentful, and feeling exploited.

In a second permutation of the four roles, participants in an ensemble-created performance who are still traumatised may slip into the perpetrator role and act out against the audience, leaving the audience feeling emotionally pummelled by the performers' raw outpouring of unprocessed feeling.

In a third variation that I have seen happen during a rehearsal process, the facilitators, the participants, and the host agency moved through several combinations of interpersonal dynamics where the roles of *perpetrator*, *victim*, *rescuer*, and *abandoning authority/bystander* were played out as variations on a theme. The original agreement was for the participants to workshop their ideas and to share them with peers and key workers within the host agency. This agreement was broken late in the rehearsal period when the host agency put pressure on the facilitators to open the performance to the public. The facilitators felt pressured and ethically compromised, because the participants were very vulnerable and the subject matter was "live" and highly personal. The end product, as originally agreed, was not meant for public audiences. The rehearsal process became fraught and unhappy, and tempers became frayed as the host agency became bullying and made ultimatums. The roles within this abusive dynamic changed several times, with people shifting between victim, rescuer, perpetrator, and abandoning authority/bystander. Phrases such as "How dare they?!", "Nobody told ME!", "You can't change the goal posts", "It's not my fault!", "What's the problem? It's not a big deal", and "Well, we'll just have to do what they say" were heard during these transactions. This round-robin exchange of roles is common within abuse dynamics. In the end, after time to reflect, the director and senior management team of the host agency met with the facilitators, and a compromise was reached in collaboration with the participants.

The stories were adjusted and fictionalised in a way that made the participants feel comfortable, and the public performances went ahead with great success.

The point here is that theatre practitioners who work with vulnerable people need to be aware of the unconscious dynamics that can inadvertently be played out during the process of workshops, rehearsal, and performance. Participatory theatre is inherently a very open form where the processes are not fixed. This openness means it is more likely that roles shift spontaneously and unconscious dynamics arise during rehearsals and workshops. While there is great potential in this, there is also inherent risk. By staying alert to the abuse dynamics, and most particularly to the dynamics inherent when the roles of *perpetrator*, *victim*, *rescuer*, and *abandoning authority/bystander* are liminally present, drama practitioners can minimise the potential for unconscious and harmful dynamics to infect the interpersonal process during drama workshops, and they can also intervene early when such dynamics begin to play out.

The Impetus for Creating the Drama Spiral: Striving for Safety When Staging Vulnerability

The Spiral emerged in the context of my investigation into the use of personal narrative in applied theatre and performance as part of a doctoral research project at the University of Exeter, UK. It also developed from my earlier work presenting issue-based, interactive performances and facilitating workshops with Geese Theatre Company (Baim et al. 2002). My international work in prisons, probation centres, forensic hospitals, and many other settings with vulnerable populations has continually shown the value of combining applied theatre approaches with techniques that utilise aspects of personal narrative, sometimes including psychodrama or psychodrama techniques (Baim 2000, 2004, 2012). This combined approach places particular emphasis on the healing potential of people telling—at many levels of implicit, metaphorical, or explicit communication—enacting, reviewing, and integrating their personal stories, using applied theatre methods within safe and supportive groups and with appropriate levels of guidance and support from facilitators. My training in traditional theatre as well as explicitly therapeutic uses of theatre has also made me acutely aware of the ethical and safety issues surrounding the use of personal disclosure and personal story, and equally aware of the many contexts in which it is inappropriate, unsafe, or unethical to elicit personal disclosure and personal narratives.

The early idea of creating the Spiral arose from enquiries from universities and drama schools, requesting that I teach about the boundaries and links between applied theatre and explicitly therapeutic uses of drama such as drama therapy and psychodrama. These workshops have shown how common the interest is among applied theatre students and practitioners in the whole range of interrelated specialisms, across the entire spectrum from fourth-wall theatre to audience-as-protagonist (psychodrama). Much of the focus of these workshops has been on how the varying methods use personal narrative and how each has techniques for maintaining safety and optimal distance.

In order to better explain these concepts and to provide students, practitioners, and educators with a useful model, I developed the Spiral as a decision-making tool for applied theatre facilitators who incorporate the personal stories of participants into their work. The Spiral represents an integration of theory and practical insights from the fields of applied theatre, psychotherapy, arts therapy, systems theory, and cybernetics (Lewin 1951), group work, experiential therapy, and attachment-based narrative approaches (Dallos and Vetere 2009). It also integrates the many well-established principles and practices of working collaboratively in the creation of devised work with groups (Heddon and Milling 2005; Govan et al. 2007).

The Spiral is intended to offer a clear and effective means for safely regulating the degree of distance and focus as required in any drama-based process, from single sessions to long-term groups. *Distance regulation* is a term used in psychology to describe how members of a family or social group regulate their emotional closeness and distance from each other (Byng-Hall and Campbell 1981). In the context of the Spiral model, I have borrowed the term and define distance regulation as the process by which a facilitator—in this case, a facilitator of applied theatre—guides a session so that the material and issues explored are pitched at the right level of aesthetic and emotional distance in order to maintain safety, ethical responsibility, and respect for personal boundaries (Rifkin 2010; Casson 2004; Jennings 2011; Bannister 1991).

Description of the Drama Spiral

The Spiral is a type of map on which one can plot the processes involved in applied theatre practice. There are six rings of the Spiral, with each ring representing a different phase of working (see Fig. 2). As one works closer to the centre of the Spiral, the topics and scenes become more personal and sensitive for the participants. The positioning of the six rings on the Spiral is indicative only, suggesting that some elements will normally be used earlier in drama processes, and some will usually come later. Facilitators can move in and out of the Spiral as needed and as appropriate at any point in a session or activity.

The image of the Spiral captures the spontaneous movement between techniques that typically occurs during applied theatre workshops. Facilitators and participants may move from one ring of the Spiral to an adjacent ring or even one further away with little or no notice, and this often works like an improvised dance or a musical jam, with themes being revisited with variations based on the needs, interests, sensitivities, resilience, and progress of the group members. When this dance is going well, everyone enjoys the process. However, even the most experienced facilitators can sometimes be tripped up by spontaneous processes that emerge during a workshop or rehearsal, and suddenly may find themselves working with very raw and vulnerable material without warning. Facilitators need simple, quick reference points that can be shared with participants, to help everyone understand the levels at which they are working. Skilled facilitators can then move nimbly from one technique or process to the next, with deft negotiation of a wide number of variables as they perceive the group process and the varying needs and levels of involvement of participants. Stating this with reference to the Spiral, facilitators "spiral in" and "spiral out" as needed and as appropriate at any point in a session or activity, in the best interests of the participants and with the overall aims of the project in mind. This process is sometimes called *rhizomatic* (Cull 2009; Deleuze and Guattari 1980), a term borrowed from botany and used to describe multiple, layered, evolving, branching, and recursive processes of human interaction and learning, as compared with more hierarchical, prescriptive, fixed, binary, or strictly sequential processes.

The Four Quadrants of the Spiral

As Fig. 2 illustrates, each ring of the Spiral also includes four important processes that are essential to working safely, transparently, and effectively with groups of people involved in ensemble-created theatre. These processes are presented in four quadrants of the Spiral: *identify*, *explore*, *present*, and *evaluate*. These four processes, and a range of subprocesses within each of them, occur at each ring of the Spiral. Some of

The Drama Spiral

Clark Baim 2015

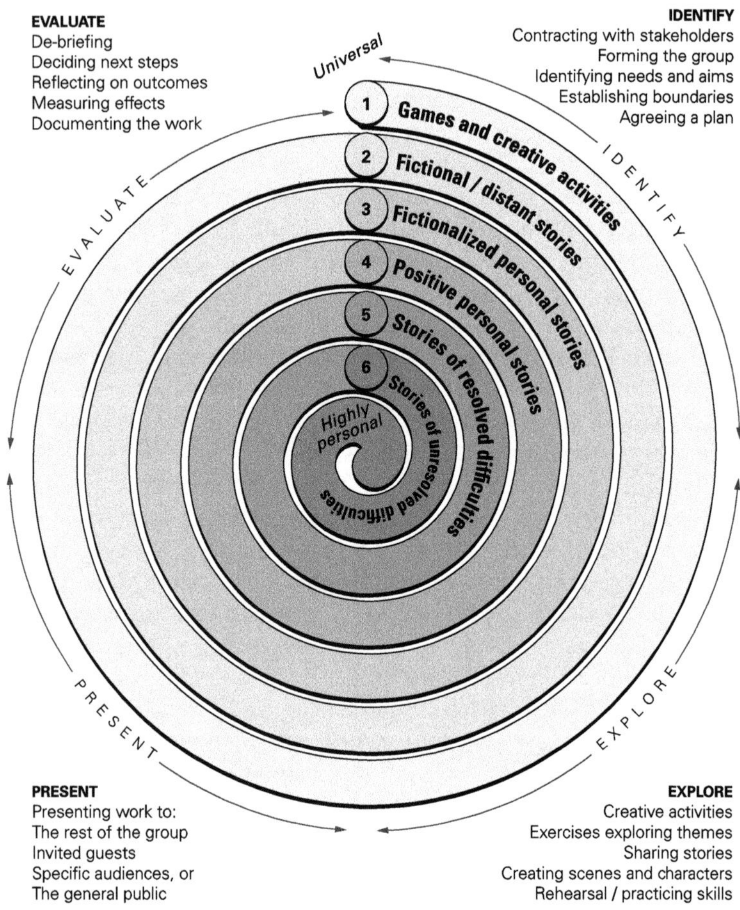

The Drama Spiral is a decision-making tool intended to help theatre and arts practitioners to work safely and ethically along the continuum from the fictional to the highly personal. In the outer rings, participants are involved in creative activities and work at the metaphorical and fictional level. As one 'spirals in' towards the centre, the rings represent stories that are increasingly personal and sensitive for the participants. Each ring of the Spiral includes four important processes: *Identify, Explore, Present and Evaluate.*

Fig. 2 The Drama Spiral: regulating distance in applied theatre and performance. Created by Clark Baim and designed by Valentina D'Efilippo (www.valentinadefilippo.co.uk)

Games and creative activities

- Group-building; warm-ups; theatre games; communication and performance skills.
- Creative activities including dance, music, song, art, writing, rhythmic movement and percussion, social and communal customs and pastimes where everyone participates.

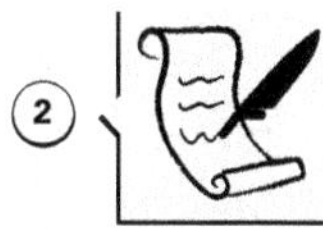

Fictional / distant stories

- Enacting stories and plays that are already written. Can include myths, fables, fairy tales and other well-known stories. Can also include watching a play / interacting with characters.
- Ensemble-created plays or improvised dramas that are wholly fictional or based on historical / news events.

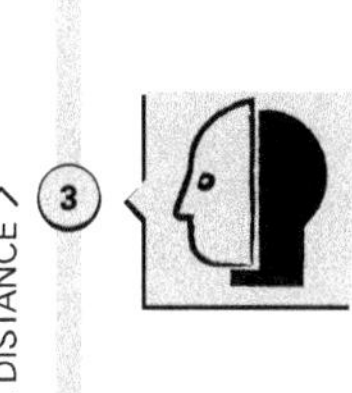

Fictionalized personal stories

- Ensemble-created drama with fictionalized scenes and characters; can include stories and themes that have arisen from more personal work.
- Metaphor is frequently used to create distance from personal stories and to contain powerful themes.

Positive personal stories

- Participants enact directly personal stories focusing on neutral, positive, safe or non-troubling topics.
- Participants may also enact situations they desire or may face in the future, i.e. 'rehearsals for life.'

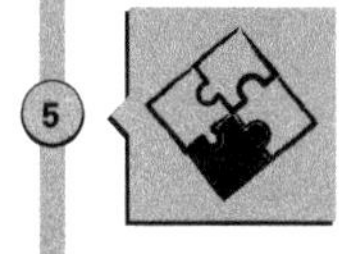

Stories of resolved difficulties

- Participants enact directly personal stories about troubling issues that are resolved – for example, stories of healing, growth, or triumph over adversity. The rehearsal process itself may be a part of the healing and growth.
- Important processes include informed consent, group support, sharing experiences, validation and witnessing.

Stories of unresolved difficulties

- Participants enact directly personal, unresolved stories for the purpose of therapy or growth. Important processes include informed consent, confidentiality, witnessing, group sharing and follow-up support.
- The focus on unresolved personal stories can make participants highly vulnerable and requires experienced facilitators and the guidance or supervision of a qualified therapist with relevant training, e.g. psychodrama, drama therapy.

Fig. 2 (continued)

the subprocesses are more associated with early stages of a group, some with later stages, and some are equally relevant throughout all stages of a group. The important point is that all of these processes are essential to applied theatre and should be borne in mind when making decisions about the appropriate level of an activity, session, or project.

To offer an example of how the four quadrants apply, we might consider how the upper right quadrant, "identify", is in part focused on "contracting with stakeholders" and also "agreeing a plan". In a context where a community theatre practitioner is, for example, engaging with a group of refugees who are service users of a charitable community centre, there is a range of stakeholders. The stakeholders may include, for example, the participants, their families, the staff and volunteers working at the centre, the potential audiences for a performance that might be produced, the funders of the charity, other service users of the charity, and so on. Whatever ideas the facilitator has regarding topics of focus, themes, or artistic concepts, or how the work should be facilitated and shared with audiences, the first step needs to be gaining the informed consent of the stakeholders and agreeing a plan regarding where the focus will be. The agreement can, of course, evolve as the project unfolds, as long as there is consent from all parties (this is accounted for in the upper left quadrant where the group and the facilitator evaluate the process as it evolves and decide the next steps). If the facilitator has objectives in mind that conflict with the aims and intentions of any of the stakeholders, this needs to be addressed and negotiated, with adjustments made as appropriate. To neglect such contracting and agreement is to increase the risk of coercive or insensitive practice, ruptures in the process, or other adverse outcomes.

First ring: Games and creative activities. The outermost ring of the Spiral includes elements such as group-building exercises, trust exercises, and related activities aimed at promoting psychological safety and deepening the communication and spontaneity of the group. This may include a wide range of theatre games, music, movement, song, physical activities, art, the enactment of cultural practices and pastimes, or other processes that encourage expression. At this ring of the Spiral, little or no personal disclosure is sought from participants.

Second ring: Fictional/distant stories. The second ring includes involvement by participants in *one-step removed* (that is, fictional or distant) sculpts, scenes, role plays, and other drama-based activities. This stage also includes rehearsal and performance of fictional plays and enacting stories and plays that are already written, that is, from the literary canon. Activities at this ring of the Spiral may also include the staging of myths, fables, fairy tales, and other well-known stories. This is only a partial list; the possibilities at this level are as limitless as drama itself.

Third ring: Fictionalised personal stories. The third ring includes fictionalised scenes and plays that are enacted at a distance from personal stories of the participants, especially vulnerable stories. For example, a scene may be performed that is based on a personal story of one of the participants, but where the setting and characters have been fictionalised in order to offer anonymity and create a safe distance in cases where the individual may feel too exposed or vulnerable to work at the directly personal level. Reminiscence theatre (Schweitzer 2007) is one form of theatre that sometimes uses this approach.

In this ring of the Spiral, personal material is typically sought during the rehearsal process, later to be fictionalised. We are therefore moving into more personal terrain, with important implications for working with sensitivity and care. This is even more important when working with vulnerable populations because traumatised individuals may not be aware of their vulnerability, and it is up to the drama practitioner to watch for this and work safely with this understanding.

When the optimal place to work is at the third ring of the Spiral, metaphor is typically used to create distance from personal stories and to contain powerful themes. An example of working in metaphor would be creating the story of an alien landing on Earth as a metaphor for the experience of refugees settling in a new country, or a former inmate resettling in the community, or a student moving to a new school. Holmwood (2014), Perrow (2012), Jennings (2009, 2011), Casson (2004), Chesner (1995), Linds (1996), and Dayton (1990) provide many examples and thorough guidance about the concept of working through metaphor, the concept of the "containing metaphor", and notions around regulating aesthetic distance. Bannister (1991) and Boal (1995) offer further useful guidance. Students and practitioners of applied theatre will be familiar with Boal's concept of "metaxis", describing the participant's encounter with the space between the world of their reality and the image of their reality, created by themselves (Boal 1995, 43). The third ring represents that part of the drama process where the "space between" is cultivated, and this can be done using all of the tools in the dramatist's and director's toolkit.

Fourth ring: Positive personal stories. At the fourth ring of the Spiral, the participants enact directly personal scenes. However, at this stage, the scenes should be on safe, neutral, or non-troubling topics, especially stories relating to strength and positive episodes from the past. Examples may include scenes of accomplishment, challenges currently being faced and dealt with, positive memories, positive relationships, significant moments or developmental transitions (example: "The birth of a new role"), celebrations, or challenges overcome. Participants may also rehearse and enact scenes they desire or may face in the future, that is, "rehearsals for life". Or participants may enact situations from their current life in order to develop positive social skills and strategies to handle personal situations (Kipper 1986; Yablonsky 1976; Baim et al. 2002).

Fifth ring: Stories of resolved difficulties. Working in the fifth ring of the Spiral, participants enact directly personal stories about troubling issues that have been resolved—for example, stories of healing, growth, or triumph over adversity. Put another way, at this ring of the Spiral we are staging vulnerability by focusing on *post-traumatic growth.* The scenes enacted may once have proved difficult for the participant to face and may even have been traumatic and unresolved in the past, but they are now resolved. Working at this ring of the Spiral taps into the insight and wisdom that participants may have gained from their life experiences and challenges they have faced, worked through, and resolved. This level of working requires shrewd judgement by the facilitator to ensure that the work stays within safe bounds. The facilitator must be skilled and experienced enough to understand how to assess whether and to what degree events that were traumatising for the participant in the past are resolved in the present. Typical examples of this form of theatre include self-revelatory performance (Emunah 2015), autobiographical theatre (Stephenson 2013; Heddon 2008), and testimonial theatre (Forsyth 2013).

Sixth ring: Stories of unresolved difficulties. The sixth, innermost ring of the Spiral is the most personal and sensitive. Here, participants are helped to stage scenes that are still difficult and unresolved for them, for the purposes of personal and communal healing, resolving fears, being witnessed, and, in some situations, advocating for social change and social justice, so that others do not have to suffer in the same way. The focus on unresolved personal stories, particularly when the stories are about painful and difficult personal material, can make participants highly vulnerable. Where the facilitator is not a trained therapist, in order to maintain safe practice and appropriate boundaries, they should have the guidance or supervision of a qualified therapist with relevant training. In any case, before entering into this terrain, the applied theatre facilitator should receive specific training in working ethically with this degree of trauma and vulnerability.

An example of a recent theatre production that could be said to have operated at the inner ring of the Spiral is Re-Live Theatre's 2014 production entitled *Memoria*, performed for public audiences at Cardiff's Chapter Theatre. *Memoria* featured the autobiographical performances of people living with dementia and also their family members and the social care professionals involved in their care. In this moving and beautifully staged production, which played to sold-out audiences, the performers shared their life stories and the challenges they face in living with dementia or caring for people with dementia. With seriousness and humour, the performers presenting their personal stories did not shy away from the stark realities of the disease, its effects on them and their families, and the struggles many patients and their families have in finding appropriate and sensitive care, support, and medical attention. The production was a powerful sharing of human experience and was also informative: many policy makers and social care and medical professionals saw *Memoria* and reflected on their learning during Q and A sessions after performances. Given the particular sensitivities of the topic and the performers, a notable feature of this production was the detailed groundwork and careful contracting done before and during the project, and the thoughtful care, support, and other forms of continued input offered to participants after the production concluded (O'Connor and Diamond 2014; also www.re-live.org.uk). Such a production serves as an exemplar of how socially engaged theatre, when carefully framed and thoughtfully facilitated by skilled practitioners operating with high ethical standards, can operate at the innermost ring of the Drama Spiral.

Conclusion

The Drama Spiral is intended as a practical tool for the theatre director, workshop leader, or applied arts practitioner who seeks to incorporate the personal stories of participants. The Spiral offers a template for decision making and structuring sessions, with the aim of improving safe practice while also giving practitioners and participants a way to share understanding about the applied theatre process. The Spiral is not a cookbook, offering a recipe for designing successful workshops. It is instead a kind of road map, featuring landmarks, possible destinations, suggested routes, sights of interest, and hazards to avoid. It is then down to the skill of the facilitator to find, in collaboration with colleagues and participants, the destination and the means and route to get there.

My intention in offering this structure is that it helps applied theatre work to stay ethical and informed, and also sensitive to the needs, vulnerabilities, and potentials of everyone concerned. I also hope that the Spiral offers applied theatre practitioners a useful practical resource to help their decision making and negotiation of risk, and prompts the exploration of new modes of working that generate new ideas and move beyond familiar tropes.

When we elicit participants' stories and work with them in a drama process, what is crucial is not really whether or not we focus on injury and risk or on only positive stories; what is crucial is the skill of the practitioner in staying focused on ethical processes, working collaboratively in transparently negotiated processes with groups. For some groups, staying metaphorical will be where they feel able to work. Other groups may wish to portray their story in direct terms. With appropriate precautions and processes in place and with a reflexive, nuanced approach, skilled applied theatre practitioners ought to be able to operate across the full spectrum of theatrical forms, from fourth-wall, fictional stories to the up-close-and-personal forms that include autobiographical performances around even the most vulnerable and risky topics.

To do this, the applied theatre practitioner must have a solid grasp of the terrain she is working within, and the demarcations within the terrain that keep the work within appropriate borders. Where drama processes directly access or explicitly refer to the personal and collective stories of participants, the theatre practitioner is obligated to work within a coherent ethical framework of practice which includes a structured, transparent approach at each stage of the process. Recognising this, the theatre practitioner working with people's personal stories needs to be conscious of how far "into the Spiral" she goes with the group. Moreover, the practitioner needs to work with the insight, broad view, ethics, and integrity to ask searching questions about the motives, aims, parameters, and potential short-, medium-, and long-term impact of the work on the participants, audiences, and wider society. This is the reason for developing the Spiral.

We need the right tools and the right skills in order to stage vulnerability without hurting people. The Spiral is an attempt to minimise risk while providing a containing framework for people to encounter vulnerability in relative safety. As such, the Spiral is proposed as a useful tool in the practitioner's toolkit.

Notes

1. This reminds us that the concept of what is "real" or "actual" (that is, "true") in a story must inevitably be contested. For our purposes in this discussion, we will use as a working definition that the "real" is what we are working with when participants share with us their perceptions of their own experiences, from their own perspective. This perception can, of course, change over time, and may even change during the course of a rehearsal process.
2. See also Giddens (1991) on the process of the reflexive construction of self.

References

Artaud, Antonin. 1977. *The Theatre and its Double*. London: John Calder.

Baim, Clark. 2000. Time's Distorted Mirror: Trauma Work with Adult Male Sex Offenders. In *Psychodrama with Trauma Survivors: Acting Out Your Pain*, eds. Peter F. Kellermann and M. K. Hudgins. London: Jessica Kingsley.

Baim, Clark. 2004. If All the World's a Stage, Why Did I Get the Worst Parts?: Psychodrama with Violent and Sexually Abusive Men. In *Theatre in Prison: Theory and Practice*, ed. Michael Balfour. Bristol and Portland, OR: Intellect.

Baim, Clark. 2012. Footsteps on the Moon: Using TSM Concepts with Offenders Who Have Unresolved Trauma. In *Healing World Trauma with the Therapeutic Spiral Method: Psychodramatic Stories from the Front Lines*, eds. Kate Hudgins and Francesca Toscani. London: Jessica Kingsley.

Baim, Clark, Sally Brookes, and Alun Mountford (eds.). 2002. *The Geese Theatre Handbook: Drama with Offenders and People at Risk*. Winchester: Waterside Press.

Balfour, Michael (ed.). 2004. *Theatre in Prison: Theory and Practice*. Bristol: Intellect.

Balfour, Michael (ed.). 2013. *Refugee Performance: Practical Encounters*. Bristol: Intellect.

Balfour, Michael, Marvin Westwood, and Maria Buchanan. 2014. Protecting into Emotion: Therapeutic Enactments with Military Veterans Transitioning

Back into Civilian Life. *Research in Drama Education: The Journal of Applied Theatre and Performance* 19 (2): 165–181.

Bannister, Anne. 1991. Learning to Live Again: Psychodramatic Techniques with Sexually Abused Young People. In *Psychodrama: Inspiration and Technique*, eds. P. Holmes and M. Karp. London: Tavistock/Routledge.

Barnes, Stella. 2009. Drawing a Line: A Discussion of Ethics in Participatory Arts with Young Refugees. In *Participatory Arts with Young Refugees*, ed. Stella Barnes. London: Arts in Education, Oval House Theatre.

Basting, Anne. 1998. *The Stages of Age: Performing Age in Contemporary American Culture*. Ann Arbor, MI: University of Michigan Press.

Blatner, Adam. 1997. *Acting-in: Practical Applications of Psychodramatic Methods*, 3rd ed. London: Free Association Books.

Blatner, Adam, and Allee Blatner. 1988. *The Art of Play*. New York: Human Sciences Press.

Blatner, Adam, and Daniel Wiener (eds.). 2006. *Interactive and Improvisational Drama: Varieties of Applied Theatre and Performance*. New York: iUniverse.

Blau, Herbert. 1964. *The Impossible Theatre: A Manifesto*. New York: Macmillan.

Boal, Augusto. 1979. *Theatre of the Oppressed*. London: Pluto.

Boal, Augusto. 1995. *The Rainbow of Desire: The Boal Method of Theatre and Therapy*, trans. Adrian Jackson. London: Routledge.

Bradley, Daniel. 2004. *Participatory Approaches: A Facilitator's Guide*. London: Voluntary Service Overseas.

Brittain, Victoria, Nicolas Kent, Richard Norton-Taylor, and Gillian Slovo. 2014. *The Tricycle: Collected Tribunal Plays 1994–2012*. London: Oberon.

Butler, Judith. 1997. *The Psychic Life of Power: Theories in Subjection*. Stanford: Stanford University Press.

Byng-Hall, John, and Donald Campbell. 1981. Resolving Conflicts in Family Distance Regulation: An Integrative Approach. *Journal of Marital and Family Therapy* 7 (3): 321–330.

Campbell, Joseph. 1949/2008. *The Hero with a Thousand Faces*. Novato, CA: New World Library.

Cantrell, Tom. 2012. *Verbatim Theatre*. http://www.dramaonlinelibrary.com/genres/verbatim-theatre-iid-2551. Accessed 1 Jul 2016.

Cantrell, Tom. 2013. *Acting in Documentary Theatre*. London: Palgrave.

Casson, John. 2004. *Drama, Psychotherapy and Psychosis: Dramatherapy and Psychodrama with People Who Hear Voices*. Hove: Brunner-Routledge.

Chesner, Anna. 1995. *DramaTherapy for People with Learning Disabilities*. London: Jessica Kingsley.

Cizmic, Maria. 2012. *Performing Pain: Music and Trauma in Eastern Europe*. Oxford: Oxford University Press.

Cossa, Maria, Sally Fleischmann Ember, Lauren Grover, and Jennifer L. Hazelwood. 1996. *Acting Out: The Workbook. A Guide to the Development and Presentation of Issue-Oriented, Audience-Interactive, Improvisational Theatre*. London: Taylor and Francis.

Coult, Tony, and Baz Kershaw. 1983. *Engineers of the Imagination: The Welfare State Handbook*. London: Methuen.

Crittenden, Patricia M. 1994. Peering into the Black Box: An Exploratory Treatise on the Development of Self in Young Children. In *Rochester Symposium on Developmental Psychopathology, Vol. 5. The Self and its Disorders*, eds. Dante Cicchetti and Sheree L. Toth, 79–148. Rochester, NY: University of Rochester Press.

Croyden, Margaret. 1974. *Lunatics, Lovers and Poets: The Contemporary Experimental Theatre*. New York: Delta.

Cull, Laura (ed.). 2009. *Deleuze and Performance*. Edinburgh: Edinburgh University Press.

Dallos, Rudi, and Arlene Vetere. 2009. *Systemic Therapy and Attachment Narratives: Applications in a Range of Settings*. Hove: Routledge.

Dayton, Tian. 1990. *Drama Games: Techniques for Self-Development*. Deerfield Beach, FL: Health Communications.

Deleuze, Gilles, and Félix Guattari. 1980. *A Thousand Plateaus*, trans. Brian Massumi. London and New York: Continuum, 2004.

Diamond, Elin. 1992. The Violence of 'We': Politicizing Identification. In *Critical Theory and Performance*, eds. Janelle G. Reinelt, and Joseph R. Roach, 390–938. Ann Arbor: University of Michigan Press.

Emunah, Renée. 2015. Self-Revelatory Performance: A Form of Drama Therapy and Theatre. *Drama Therapy Review* 1 (1): 71–85.

Evreinov, Nikolai. 1927. *The Theatre in Life*. New York: Harrap.

Feltham, Colin, and Ian Horton (eds.). 2012. *The Sage Handbook of Counselling and Psychotherapy*, 3rd ed. London: Sage.

Fischer-Lichte, Erika. 2008. *The Transformative Power of Performance*. London: Routledge.

Flyvbjerg, Bent, Todd Landman, and Sanford Schram (eds.). 2012. *Real Social Science: Applied Phronesis*. Cambridge: Cambridge University Press.

Forsyth, Alison (ed.). 2013. *The Methuen Drama Anthology of Testimonial Plays*. London: Bloomsbury.

Forsyth, Alison, and Chris Megson. 2009. *Get Real: Documentary Theatre Past and Present*. New York: Palgrave.

Foster, Hal. 1996. *The Return of the Real: The Avant-Garde at the End of the Century*. London: MIT Press/October Books.

Freud, Sigmund. 1953/1986. *The Essentials of Psychoanalysis*. London: Penguin.

Gardner, Lyn. 2010. Lifegame. *The Guardian* online (12 July 2010). https://www.theguardian.com/stage/2010/jul/12/lifegame-review. Accessed 27 May 2016.

Giddens, Anthony. 1991. *Modernity and Self-Identity: Self and Society in the Late Modern Age*. Cambridge: Polity Press.

Ginkas, Kama, and John Freedman. 2003. *Kama Ginkas Directs*. Hanover, NH: Smith and Kraus Inc.

Govan, Emma, Helen Nicholson, and Katie Normington. 2007. *Making a Performance: Devising Histories and Contemporary Practices*. London: Routledge.

Haedicke, Susan, and Tobin Nellhaus (eds.). 2001. *Performing Democracy: International Perspectives on Urban Community-Based Performance*. Ann Arbor, MI: University of Michigan Press.

Hammond, Will, and Dan Steward (eds.). 2008. *Verbatim Verbatim: Contemporary Documentary Theatre*. London: Oberon Books.

Heddon, Deirdre. 2008. *Autobiography and Performance*. London: Palgrave.

Heddon, Deirdre, and Jane Milling. 2005. *Devising Performance: A Critical History*. Basingstoke: Palgrave.

Holmwood, Clive. 2014. *Drama Education and Dramatherapy: Exploring the Space Between Disciplines*. London: Routledge.

Hudgins, Kate, and Francesca Toscani (eds.). 2013. *Healing World Trauma with the Therapeutic Spiral Model: Psychodramatic Stories from the Front Lines*. London: Jessica Kingsley.

Innes, Christopher D. 1972. *Erwin Piscator's Political Theatre: The Development of Modern German Drama*. Cambridge: Cambridge University Press.

Itzin, Catherine. 1980. *Stages in the Revolution: Political Theatre in Britain Since 1968*. London: Methuen.

Jaynes, Julian. 1976. *The Origin of Consciousness in the Breakdown of the Bicameral Mind*. London: Penguin.

Jennings, Sue (ed.). 2009. *Dramatherapy and Social Theatre: Necessary Dialogues*. Hove: Routledge.

Jennings, Sue. 2011. *Healthy Attachments and Neuro-dramatic Play*. London: Jessica Kingsley.

Jennings, Sue, and Ase Minde. 1993. *Art Therapy and Dramatherapy: Masks of the Soul*. London: Jessica Kingsley.

Johnstone, Keith. 2015. *Lifegame*. http://www.keithjohnstone.com/formats. Accessed 1 Jul 2015.

Jones, Phil. 1996. *Drama as Therapy: Theatre as Living*. London: Routledge.

Karpman, Stephen. 1968. Fairy Tales and Script Drama Analysis. *Transactional Analysis Bulletin* 26 (7): 39–43.

Khaiat, Kalanthe. 2011. Accountable and Theatrical Acts of Witness: Queen's University DRAM 476 Testimonial Project Pieces 2010. *Canadian Theatre Review* 147: 86–88.

Kipper, David. 1986. *Psychotherapy Through Clinical Role Playing*. New York: Brunner/Mazel.

Kumiega, Jennifer. 1987. *The Theatre of Grotowski*. London: Methuen.
LaFrance, Mary. 2013. The Disappearing Fourth Wall: Law, Ethics, and Experiential Theatre. *Vanderbilt Journal of Entertainment & Technology Law* 15 (3): 507–582.
Landy, Robert, and David T. Montgomery. 2012. *Theatre for Change: Education, Social Action and Therapy*. Basingstoke: Palgrave.
Leffler, Elliot. 2012. Replacing the Sofa with the Spotlight: Interrogating the Therapeutic Value of Personal Testimony Within Community-Based Theatre. *Research in Drama Education: The Journal of Applied Theatre and Performance* 17 (3): 347–353.
Lewin, Kurt. 1951. *Field Theory in Social Science: Selected Theoretical Papers*. New York: Harper & Row.
Linds, Warren. 1996. Metaxis: Dancing (in) the In-between. In *A Boal Companion: Dialogues on Theatre and Cultural Politics*, eds. Jan Cohen-Cruz and Mady Schutzman, 114–124. London: Routledge.
McAvinchy, Caoimhe. 2011. *Theatre and Prison*. Basingstoke: Palgrave.
McConachie, Bruce. 2013. *Theatre and Mind*. Basingstoke: Palgrave.
Malaev-Babel, Andrei. 2013. *Yevgeny Vakhtangov: A Critical Portrait*. New York: Routledge.
Martin, Carol (ed.). 2012. *Dramaturgy of the Real on the World Stage*. Basingstoke: Palgrave.
Martin, Carol. 2013. *Theatre of the Real*. Basingstoke: Palgrave.
Mattingly, Cheryl. 1998. *Healing Dramas and Clinical Plots: The Narrative Structure of Experience*. Cambridge: Cambridge University Press.
Milling, Jane, and Graham Ley. 2001. *Modern Theories of Performance*. Basingstoke: Palgrave.
Moreno, Jacob L. 1924. *Das Stegreiftheatre*. Vienna: Gustav Kiepenheuer Verlag. Published in 1947 as *The Theatre of Spontaneity*. New York: Beacon House.
Moreno, Jacob L. 1946/1972. *Psychodrama*, vol. 1. Ambler, PA: Beacon Press.
Moreno, Jacob L., and Zerka T. Moreno. 1975. *Psychodrama*, vol. 2. Beacon, NY: Beacon House.
Moreno, Jacob L., and Zerka T. Moreno. 1969/2012. *Psychodrama, Vol. 3: Action Therapy and Principles of Practice*. Merseyside: North West Psychodrama Association, Lulu.com.
Moreno, Jonathan D. 2014. *Impromptu Man: J.L. Moreno and the Origins of Psychodrama, Encounter Culture, and the Social Network*. New York: Belleview Literary Press.
Neuringer, Charles. 1992. Freud and the Theatre. *Journal of the American Academy of Psychoanalysis* 20 (1): 142–148.
Nicholson, Helen. 2014. *Applied Drama: The Gift of Theatre*, 2nd ed. Basingstoke: Palgrave.

Nolte, John. 2014. *The Philosophy, Theory and Methods of J.L. Moreno: The Man Who Tried to Become God*. London: Routledge.

O'Connor, Alison. 2015. Abandoned Brothers, Life Story Theatre with Veterans and Their Families. *Arts & Health: An International Journal for Research, Policy and Practice* 7 (2): 151–160.

O'Connor, Alison and Karin Diamond. 2014. Re-live: Theatre, Life Story Work and Dementia. *Signpost: Journal of Dementia and Mental Health Care of Older People* 20 (2): 15–20.

Pendzik, Susana, Renée Emunah, and David Read Johnson (eds.). 2016. *The Self in Performance: Autobiographical, Self-Revelatory, and Autoethnographic Forms of Therapeutic Theatre*. New York: Palgrave.

Perrow, Susan. 2012. *Therapeutic Storytelling: 101 Healing Stories For Children*. Stroud: Hawthorn Press.

Prendergast, Monica, and Juliana Saxton (eds.). 2009. *Applied Theatre: International Case Studies and Challenges for Practice*. Bristol: Intellect.

Prentki, Tim, and Sheila Preston (eds.). 2009. *The Applied Theatre Reader*. Abingdon: Routledge.

Rancière, Jacques. 2009. *The Emancipated Spectator*. London: Verso.

Richards, Thomas. 1995. *At Work with Grotowski on Physical Actions*. London: Routledge.

Rifkin, Frances. 2010. *The Ethics of Participatory Theatre in Higher Education: A Framework for Learning and Teaching*. York: Higher Education Academy (Research Report).

Rohd, Michael. 1998. *Theatre for Community, Conflict and Dialogue: The Hope is Vital Training Manual*. Portsmouth, NH: Heinemann/Reed Elsevier.

Salas, Jo. 1993. *Improvising Real Life: Personal Story in Playback Theatre*. New Paltz, NY: Tusitala.

Saldana, Johnny (ed.). 2005. *Ethnodrama: An Anthology of Reality Theatre*. Walnut Creek, CA: AltaMira Press.

Saldana, Johnny. 2011. *Ethnotheatre: Research from Page to Stage*. Walnut Creek, CA: Left Coast Press.

Salverson, Julie. 1996. Performing Emergency: Witnessing, Popular Theatre, and the Lie of the Literal. *Theatre Topics* 6 (2): 181–191.

Salverson, Julie. 2001. Change on Whose Terms? Testimony and an Erotics of Inquiry. *Theatre* 31 (3): 119–125.

Schank, Roger C. 1990. *Tell Me a Story: A New Look at Real and Artificial Memory*. New York: Charles Scribner's Sons.

Schechner, Richard. 1988. *Performance Theory*. London: Routledge.

Scheiffele, Eberhard. 1995. *The Theatre of Truth: Psychodrama, Spontaneity and Improvisation: The Theatrical Theories and Influences of Jacob Levy Moreno*. PhD dissertation, University of California at Berkeley.

Schneider, Rebecca. 2011. *Performing Remains: Art and War in Times of Theatrical Reenactment*. Abingdon, UK: Routledge.

Schutzman, Mady, and Jan Cohen-Cruz (eds.). 1994. *Playing Boal: Theatre, Therapy, Activism*. London and New York: Routledge.
Schweitzer, Pam. 2007. *Reminiscence Theatre: Making Theatre from Memories*. London: Jessica Kingsley.
Sepinuck, Teya. 2013. *Theatre of Witness: Finding the Medicine in Stories of Suffering, Transformation and Peace*. London: Jessica Kingsley.
Shailor, Jonathan (ed.). 2011. *Performing New Lives: Prison Theatre*. London: Jessica Kingsley.
Smith, Anna Deavere. 2001. *Talk to Me: Travels in Media and Politics*. New York: Anchor Books.
Smith, Anna Deavere. 2006. *Letters to a Young Artist: Straight-Up Advice on Making a Life in the Arts—For Actors, Performers, Writers, and Artists of Every Kind*. New York: Anchor Books.
Stanislavski, Constantin. 1961. *Creating a Role*. New York: Theatre Arts Books.
Stephenson, Jennifer. 2013. *Performing Autobiography: Contemporary Canadian Drama*. Toronto: University of Toronto Press.
Thompson, James. 1998. *Prison Theatre: Perspectives and Practices*. London: Jessica Kingsley.
Thompson, James. 2005. *Digging Up Stories: Applied Theatre, Performance and War*. Manchester: Manchester University Press.
Thompson, James. 2009a. The Ends of Applied Theatre: Incidents of Chopping and Cutting. In *The Applied Theatre Reader*, eds. Tim Prentki, and Sheila Preston. Abingdon: Routledge.
Thompson, James. 2009b. *Performance Affects: Applied Theatre and the End of Effect*. Basingstoke: Palgrave.
Van der Kolk, Bessel. 2014. *The Body Keeps the Score: Brain, Mind, and Body in the Healing of Trauma*. New York: Viking.
Wake, Caroline. 2013. To Witness Mimesis: The Politics, Ethics, and Aesthetics of Testimonial Theatre in Through the Wire. *Modern Drama* 56 (1): 102–125.
Walsh, Fintan. 2013. *Theatre and Therapy*. Basingstoke: Palgrave.
Warner, Marina. 2012. *Stranger Magic: Charmed States and the Arabian Nights*. Cambridge, MA: Harvard University Press.
Wasilewska, Ewa. 2000. *Creation Stories of the Middle East*. London: Jessica Kingsley.
White, Michael. 2007. *Maps of Narrative Practice*. New York: Norton.
Yablonsky, Lewis. 1976. *Psychodrama: Resolving Emotional Problems Through Role-Playing*. New York: Basic Books.
Zarilli, Phillip B., Bruce McConachie, Gary Jay Williams, and Carol Fisher Sorgenfrei. 2010. *Theatre Histories: An Introduction*, 2nd ed. London: Routledge.

PART II

Performing Intimacies: Flirting, Whispering, and Sharing Stories in the Dark

Dance with a Stranger: Torque Show's *Intimacy* (2014) and the Experience of Vulnerability in Performance and Spectatorship

Matt Hargrave

You are invited to join the actor on stage. You do so, only half grudgingly. You know that this moment has been coming. Strange but inevitable. You felt it as you were entering the auditorium. Like you were being vetted. What kind of a person are you? Did they see in you some secret desire, a need to perform? Were you "asking for it", so to speak? "It": this intrusion. At the invitation, midway through the show, you stand up, like you are at the poolside, about to take a dip. You are wearing Birkenstocks. You shuffle them off. This gets a laugh. What caused that? This minor act of stripping, from one self into another, from audience to performer? Perhaps it is the slightly weary way you make this gesture: Oh no, not participation! *You walk on stage. Barefoot. Minutes later you are asked to cuddle a male performer in a sleeping bag. This also gets a laugh. You're cuddling him on the floor, he in his sleeping bag, you outside it. He asks you for touch, for warmth. You are*

M. Hargrave (✉)
University of Northumbria, Newcastle-upon-Tyne, UK
e-mail: matt.hargrave@northumbria.ac.uk

© The Author(s) 2017

A. O'Grady (ed.), *Risk, Participation, and Performance Practice*,
DOI 10.1007/978-3-319-63242-1_5

a middle-aged man spooning a younger man on stage. Later, you build an imaginary campfire. You avert your gaze for a second and get another laugh from the audience. Vincent has dropped his sleeping bag. The laugh comes because of the assumption—wrong, as it turns out—that Vincent will be naked. You missed the big reveal, because you were ... participating, carrying out some function in the narrative, thus not able to see what the others see. You feel disappointed for a second. You are looking into someone else's eyes, another spectator turned actor. You didn't think it would turn out this way.[1]

"'I didn't think it would turn out this way' is the secret epitaph of intimacy", says Lauren Berlant, speaking of "the attachments [that] buttress 'a life' ... of constant, if latent, vulnerability (1998, 281–282). She is talking here of the intimate life: the sustaining normative of "the couple", who support each other over a life. The normative model of intimacy is riven with tacit exclusions: what of those encounters that don't lead to "a life"? How does a drama of desire that sidesteps the couple play out? What does the individual left out of this ideal "canon" have left to believe in? And how might sexuality be reframed in the event of bodies that cannot manifest their desire unsupported? Michelle Ryan's "character" in *Intimacy* appears to have been thrown out of her previous life, the life she expected to live: a continuation of professional dancer, choreographer, lover, and partner. Yet the power of *Intimacy* lies in the way that Ryan's vulnerability spills out to affect the entire aesthetic, and thus the audience. The aesthetic confronts several audience members, as the opening voice (my own in raw form) suggests, with their own vulnerability in surprising ways.

This chapter investigates the meaning of vulnerability in relation to performance. It argues that performance as vulnerability/vulnerability as performance is a shifting dynamic rather than a simple binary. Theoretically, this chapter is grounded in the aesthetics of disability (Seibers 2010; Davidson 2008; Hadley 2014); extends insight into the poetics of disability (Hargrave 2015); and builds on a platform of critical disability studies, which distances itself from both medical and social models of disability (Shildrick 2009) and focuses on disability through the lens of vulnerability: this is in order to highlight the interconnectedness, rather than the exclusivity, of corporeal diversity. I deliberately use the terms disability and vulnerability interchangeably in this chapter, not because they are the same thing, but because the ambiguity between the two can open up a new critical space, a frame that continually undoes the (singular, monolithic) frame: I am disabled/you are not.

Too often the debate about disability and disability art falls back on an outmoded binary between different models (social, medical, or affirmative). *Intimacy* represents a critique of such binaries because it asks the spectator to engage in the intimate sphere, always an intersubjective realm, not an either/or one of fixed identity positions. In this chapter I will argue for a poetics of vulnerability: that vulnerability is an interruptive value, both socially (because it upsets the myth of the autonomous self) and aesthetically (since it opens up the closed aesthetic artefact); that it invites spectators' complicity; that vulnerability reavows structural support; and that it places both fixed identity and fixed judgement in doubt.

In what follows I engage closely with Erin Gilson's work on vulnerability (2013)—with her refusal to accept the normative frame of vulnerability as a given, but rather to examine how vulnerability is constructed as a problem. The primary question of this chapter is: How can we theorise vulnerability? A second question is: What theatrical forms might arise, taking vulnerability as their starting point? Furthermore, how can the rich ethical implications of vulnerability be conveyed within the aesthetic? Vulnerability is, after all, built into the fabric of theatre. Public performance does away with the safety net of script and rehearsal room and transports its actors into places unknown: strange buildings, new people, watchful eyes, friendly at first yet expected to cast a critical eye. The liveness of theatre means that it shares with Ryan the fact of corporeal contingency. Performers on stage are always vulnerable, prone to errors in sequencing, lapses in the display of continuity; yet Ryan's vulnerability, as with all artists who acquire impairment, engages her in a new relationship with (her former) virtuosity. The normative "former self" becomes a ghostly reference point not only for loss and grief but also for normativity itself. Gilson's eloquent and exhaustive *Ethics of Vulnerability* (ibid.) explores the implications of three assertions: firstly, that the normative equivalence of vulnerability with weakness (as well as with liability and powerlessness) devalues vulnerability as something socially "bad", to be disavowed where possible; secondly, that vulnerability can be viewed as an ethical resource that helps manifest virtues of empathy, compassion, and community; and thirdly, that there is often a negative, as yet critically underexamined, relationship between risk and vulnerability, one that reduces vulnerability to a state of perpetual risk (as opposed to the ambiguous, multifaceted, and productive experience it has the potential to be). I argue that a fourth implication arises from this critical work: that vulnerability is an aesthetic resource.

In order to explore these theoretical questions, the chapter utilises a single case study: *Intimacy*, a show by Australian company Torque Show in collaboration with Michelle Ryan. The piece, directed by Ingrid Weisfelt, which made its international debut at Unlimited 2014, is part confessional, part cabaret, and part flirtatious dance with an audience seduced into participating. Ryan, accompanied by musician Simon Eszeky, singer Emma Bathgate—collectively Lavender Vs. Rose—and a male dancing partner (Vincent Crowley), is at the centre of the work. The piece deals with the reality of her life living with multiple sclerosis (MS), a condition that first affected her at the age of thirty, when she was at the prime of her dancing career. *Intimacy* invites spectators to witness the emotional fallout of her MS: her marital break-up, the loss of physical capacity, the need for constant support, and the appearance of an array of unsuitable men. The musical score creates a playful cabaret atmosphere; Ryan's dreams are surreal, savage yet funny; comedy arises too from frequent audience interaction. At one point Ryan asks for help changing her dress; three men are enlisted to help. Others are called on to create a campfire scene, helping Ryan's fictive partner (Crowley) overcome his resistance to intimacy. Performers and spectators hold each other, gaze into one another's eyes, flirt publicly, embarrass easily. This work is about the risk of vulnerability; it is also about teasing, playing at the edges of commitment. This chapter explores both and argues that their juxtaposition—in performance—is what generates new knowledge and models what Jen Harvie has described as "alternative ways of being which preserve principles of social collaboration and interdependence" (2014, 193).

I saw *Intimacy* at the Unlimited festival at the Southbank Centre in 2014, where it had been brought in by the Southbank producers to add an international dimension to the festival, which features new works by UK-based disabled artists. This chapter explores *Intimacy* through the lens of vulnerability, not in order to validate the bravery of the performer or to exoticise the elements of risk, but rather to examine what vulnerability looks and feels like; in this case, it is anything but uniform, tragic, or weak. In the case of *Intimacy*, it is the sensuousness of vulnerability that makes itself felt, its openness to feelings the spectator cannot control. *Intimacy* could just as well be titled *Flirtation*, in the psychoanalytic sense: an experimental approach to life that "does not make a virtue of instability but a pleasure" (Phillips 1994, xii). Likewise, it is pleasure that invites consideration in this work: of relationships (as opposed to distinctions) between bodies; of touch, care, support; of irreverence; and of the potential for vulnerability to act not as another master narrative but as a holding frame for alternatives to shaming. My beginning intention, then, is to closely examine the formal properties of the work and the affective experience of being a spectator (and, however briefly and strangely, a co-performer); I do so in the belief that the theatrical frame can lead to an analysis of the frame of vulnerability itself, how it is constructed, and how it might be otherwise.

Dreaming and Framing: Vulnerability as an Interruptive Value

[Ryan turns to Crowley. They pretend to be two friends, having a drink in a bar.]

I have very vivid dreams about men. In my last dream there were two men. Both men were in love with me, and I loved both men. So the two men decided they would take things into their own hands ... We met in a café; they both had beautiful brown shoes on, and each one had a beautiful brown hat. One took his hat off and placed it on the table and the other man left his hat on. They started to kick each other; they started to fight to the point where they started to bleed. So they went outside, and continued to fight, and the fighting went on for three days and three nights, and by the end of the third night they were just exhausted and covered in blood. They went back inside but there was still the problem of what they were going to do about me. So one man decided that he would turn me into a chicken. The other man prepared me by putting beautiful herbs and spices all over me, and he placed me in the oven. And when I came out I had crispy brown skin and succulent flesh. But there was still the problem of who was going to have me. So they decided that they would cut me down the middle. The first man, who wanted all of me, took his half and just devoured me. The second man, he decided that he didn't want his half, so he just ripped off my leg, took a bite of my flesh, and threw the rest of me away.

Dreaming reframes reality. It reconfigures how we think of our lives in surprising ways—as does disability. Disability upsets the dramaturgy of everyday life. Disability reframes the normative world, estranging one from what "just is": a staircase, a career, a lover. *Intimacy*'s dramaturgy is a dreamscape, a weirdly logical juxtaposition of song, movement, storytelling, dramatic dialogue, and audience interaction. Ryan, as above, speaks her dreams in the play. These are dreams within a dream. The formal properties of the work play with the problem of framing: the play is a dream from which Ryan cannot awake.

The structure of the work is broadly that of postmodern dance theatre, in which the performers and musicians move from song to dance, to conversation, to audience interaction. The deployment of a traverse stage places the performers between two sets of spectators and enables those spectators to watch each other: the audience are constantly watching themselves watching the show; one's point of view is dependent on where one sits and who else is present at a given performance. This is highlighted in recorded versions of the piece: the camera continually goes in and out of focus. Its gaze never settles on a unitary point. *Intimacy* breaks with the unity of the proper or the orderly and composes itself via juxtaposition and interruption. It achieves its effects by continually undoing the frame. This is the first principle of what I will call the poetics of vulnerability: that vulnerability is an interruptive value. The context for the above dream, for example, is Ryan acting out a conversation in a bar with Crowley, who looks ever more uncomfortable as the dream unfolds. The dream is not presented as direct address: it is received by an interlocutor who reacts, not with earnest encouragement but with ironic distance. This is an important aspect of the piece: it continually ironises feeling. Very few speeches or perspectives are free of juxtaposition with conflicting feelings or ideas. Following an earlier dream, in which Ryan breaks a tooth, Bathgate immediately begins a raucous version of *Accentuate the Positive*. These constant shifts of mood and perspective not only undo the aesthetic but point also to vulnerability as a frame, that is, a fixed, uninterrupted idea about how the world is. They enhance, rather than undermine, vulnerability, since they demonstrate how survival, as in everyday life, is so often supported by dark comedy and distanced perspective.

Judith Butler argues that frames—intellectual frames: how we view the world—provide conditions of intelligibility and thus "organise visual experience" (2009, 3). Dramaturgical choices frame the way one views a work, but prior to this one already has a view of what the frame should be. Normative ideas about vulnerability—weakness, individual tragedy—frame the way we look at vulnerability: the frame is not neutral. Thus, the ethical job of criticism is to lay bare the device, so to speak, to reveal what is usually taken for granted. I argue that *Intimacy* already does this. By speaking intimate dreams in public, by opening up the structure of the show to risk audience participation, by having Bathgate sing songs that often contradict the mood of the preceding scene, the frame allows itself to be continually undermined. One of the key tenets of Butler's work on vulnerability is that she seeks to avoid judgements arrived at without critical thought. The example she gives is "terrorist violence", a term that closes down debate as soon as it is uttered: it is simply wrong, and its "wrongness" is not seen as a matter for debate (ibid., 153). The frame of the Unlimited festival, where I viewed the work, was "disability art". I am not suggesting a direct correlation between "terrorist violence" and "disability art": I do, however, argue that the framing of work as "disability art" is not neutral. As a contemporary report articulates it: "Whether external reviewers tend to be more generous with the work of disabled artists is a question worth asking. It may be that conventional approaches to criticism are inadequate for some reviewers and they opt for the safer option of offering a critique that examines but does not judge" (AQA report 2014). It struck me when I first saw *Intimacy* that I was not seeing a piece of work *about* disability but rather a work about the human need to connect, a theme that transcends differential categories. And furthermore, the pleasure I took in the work *demanded* that I judge it, because, to quote Edmund Husserl: "Within the joy we are intentionally (with feeling intentions) turned toward the joy-Object as such in the mode of affective 'interest'" (quoted in Ahmed 2010, 31). In art, pleasure and judgement are one.

One way of judging the "meaning" of Ryan's dreams is to not dwell on the subject of those dreams but rather to notice the form of their telling. The dream of being eaten is both horrible and funny because of the pure, disembodied gaze via which she observes her demise. The ultimate fantasy in a Lacanian sense is to see ourselves as others see us, or indeed to see the world *without ourselves*, as if we were dead. Equally, as Žižek playfully points out, "all dreams have a hidden sexual meaning, except the overtly sexual ones" (2014, 26). The subjects of Ryan's dreams are less important than their function *as dreams*. This is important in two ways: firstly, they break the taboo of public exposure, and secondly, they point to the destruction of the frame as such. Vulnerability, as the "viral" success of popular psychologist Brené Brown's lectures attests, is a very difficult thing to talk about: a taboo of a kind. Ryan's public speaking is going further than Brown: she is speaking her unconscious out loud. Žižek argues that the point of psychoanalysis is not to step outside fantasy but rather to traverse it, to shatter its foundations. Fantasy, here, is meant as the sense of reality one maintains in order to adhere to normative boundaries. If we view the frame of vulnerability—or, rather, the myth of invulnerability— carefully, its power is revealed as entirely derived from unspoken assumptions: for example, vulnerable people are a risk to themselves and others, they are a burden on the invulnerable majority. If, as Žižek maintains, "fantasy is a dirty intimate secret which cannot survive public exposure" (ibid., 30), the persistent occurrence of dreams in *Intimacy* is a clue to an open secret: our shared vulnerability. An ethical criticism, then, is one that always seeks to name unspoken assumptions, hidden subtexts. If Ryan's dreams point to melancholia—unresolved mourning and attachment to a lost object (her former self or her former intimacies)—the question arises, to what extent does the normative frame encourage and even incite the tendency to mourn disability? Disability, perhaps especially the suddenly acquired impairment, is rarely viewed as a positive outcome in the life narrative, just as the birth of a disabled child is rarely met with uncomplicated celebration. As Sara Ahmed has written, the queer child upsets her parents not necessarily on the basis of sexuality but rather because her choice of sexuality is seen to preclude her future happiness:

> [F]or a life to count as a good life, it must return to the debt of its life by taking on the direction promised as a social good, which means imagining one's futurity in terms of reaching certain points along a life course. The promise of happiness thus directs life in some ways rather than others. (2010, 41)

The promise of happiness rarely seems to coincide with disability or vulnerability, yet any human life will inevitably involve both, sooner or later. To think of vulnerability as one facet of life among many is simply a shift of perspective, yet it is a difficult one to maintain when the frame of invulnerability—the persistent fiction of complete autonomous personhood—remains, in virtually every aspect of daily and public life, so pervasive. Furthermore, as Ahmed argues, the correlation between good feelings and a progressive attitude—and between bad feelings and backward, regretful ones—closes down human diversity; this is what *Intimacy* achieves: an art work that affirms vulnerability as one facet of a pleasurable aesthetic whole.

Joining in: Vulnerability as Complicity

Bathgate, who has been carrying Ryan piggyback style, leaves the stage, leaving Ryan supported by an audience member: "She usually comes back, but it's not looking good today," says Ryan. "While you're up would you mind helping with this dress? Thanks. And you, could you help as well? Would you mind just taking my shoes off? And can you pull my pants down for me? Could you just grab my other shoes ... I feel really bad, thanks. And if you could give me a little neck rub? Thank you very much for your help, I really appreciate it."

Intimacy complicates the meaning of vulnerability, and this complication develops not just ethical resource but also aesthetic potential, not least in relation to audience participation. Any singular, and thus reductive, meaning of vulnerability is ruptured by the constant interaction between Ryan and her co-performers and between both and the audience. A normative reading (or performing) of vulnerability would single out Ryan as the "vulnerable one", different from the autonomous, invulnerable spectators—or indeed the sovereign, always in control, male dancer—a victim of injury, to be gazed upon with pity and assumed to be prisoner of a fixed (always vulnerable) state. Such a reading would be wholly in keeping with normative assumptions that seek to close down a nuanced engagement with the subject of vulnerability. *Intimacy* circumvents this model in several ways. *Both* performers and spectators are placed in vulnerable states, in the best sense: they are, if they so choose, open, engaged, affected, alert. It could be you next; *you are both darer and carer.* This kind of audience participation is quite unlike, say, Boalian practice where spectators are asked to consider a particular dramatic deadlock and suggest a rational solution. The kind of participation in *Intimacy* does not feel like autonomous action. It is more like a series of questions asked of a body (my body/your body) as it responds to the need of another, an acknowledging of the other, and a giving in. This did not appeal to all spectators. As Weisfelt explains: "The audience member that Vince invited to sit by the fire with him at one point, half way through the scene, decided that they didn't want to be involved any more and just got up and left him there alone! [It] shows how tenuous the audience/performer conceit is" (pers. comm., 5 November 2015). Above all, the show challenges the ideal of the self as an autonomous chooser of experience. Rather, it suggests, in its microcosmic playful dream world, that relationality (or intersubjectivity) is the proper mode of human conduct, the secret that we need to keep sharing. Our choices to "act" during *Intimacy* are more instinctive than rational, more collaborative than goal orientated. The moment in the play when Ryan asks for support in dressing and undressing is a good example of how the aesthetic transgresses boundaries of touch and intimacy, yet does so in the most gentle, courteous of ways, often catching the audience unawares, with little time to make a considered choice. It is important to note that if this sounds rather intimidating on paper, the pervasive mood of the spectators during live and recorded performance is of shared mirth, as if these sudden intimacies release a deep pleasure: pleasure in seeing unsuspecting performers placed in new roles, and pleasure that these "para-performers" feel in having contributed.

Margrit Shildrick argues that the normative ideal (corporeal and psychic wholeness) is based on denial of our always vulnerable selves. From a psychoanalytic perspective, the infant is a vulnerable being before s/he is a sexual one: s/he is beset by the terrors of castration and mutilation, of dislocation and evisceration. In order to construct a workable identity, the child must disavow these realities and construct a unified, stable self. From this viewpoint, several logical possibilities emerge: identity is defined by contingency and vulnerability; this vulnerability must remain repressed or unacknowledged in order for the "autonomous" self to defend (the illusion of) wholeness; and those persons "marked" by vulnerability present a profound challenge to this status quo. The disabled body troubles and extends the meaning of a desiring subject, in the sense that disabled bodies disrupt "the putative norm of the autonomous subject", heteronormative and free from external interaction (Shildrick 2009, 179). Shildrick utilises Deleuze to suggest that, far from seeing the precarious or disorganised body as lacking, it is an opportunity that produces an excessive network of energies or flows. *Intimacy* plays, perhaps unconsciously, with the "implicit confusion of boundaries between one body and another" (ibid., 129) and the inherent risk involved in touch. Touch is risky because it undermines the "illusion of purity and self-sufficiency" (ibid.).

Shildrick's concern, in *Dangerous Discourses*, is partly with the performativity of the sexual self: how disabled bodies undermine the notion of autonomous desire. Her examples are the use of prosthesis and the involvement of carers who support sexual acts by disabled clients. I make no direct correlation here between *Intimacy* and supported sex; rather, I want to transport ways of thinking about the subject back into performance. The moments when Ryan asks for audience support evoke Shildrick's remark that the "disabled woman performer who relies on an assistant to prepare for a sexual encounter … is not different in kind from other women, but only engaged more overtly in … networks … [characterised as] desiring production" (ibid., 138, my substitutions). Such moments deconstruct the meaning of the isolated sovereign performer, pursuing a fixed desire line. They open up an array of relationships that trouble the binaries of active/passive and invite new ways of interconnectedness. I invite the reader to consider Shildrick's words and to replace "woman" with "performer"; "sexual encounter" with "staged encounter"; and "desiring production" with "performance production". By involving the audience in acts of intimate care, Ryan produces an aesthetic that interrupts the mechanisms of performance production and creates a complex complicity. Such blurring of performance roles are, like mediated sex, perhaps "risky and uncomfortable" (ibid., 144), but they open up a world of "differential ... exploration rather than silence and shame" (ibid., 145). This is a further component of a poetics of vulnerability. It does more than interrupt the aesthetic: it makes the audience complicit in the act.

Propping Up: Vulnerability as Structural Support and Identity Work

The risk of potentially looking foolish on stage for one brief moment in their life is nothing compared to the risk and charm offensive that Michelle performs daily to get a taxi to work. Michelle has to concoct these moments of intimacy, collusion and flirtation with complete strangers every day. (Weisfelt, pers. comm., 16 December 2014)

The performance involves several props: chairs, sleeping bags, a fire, wine glasses, and bottles, but in a very concrete sense, the audience are props too: "warm props", as the old joke designates actors, who support and act as thinking prostheses, not just for Ryan but for other elements in the production. Prosthesis is a way of adjoining flesh to some other mechanism; it may enhance or replace a habitual function, but it may also radically subvert the use of them. In an uncanny way such props trouble the safety of the binary between the body and the thing, or between the active and passive self. As Shildrick maintains:

> The emphasis shifts from the integrity of the whole organism to focus instead on the material and momentary event of coming together of disparate parts, bodies [therefore] need no longer be thought of as either whole or broken, able-bodied or disabled, but simply in a process of becoming though the unmapped circulation of desire. (2009, 135)

I want to underline "event" here. Žižek defines the basic feature of an event as "the surprising emergence of something new which undermines every stable scheme" (2014, 6). The immediate onset of MS is an event: that of becoming disabled. So too is *Intimacy* the show: becoming relational, unlocking the potential of disparate bodies. My concern here, once again, is not simply the ethical injunction to "support others" but also the aesthetic potential of support: vulnerability as form. Firstly, vulnerability invites innovative ways to support not just the central actor but the entire aesthetic structure. Even in large sections of the show that do not feature Ryan directly, the constant sense of her—and our—vulnerability is felt. *Intimacy* would make sense without audience support. The dreams, stories, songs, and choreography work in and of themselves but without intervention they would be flattened, diminished. This is another principle of the poetics: vulnerability *reavows* structural support. *Intimacy* is a teaming heteronomous interplay, which upsets the ideal of both autonomous artwork, and autonomous self: its openness to contingency is an experiment in aesthetics and an implicit critique of the ideology of what Gilson terms "entrepreneurial subjectivity", the now prevalent mode of citizenship which promotes competitive self-seeking rationality. *Intimacy*, in Shannon Jackson's words, "foregrounds performance as a series of supporting relations" (2011, 42). Many of the supporting structures that make the show possible, of course, are *not* seen. An audience does not expect to see preparation, planning, and orchestration in the normative theatre ecology. Yet, as Weisfelt's comment about Ryan above indicates, the spectator is encouraged to see beyond the *mise en scène* into the everyday life of the performer. Weisfelt makes the point that Ryan's training as a performer enabled her to manipulate her vulnerability on stage during a career in a dance company—"does the director/choreographer/my colleagues like the creative decisions that I am making and therefore validate me as an artist?" (pers. comm., 16 December 2014)—and has enabled her to "charm, flirt with and emotionally manipulate people constantly to be able to do what she wants or needs to do" (ibid.). The moments when Ryan cajoles and teases audience members into "helping" take on a different meaning in this light: it suggests performance as vulnerability/vulnerability as performance, a shifting dynamic rather than a simple binary. This extends Gilson's argument about the multifaceted nature of vulnerability. On stage, as in life, Ryan has become expert at using physical weakness to survive, again echoing Adam Phillips's point: making not "a virtue of instability but [at least a] pleasure" (Phillips 1994, xxiii).

Secondly, the facilitative living prop troubles the binary of the audience–performer relationship. Such props become a "third actor", undermining the fixedness of who and who is not a performer, and what should or should not be seen on stage. As soon as I entered the stage to "support" Crowley, I was read aesthetically, a capacity that is *both* vulnerable and powerful. I could literally change the course of the show. Every action shifted the meaning of what came next. I am struck by the irony of Andrew Sofor's remark, "A prop is something an object becomes rather than something an object is" (quoted in Jackson 2011, 80). He is paraphrasing Winicott's essay on babies and is referencing the fact that all props are read within the semiotic system. The truth is that the spectators invited to take the leap are persons that *become* props, in the sense that they hold Ryan up and also enter into the semiotic system. Of course, in a very real sense, Ryan has become disabled by MS—she has acquired an impairment—but she can only truly *become* disabled by the gaze and naming of others, by the frame of disavowal that "reads" that impairment. My point is that any linear, reductive reading of disability—that is, some people have it, others do not—is placed in doubt by the constantly shifting interplay of actors and spectators. This is another principle of the poetics: what disability or vulnerability "is" is placed in doubt for the duration of the performance.

Writing Up: Vulnerability as a Method

He puts off writing about this show. Writing makes one vulnerable to attack, from other scholars, but also to the nagging, guilty sense that one will not do the work justice. Sources, evidence, methods, theories are strategies for critique but also avoidance: ways of sidestepping vulnerability, of bolstering the scholar's defences, of backing up, or covering up. Criticism at its most productive is an act of deep appreciation, a way of warding off disappearance. It keeps what should not be forgotten alive. At its worst, it is a way of closing down, finishing something that should remain open. (Author's journal, 2 May 2015)

Intimacy, like other works that seem to push vulnerability to the forefront of consciousness, demands a supple and reflexive criticism. It asks us to reflect on the act of critical engagement as a relational and cooperative method. Part of this method is to acknowledge one's own vulnerability, to acknowledge the truth of Elspeth Probyn's insight: "The risk of writing is always that you will fail to engage readers ... There is shame in being highly interested in something and unable to convey it to others" and that "[d]isappointment in yourself looms large" (Probyn 2010, 72). Perhaps a necessary part of engaging with questions of vulnerability is the tendency to become hyper-alert to one's own anxieties. What would a vulnerable writing method look like? Gilson outlines the components of "epistemic vulnerability": an openness to not knowing (often considered a form of intellectual weakness); venturing ideas without fear that they may be considered "wrong"; putting oneself in the way of vulnerability by trying out new situations; calling attention to embodied knowledge and affective response; and being open, not just to new ideas or beliefs but also to a different sense of self, one that privileges the affecting of, and being affected by, others (Gilson 2013, 93–96). *Intimacy*, furthermore, requires a poetics of vulnerability: a mode of address that privileges its existence as something made, an artefact designed to evoke thought and pleasure. A poetics takes the work seriously yet is itself playful, that is, descriptive rather than prescriptive, as much an attitude—a sensibility—as a model. A model implies something fixed and correct; an attitude, on the other hand, like the way a jazz musician approaches a theme, is less about what is said than how it is said. Rather than seek to finalise knowledge into intellectual paradigms, a poetics seeks to provoke heightened response, nuance, and ambiguity.

I argue that precisely by withholding fixed outcomes, refusing to make final claims, and resisting instrumental knowledge, vulnerability and performance can upset the foundations of what Gilson calls "entrepreneurial subjectivity" (ibid., 98–127). Such subjectivity reduces life to competitive rational individuals pursuing autonomous goals, dependent on the deep background of market forces. Vulnerability as performed in *Intimacy* acts as a mode of resistance. In a sense, the moment when the audience member chose to abandon Vincent is the most powerful example. *Intimacy* does not suggest that works of art will make things "better", but they do make us think differently about the support we need and moments when we refuse to give it (or remain unaware that we have done so). The fact that Ryan's vulnerability makes the materials of support visible and transparent is a contribution to a shift in knowledge; it outs the support structures that are usually hidden, countering the myth of the unsupported artwork/genius artist. This is not to say that criticism should not be rooted in a recognition of fundamental inequalities. As Stuart Hall argues: "One needs to be able to offer … critical judgement and to argue it through, to have one's mind changed, without undermining one's essential commitment to the project of the politics of black [or, in this case, disabled] representation" (1987, 10). It is not my intention here to draw a simplistic parallel but rather to highlight the tension involved in critiquing artworks which are—or are for the duration of the Unlimited project—part of a burgeoning movement. Hall's first steps in struggling to name the "politics of representation" (critical, shifting, perpetually repositioning) as distinct from the "burden of representation" (essential and fixed black/white subjects) resonates over twenty years later as disabled artists, whose work was commissioned for Unlimited, faced leaving, in Hall's terms, "the age of critical innocence" (ibid., 10). These questions of aesthetic judgement are precisely those Hall engaged in from "*inside* a continuous struggle and politics around black representation" and which he was at pains to admit were "extremely tricky" because the "mode" of address was *as important* as the particularity of the judgement itself (ibid., 10). As Hall concludes, the job of criticism is to "get both things right", a challenge that is evoked again by *Intimacy*.

I argue, however, that *Intimacy* does not require "bracketed" criticism, a defence of its aesthetic qualities, in relation to the *subject of* disability. In art theorist Bruce Baugh's words, *Intimacy* "commands our assent" and can be "held back" only "due to misunderstanding, ignorance, or a refusal to judge the work aesthetically" (1988, 482). For Baugh, "works of art have a 'world' that they can make 'their own' by revealing it in a singular manner and … it is in this that artistic authority consists" (ibid., 479). Art does more than simply represent: it transforms the spectator. It does so paradoxically, not by the intended transmission of a "message" but conversely by suspending the need for such a definitive outcome. *Intimacy* is a "made thing", something that is intentionally willed into existence. It is precisely this intention that allows it to be perceived as art. The show also *defined* its own world: it created an opportunity for a new space to emerge outside existing social constructions. Baugh argues that an artwork transforms our experience when we "adopt what we take to be the work's organizing principle, and allow it to order our experience" (ibid., 480). This distinction between *our own ends* and the *ends of the work* is crucial but complicated by the blurring of self and artwork that occurred during the show. Only by relinquishing a wish for the work to be "useable", Baugh argues, can spectators truly allow themselves to be transformed. Equally, in the case of *Intimacy*, it is only through spectators' willingness to be used that the work can be realised. The end of the work cannot be known by the makers or by the recipient but only experienced in the moment of the work's reception and/or participation. I am struck by the tendency in criticism to forget the pleasure of being present at a work. Watching the recorded versions reminds me how much sheer fun is to be had in this performance, how much laughter it inspires, how unlike any other performance it is. Above all, however, it commands us to judge, to engage in careful aesthetic critique, which in itself is a vivid contribution to reframing vulnerability.

By sidestepping the "subject" of disability for most of this essay I have deliberately sought to open up a new critical space that foregrounds not bodily or cognitive difference per se but rather shared vulnerability, realised in aesthetic form. Ryan's situation could be my situation, or yours, tomorrow, but the show will remain as a shared language, an art object that continually undoes any fixed notion of vulnerability.

Closing

Bathgate, accompanied by Eszeky on guitar, sings a sultry jazz ballad, often close up on Ryan as she emerges from a sleeping bag to perform a final dance solo. Stripped down to black underwear, she sits on a bench in dialogue with the music and her own lower body; she stands, she sits, she continually picks up her legs and places them in new positions, she lies down. Alone. The lights fade on Ryan.

Performance, like an "event", is not just something that happens "in the world": it is a change in "the very frame through which we perceive the world and engage in it" (Žižek 2014, 10). It is the potential for reframing that vulnerability—especially sudden vulnerability—shares with performance. Vulnerability itself is not the problem. The problem is the way we—the normative we—think about vulnerability: as a pervasive injury as opposed to a creative and receptive state. *Intimacy* breaks the frame of vulnerability by breaking the frame of performance. The spectator is never quite sure if the textual material is dream or reality, if he or she will be called upon to enter the frame. The frame, furthermore, is both inside and outside the performance: it is both the leaky boundaries of the performance itself—its beginning, middle, and end—and the very limits of intelligibility surrounding it that "organize visual experience" (Butler 2009, 3). In this chapter I have argued for a poetics of vulnerability: that vulnerability is an interruptive value, both socially (because it upsets the myth of the autonomous self) and aesthetically (since it opens up the closed aesthetic artefact); that it invites spectators' complicity; that vulnerability reavows structural support; and that it places both fixed identity and fixed judgement in doubt. In this chapter I have blurred the distinction between disability and vulnerability. This is done deliberately as a means of opening up a relationship between (sometimes necessarily) fixed ways of thinking about disability and the construction of new, shared ways of tackling the barriers to human flourishing. One way of defining disability, vulnerability, and performance is to view all three as an openness to affect, to being affected by pain, pleasure, art, care, and touch, in ways we cannot control and that enrich our sense of being alive, in relation to others. As *Intimacy* reveals, vulnerability is both a deeply theoretical problem (because it is misunderstood and because these misunderstandings frame our world) and a subjectively lived experience. What began as a personal experience of Michelle Ryan's has become a rich aesthetic artefact that makes other readings of vulnerability possible.

Note

1. Excerpt from field notes (9 September 2014). Throughout this chapter I head each section by including observations, field notes, and quotations from and descriptions of the play. I want to give the reader a sense of being present at the work, to validate the act of spectatorship as an intersubjective experience, and to add richness to the texture of the writing: other voices heard slightly at a distance from the unitary scholarly narrative. Academic writing can risk overvalidating the theoretical at the expense of a more exploratory, sensory engagement: our senses, the pleasures we seek in a work, are, for me, the point of entry to intellectual judgement.

References

Ahmed, Sara. 2010. Happy Objects. In *The Affect Theory Reader*, ed. Melissa Gregg and Gregory J. Seigworth, 29–51. Durham, NC: Duke University Press.

AQA (Artistic Quality Assessment) Report, quoted in personal correspondence with Jo Verrent, senior producer, Unlimited (14 June 2014).

Baugh, Bruce. 1988. Authenticity Revisited. *The Journal of Aesthetics and Art Criticism* 46 (4): 477–487.

Berlant, Lauren. 1998. Intimacy: A Special Issue. *Critical Inquiry* 24 (2): 281–288.

Butler, Judith. 2009. *Frames of War: When Is Life Grievable?* London: Verso.

Davidson, Michael. 2008. *Concerto for the Left Hand: Disability and the Defamiliar Body*. Ann Arbor: University of Michigan Press.

Gilson, Erinn. 2013. *The Ethics of Vulnerability: A Feminist Analysis of Social Life and Practice*. London: Routledge.

Hadley, Bree. 2014. *Disability, Public Space Performance and Spectatorship: Unconscious Performers*. London: Palgrave.

Hall, Stuart. 1987. Texts About Handsworth Songs by Salman Rushdie, Stuart Hall, Darcus Howe, Isaac Julien & Kobena Mercer. http://www.diagonal-thoughts.com/?p=1476.

Hargrave, Matt. 2015. *Theatres of Learning Disabilty*. London: Palgrave.

Harvie, Jen. 2014. *Fair Play—Art Performance and Neoliberalism*. London: Palgrave.

Jackson, Shannon. 2011. *Social Works: Performing Art, Supporting Publics*. London: Routledge.

Phillips, Adam. 1994. *On Flirtation*. London: Faber & Faber.

Probyn, Elspeth. 2010. Writing Shame. In *The Affect Theory Reader*, eds. Melissa Gregg and Gregory J. Seigworth, 71–92. Durham, NC: Duke University Press.

Shildrick, Margrit. 2009. *Dangerous Discourses of Disability, Subjectivity and Sexuality*. London: Palgrave.

Siebers, Tobin. 2010. *Disability Aesthetics*. Ann Arbor: University of Michigan Press.

Žižek, Slavoj. 2014. *Event: Philosophy in Transit*. London: Penguin.

Risking Intimacy: Strategies of Vulnerability in Vertical City's *All Good Things* and *Trace*

Bruce Barton and Pil Hansen

It is a cliché and a statement of fact to say we live in an era of risk. If this was not a globally accepted reality before the melodramatic fear-mongering of the recent US election campaign, any last vestige of innocence in this regard has since been irrevocably lost. Risk is a threat and a promise, a brokered commodity and a "kind of background radiation saturating experience" (Massumi 1993, 24) that provides a key context for and contradiction of contemporary experience. It is hardly surprising, therefore, that risk also plays a central role in contemporary performance aesthetics—at times as a sincere expression of alternative, countercultural resistance, at others as an all-too-reassuring investment in a generalised, persistent preoccupation.

A surge in the scholarly attention directed toward the concept of risk has accompanied its growing instrumentalisation across a wide range of disciplines. Yet these dynamics increasingly coincide with a commonplace conflation of risk with related but distinct concepts such as *uncertainty* and even *danger*, rendering elusive any stable and transferable understanding of the term. However, as Deborah Lupton has noted, this

B. Barton (✉) · P. Hansen
University of Calgary, Calgary, Canada
e-mail: bruce.barton@ucalgary.ca

© The Author(s) 2017

A. O'Grady (ed.), *Risk, Participation, and Performance Practice*,
DOI 10.1007/978-3-319-63242-1_6

semantic slippage is a relatively recent development. With early Western modernity's adoption of statistical calculation (and the not coincidental rise of the insurance industry), risk was initially differentiated from uncertainty through its association with known and quantifiable conditions (Lupton 2013, 7), with the aim of maximising productivity by anticipating and steering clear of risk. In contemporary popular use, the term has lost much of this specificity and now generally evokes "a threat, hazard, danger or harm" (ibid., 10). But as "the myth of calculability" (Reddy 1996, 237) has evolved, risk has also shifted from being something to be avoided at all costs and has become an integral, even sought out element to be estimated and assessed with an eye to maximising investments.

This "risk opportunism" is clearly evident in current efforts to understand contemporary spectatorship. One such analysis emerging out of the UK, *The Audience Experience* (Radbourne et al. 2013), locates risk among four key attributes of an audience's experience in the performing arts, along with knowledge, authenticity, and collective engagement (ibid., 8). Within this study, risk takes multiple forms: "economic risk (Have I wasted my money?), psychological risk (Will I feel okay about the experience?), or social risk (Will I fit in?)" (ibid., 8). Of particular significance for my argument in this chapter, the authors propose that risk "can be seen as the gap between expectation and perception … it tells us about the audience's state of 'readiness'".

What does it mean, in the twenty-first century, to say an audience is "ready" (or that it is not)? How is "readiness" achieved and/or assessed? These are, of course, context-specific questions with a wide range of determining criteria. But in an era of "risky aesthetics" and rapidly evolving performance modes in live and mediated artistic practices, these questions emerge as critical and unavoidable. One possible answer is that audiences are increasingly ready for *failure.*

It would be difficult to challenge the assertion that one of the most commonly perceived risks of performance, for both an event and its audience, is failure. What constitutes failure, however, is a site of considerable difference of interpretation. While a substantial mainstream theatre sector may still measure success in terms of product standardisation and precision repeatability, the interrogation of these same aesthetic priorities as the expression of a corporate-driven consumerist model is widespread within contemporary performing arts practice. Equally familiar, what Sara Jane Bailes has recently articulated as "the poetics of failure" underpins a broad-based response to popular entertainment frameworks, prioritising disjunction and discontinuity as interwoven aesthetic and ideological values. For Bailes, the multiplicity of possible futures afforded by failure represents "an aperture, an opening onto several (and often many) other ways of doing that counter the authority of a singular or 'correct' outcome" (Bailes 2011, 2). This understanding of what Emilyn Claid has called "creative failure" is embraced by a broad range of contemporary performance makers as a "letting go of fixed things; where uncertainty, un-knowing, between-ness and here-and-now process breathe different energy into performance making" (Claid 2016, 259). Thus, although failure often manifests in a "breakdown" (Bailes 2011, 2), it also "indexes an alternative route". While ostensibly a "wrongdoing", it is first and foremost "a function of *doing*" (ibid., 12, emphasis added), and thus asserts "performance's promise, its potentiality and its present continuous ambition".

Ultimately, Bailes suggests, it is *hope* that lies at the beating heart of failure, and in this she joins a long tradition of intentional and ultimately idealistic irony. As Inéz Katzenstein has queried, "Is it not in the failed enterprises and dead ends that one can better perceive the exorbitance of individual obsessions and, therefore, the prospect of utopia?" (Katzenstein 2004, 189). However, at what point does the fact that "[f]ailure works" (Bailes 2011, 2) limit or even contradict the idealist oppositional work here attributed to it? When does a poetics of failure become so thoroughly embraced and enacted as to lose its status as "wrongdoing"—and thus effectively (all too effectively) become compromised by its own assumed authority? With an eye to the prominent stature of Bailes's primary case studies (none other than Forced Entertainment, Goat Island, and Elevator Repair Service), at what juncture does the risk of failure surrender to the risk of its own success?

A pronounced litmus test for this relationship between risk and failure (and, by extension, success) can be found in immersive performance contexts, particularly those that invite audience participation. Like several of the categorical terms identified above, "immersive" is a much discussed and much contested idea these days, but most definitions include the core elements described by Josephine Machon in her popular volume *Immersive Theatres: Intimacy and Immediacy in Contemporary Performance* (2013). While several of the ingredients that Machon proposes as common to all immersive performances represent the staples of virtually all collaboratively composed performance creation ("Space",

"Sound", "Bodies", etc.), immersivity emerges as distinct in that "the audience-immersant is *always* fundamentally complicit within the concept, content and form of the work" (ibid., 98, emphasis in original). Furthermore, Machon asserts, immersive performances involve a "contract for participation" (ibid., 99) that "invite[s] varying levels of agency and participation, according to how far the audience-participant is prepared to go" (ibid., 100). Intriguingly, for Machon immersivity is not merely a product of intention but demands a sufficient level of *expertise* to guarantee "the artist or the company an authoritative grasp of the artistic potential and creative constraints of the form and of the 'contract of participation' in order to enable the participant in the event to have a full, undeniable immersive experience" (ibid., 100).

Arguably, the necessary expertise to navigate the risky business of audience participation represents the crux of the authority asserted and exerted within much contemporary immersive performance. Virtually all critiques of an easy or thorough endorsement of immersive theatre, particularly that involving audience participation, focus on the balance of control and agency. More specifically targeted is the quick presumption that participatory performance contexts cede an uncommon degree of agency to the audience. Such unqualified assertions tend to employ an often oversimplified theatrical version of Bourriaudian relational aesthetics in an awkward and ill-fitting, if superficially empowering, grasp towards Rancière's emancipated spectator. Alan Read (who is guilty of no such thing) has proposed that "the holy grail of interactivity" (Read 2013, 24) could, ultimately, mark the end of what he refers to as our enduring "Ceramic age" of theatre practice, with its "surfaces at work rather than volumes to be entered" (ibid., 26). But in her interrogation of some of the most high-profile examples of twenty-first-century immersive projects, Helen Freshwater has suggested that the "model of interaction presented is one in which freedom to choose is profoundly compromised by the limitations of the system in which choices are made" (Freshwater 2009, 70). "Is there any seriously democratic thread to this process", Freshwater asks, "or does the artist merely establish a benevolent dictatorship with him or her at the apex?" (ibid., 72).

Adam Alston's recent effort to theorise this operative ambivalence attempts to shift the current discourse *beyond* either blanket endorsements of immersive experience or localised critique of practitioner motivations. Instead, Alston offers a sophisticated analysis of the entwining of risk, affect, and emotion in immersive performance contexts that regularly places artists as well as audiences in the service of neo-liberal productivity. In discussing his own experience of Lundahl & Seitl's performance *Rotating in a Room of Images* (2007–), he notes,

> [Our] role as productive participants is therefore complicated by a binding of risk and trust that opens out as much toward neoliberal value as it does toward alternative, more socially minded values ... While nuanced, productive participation remains as a resource in the production of an immersive theatre aesthetic. (Alston 2016, 105)

A helpful framework for negotiating these complex tensions between control and agency in participatory performance is offered by Jean-Luc Nancy, who marks a clear distinction between what he terms being "common" and being "in-common". As Eirini Nedelkopoulou has noted, while the former valorises "models of social relation and community that either fetishize a myth of a unified singularity and thereby obliterate difference or propose an unresolved multitude" (Harvie, quoted in Nedelkopoulou 2015, 159), the latter proposes a liminal space of negotiation "between those communicating, between the I and its other, between you and me, between us" (ten Kate and Nancy, quoted in Nedelkopoulou 2015, 158). As Nancy succinctly proposes, in such a model community is "what happens to us" (Nancy, quoted in Nedelkopoulou 2015, 159). Precisely because in this space "anything can happen ... peace and violence, order and disorder, cohesion and destruction" (ibid., 158), immersive performance is, perhaps first and foremost, a space of negotiation in which the primary thing being negotiated is the means by which the negotiation will take place.

Ultimately, it would seem, as Freshwater contends, "Anxiety and apprehension are central to many of the effects and affects evoked by participatory performance" (ibid., 65). And as I have noted elsewhere (Barton 2014, 66), considerable attention has of late been turned towards the relationship between invitation and risk in participatory performance. Gareth White, in his articulation of what he terms an "aesthetics of invitation" in participatory theatre, asserts that although "there is not necessarily a directly proportional relationship between risk and agency, there are connections between the perception of the investment of the self in a performance and its apparent risk" (White 2013, 177). In fact, White suggests that a large part of facilitating participatory performance lies within the realm of what might be called "risk management".

> [A] horizon of risk, as a dimension of the horizon of participation as a whole, is given structure by the negative impulses of the audience participant, and the positive exertions of the procedural author who tries to anticipate, elide, ameliorate and/or overcome these perceptions. It is also where the landscape within the horizon is given further shape and character by felt responses of a negative kind, by anxiety or trepidation. (ibid., 83)

However, as I have also proposed (Barton 2014, 66), overcoming audience anxiety and trepidation is only one aspect of an invitation to participation. Arguably, the authoritative management of audience agency remarked upon by Freshwater is a direct expression of immersive practitioners' awareness of the two-sided coin of audience participation. As Alice O'Grady has observed, "The skills needed by artists if they are to truly loosen control over the audience, but still share their pleasure, are perhaps less like the traditional art skills, and more like the social interaction skills of 'throwing a good party'" (O'Grady 2011, 169). By extension, "[a]nything flexible or open runs the risk of collapse … what happens when you have gatecrashers or plates start to get smashed?" (ibid., 169). Conceived of in this manner, facilitated participation requires neither oppression nor abdication and takes the form of neither crowd control nor incited chaos. Rather, in this revised context, the relationship between risk and failure involves "a constant negotiation between maintaining a structure and allowing for fluidity … If you invite people to play with you, there has to be some negotiation of rules" (ibid., 169).

In the remainder of this chapter I want to trace the various strands of this current discourse as they relate to two currently touring productions of Vertical City, the interdisciplinary hub of which I am the artistic director: *All Good Things* (2013–) and *Trace* (2014–). My aim is to tease out some viable and generative options for performers and audience members, as well as the positions from which they may actually negotiate power, authority, and agency. How can a performance acknowledge not just its own indeterminacy but also its ambivalence and anxiety about that indeterminacy? How can it ensure and display its own vulnerability to *both* failure *and* success as a promise—a performed contract—of shared safety and shared risk with its audience?

Vertical City is an interdisciplinary performance hub consisting of me, the Danish-Canadian performance dramaturg and scholar Pil Hansen, and an evolving group of artists exploring the relationship between traditional theatrical performance and guided audience interaction. Drawing on a spectrum of approaches, including installation, spatial engineering, aerial movement, soundscape design, and intermediality, Vertical City works on a wide scale of proportions, from large architectural landscapes to participatory one-to-one encounters. All our work begins with a preoccupation with "navigation" and explores both the function of gravity and the possibilities for balance in the performance of urban life. Our projects emerge out of a desire for intimacy—within the performance context and between the performance and its audience ("About VCP").

I have elsewhere noted (Barton 2014, 64) that *Trace* is an attempt to solve a dilemma. However, I have since come to think of the circumstances involved as more of a puzzle than a dilemma (with an intention of shifting the focus, in the process, from anxiety to speculation). My earlier published thoughts on *Trace* emerged out of our preparation and preliminary aspirations for the piece; this chapter offers reflections that follow upon the creation and staging processes of its premiere production, and as we enter a revisiting of the performance in advance of its next festival iteration.

Trace's immediate predecessor in Vertical City's efforts is the micro performance *All Good Things*—which is, in some ways, the most explicit expression of the puzzle that *Trace* is an attempt to solve/resolve. *All Good Things* (AGT) was originally commissioned by Toronto's Buddies in Bad Times Theatre as part of its 2013 Rhubarb Festival of new performances. A feature of that year's programming was a series of one-to-one performances hosted offsite in the 519 Community Centre located in Toronto's socially diverse and economically challenged Church Street neighbourhood. Amid the Centre's defiantly inclusive and regularly animated daily activities, a half-dozen markedly different performances claimed as many distinct locations in the building over the first week of the festival. Each offered Rhubarb's heartiest and most adventurous patrons a unique and uncommonly intimate encounter, and the performances included a multi-hour Reiki session, "clothes tattoos" embroidery, and a blindfolded close dance with a giant mole (to a glacial version of Springsteen's *Dancing in the Dark*).

The precarity of the venue was clearly intentional on the part of the series curator, Laura Nanni. The volunteer front-of-house staff amicably negotiated the multiple intentions playing out in and between the various spaces as they managed contrasting schedules, differing degrees and requirements of audience preparation, and a diversity of site sensitivity. At the same time, they were called upon to respectfully acknowledge and interact with—and, on occasion, intercept and deflect—unanticipated contributions from visitors to the Centre who were not directly associated with the performances (although certainly, if indirectly, these individuals were fully anticipated within the overall series design). This combination of tasks—welcoming and facilitating, engaging and controlling—neatly paralleled the dynamics of most, if not all, of the performances, and most certainly those of AGT.

While, as mentioned, the series featured a broad range of approaches to performance and audience engagement, AGT was conspicuous in the degree to which it incorporated and interrogated a variety of traditional theatrical elements. Of its approximately thirty-five-minute running time, about twenty to twenty-five minutes are fully scripted; the solo performer adopts many qualities associated with a fixed "character", and the piece traces a pre-established narrative arc through every complete performance. In part, then, the success of the piece, and of each of its performances, can be measured in terms of its consistency, its repeatability, and its emergent pull to completion and closure.

At the same time, however, AGT is intended to perform its own dissatisfaction with the efficiency of these elements and a resistance to its own conventional containment. Perpetually complicating its engagement with traditional theatrical dynamics are aspects designed to frustrate their straightforward consumption. Indeed, one of AGT's primary offerings is a gentle discourse on risk. Its narrative is based on an autobiographical experience of near-drowning that I survived only because a fisherman in a small boat grabbed onto my hand as I was slipping under the surface of the water and held on long enough to pull me to shore. AGT's initial catalyst lies in its fundamental preoccupation with physical contact as an actual and existential "lifeline". Several simple questions served as the basic inspiration for the piece: What would it be like to hold hands with a stranger for half an hour? What is the effect of the performer holding the audience member in his hands—of *being held* by the audience member—physically, as well as metaphorically and emotionally? As the promotional material for the piece suggests, "In the end, however, *All Good Things* is about holding hands. As if your life depended on it. Because it did, and it does, and it will again" ("All Good Things").

AGT thus features a set text that employs the familiar dramatic strategies of allusion and abstraction, poetic language utilised in the service of a strategically circuitous narrative construction, accumulative characterisation, and—ultimately—a thoroughly Aristotelian plot construction (albeit with an intentional concluding ambivalence). Yet this conventional dramaturgy unfolds in a context of pronounced and relentless intimacy, spatially imposed and materially sustained, with the audience member seated across a small table from the performer, holding hands in a darkened room. The performer accompanies his spoken dialogue with subtle hand choreography, affectively prompting and guiding the audience-participant but also spontaneously responding to and conversing with that individual's own "hand language". In addition, the pre-established narrative opens up repeatedly to improvised exchanges that emerge out of the character's preoccupations, and these moments partake of an intentionally unresolved (perhaps unresolvable) hybridity as both narrative digressions and the fundamental establishment of the piece's "in-its-own-worldness" (Machon 2013, 93), one that extends well beyond its fictional parameters.

I have written (Barton 2014) about what I see as the foundational tension between interpretation and affect that is put into play by this set of performance conditions—and which is largely sustained beyond the conclusion of the piece through its strategic indeterminacy. But it is equally instructive (at the very least for its creators) to reflect upon the performance's generative engagement with the risk of failure—and, equally, the risk of success. As has been repeatedly proposed in writing about interactive performance, the effective facilitation of spectator agency regularly requires a complex infrastructure to buttress the inevitable increase in uncertainty associated with audience participation. But while much has been discussed about the nature and function of risk for spectators in immersive performance, a primary *and defining* risk at play in many of these projects is that to the performance itself. And while these two categories of risk are obviously interwoven, it is productive to shine a focused light on the latter.

Given the intimate situation established by AGT, one would anticipate that its dynamic would be quite fragile. However, the piece has been remounted four times, each in a markedly different configuration, almost entirely without the loss of its participatory equilibrium. The second production saw the original one-to-one staging expanded for an audience of ten spectators who sat huddled on the edge of the visible playing area in a small, otherwise darkened micro performance space in Vancouver. The third production extended this process of opening up and was placed at the side (and, ultimately, within) a filled indoor hotel swimming pool as part of an all-night live art festival in Halifax, playing throughout the evening to audiences of approximately 100 spectators. The most recent production, staged in Calgary in May 2016, recreated all three configurations, performing to audiences of one, eleven, and 100 in rotation. To our surprise, the piece was able to consistently achieve and sustain a high level of intimacy between the performer and the central audience-participant, despite the wide range of audience capacities. Yet at the same time, virtually all participants also commented on the dual nature of that intimacy, with a strong and immediate personal connection with the actor being combined with the sense of having witnessed a private showing of a prepared performance.

While intimacy is regularly invoked in writing about performance, it is often utilised as a taken-for-granted shared value, either the by-product or the catalyst of the conventional "communal" function of shared space experiences. In the hands of accomplished scholars, intimacy has been employed strategically with either elusive abstraction (see Read 2009) or reductive materialism (see Auslander 1999/2008) as a response to the commodification of mediatised experience. In my own work related to intimacy in performance (see Barton 2007, 2009, 2010, 2014), I have drawn from an interdisciplinary spectrum of scholarship, including psychology, sociology, philosophy, and communications, in addition to the fine and performing arts, in pursuit of precision in both interpretation and application.

One of the most commonly referenced articulations of the conditions of intimacy emerges out of the work of psychologist Karen Prager (1995, 2004, 2014). Constant throughout Prager's scholarship is the identification of three necessary conditions for intimacy: deep and significant self-disclosure; positive, mutual involvement; and accurate, mutual understanding (2013, 2–3). And while sociologist Lynn Jamieson has distinguished the late twentieth-century attraction to self-disclosure (a dynamic that has increased exponentially within the first decades of the twenty-first) as "an intimacy of the self rather than an intimacy of the body" (1998, 1), contemporary philosopher Kim McLaren calls on phenomenology to posit a basic "ontological intimacy" as a basic human condition: it is "as if we have come to embody the other's perspective, or as if they have come to be incorporated into our own ways of perceiving. Others become, as it were, an extended form of our embodiment" (2014, 58).

Prager's work is also particularly helpful in its differentiation between "intimate interactions" and "intimate relationships". While relationships "exist in a much broader, more abstract space-and-time framework [and] continue in the absence of any observable behavior between partners", interactions "refer to dyadic behavior that exists within a clearly designated space-and-time framework" and are highly influenced by the immediate context in which they occur. Indeed, intimate disclosures may occur in interactions between strangers precisely "*because* of the unlikelihood of a further relationship and the attendant opportunities for betrayal" (2004, 19). This spectre of betrayal—further intensified within a fully embodied understanding of intimate exchange—has come to figure prominently in my own approaches to intimacy, both scholarly and creative, and represents something of an event horizon—a point of no return—within *Trace*'s dramaturgy of embrace.

I noted above that the piece has "almost entirely" retained its participatory equilibrium throughout its production history. The single exception offered us perhaps the most instructive moment across the now thirty-nine times it has been publicly performed. In one instance early in its performance history—the first appearance in its one participant/ten spectator configuration—we discovered after the fact that the audience-participant turned out to be a local theatre critic. It was clear from the outset of the performance that this individual's intention *and attention* had little to do with an open reception of the piece or with the possibility of exchange or collaboration; rather she had arrived *to perform*. Participating before her peers (the small audience was disproportionately populated by the city's print and digital reviewers), she consistently attempted to be comical and clever, to alter and contradict the performer's narrative trajectory, and to short-circuit AGT's delicate dramaturgy. Finding himself in contested territory, our performer/co-creator Martin Julien saw no option other than to, himself in turn, move into "performance mode". In response he unilaterally attempted to contain the piece's narrative parameters and impose a structural and interpersonal authority within the exchange—to, effectively, corral and shepherd his unruly play partner towards a workable progression and coherent conclusion.

There were several lessons we took from this experience, all of which relate to the issue of *readiness*. The critic-participant's intention, attention, and actions—her desire to derail the production's dynamic—make up an entirely legitimate response to the performance's invitation.

While not the one *we* desired and facilitated, it should hardly have caught us by surprise. The combination of rehearsed and spontaneous performance, in a sense, invites precisely this kind of audience intervention, lays its own trap, and waits to see if the participant will spring it. What *is* surprising, therefore, is that the other thirty-eight performances have been so thoroughly engaged and reciprocal. What this critic was ready for, what she came prepared to accomplish—in Prager's term, her *betrayal* of the AGT's offer of intimacy—sits fully within the range of anticipated audience options. It was the performance that was not, in a sense, ready for that response—providing Martin no option other than a reciprocal betrayal of his own. By this I am not suggesting it was under-rehearsed; rather, it was not yet robust enough in its own reaction "toolkit" to meet this complication on the level of sustained interpersonal exchange, as a challenge to be exploited on its own terms.

We have continued to explore response strategies and to develop more subtle manoeuvres to be employed in the face of this kind of challenge. But we are also attentive to the other primary lesson served up by this instance. For perhaps more illuminating than the disruption it caused is the fact that it is, to date, unique in our experience. While participant responses have been widely varied in mode of expression, all others have been deeply grounded in direct engagement. This is, no doubt, in part due to the lottery process we employ to select the solo audience-participant (which effectively identifies individuals with a clear resistance to participation while largely winnowing out individuals who are overtly keen to find themselves onstage). Beyond such logistical strategies, however, the carefully constructed conditions of the performance itself seem to provide a reliable conduit to an uncommonly deep performer–participant connection, one both built and reliant on the performer's shared vulnerability to risk. A critical element here, I believe, is that the performer's vulnerability is actual—and is perceived as such; it is affectively and unequivocally experienced as a condition of the performance's environment. By extension, then, if the performer were less vulnerable to audience disruption, if he had confidence that he could accommodate any possible participant response … if he were relatively certain he *could not fail* … under those conditions I believe it would be impossible for AGT to succeed. These are the conditions that provide the basis for what I refer to as a "dramaturgy of embrace", which I will discuss more fully in the next section. For it is only in its embrace of the risk of failure (as opposed to the pursuit of failure) that AGT also runs the risk of success.

Trace is borne out of a desire to move beyond the hybrid nature of AGT and more closely approaches what I have referred to as a dramaturgy of embrace (Barton 2014, 67). The phrase is, in part, an explicit effort to bypass the culture of exploitation and manipulation that characterised so much early twenty-first-century participatory performance, but also a conscious gesture to acknowledge and extend the “dramaturgy of care” employed by the German company Rimini Protokoll (see ibid., 67). I offer “embrace” as a mutuality of both desire and concession, a “twin(ing) around” that is entered “readily and gladly” (Merriam-Webster, web). To initiate an embrace, one must first open one’s arms widely, figuratively if not in every case literally, and then wait for the other to do the same before entering into a shared experience. Given this complexity, a dramaturgy of embrace is a durational process that involves patience, assessment, a call-and-response negotiation that opens space for evaluation, reconsideration, and, if successful, confident engagement. The definitions of embrace I am calling on are specific and signal the pursuit not simply of *equity* but also a form of *equivalence* (Dictionary.com, web) between performers and audience members, suggesting not only shared agency but also a correspondence and similarity between their experiences of the performance, one made all the more conspicuous by their fundamentally different entry points and enduring functions.

Trace begins with a fascination with the workings of memory, with the ways that both apprehensions and aspirations are equally rooted in the past and projected into the future. It reflects an impression that much in human behaviour is mapped out adjacent to the traces that these interwoven fears and hopes deposit along that temporal journey, making it extremely difficult to be present (in the many senses of that term). In the creation process for *Trace* we drew upon the genre conventions of ghost stories—we refer to the performance as a “ghost telling”—both to call into play a body of broadly shared cultural experience and to provide a store of ready narrative content and strategies. These are, most obviously, storytelling conventions—tropes, patterns, rhythms—but adopting this frame also introduces conventional practices associated with (a) the fostering, shaping, and rewarding of imagination, (b) the demarcating and reaffirming of cultural beliefs and contracts, and (c) confirming an investment in both solemnity and levity, seriousness and playfulness. The “ghost telling” frame thus gave us quick access to recognisable gestures and modes of movement, both literal and conceptual, and resulted in a welcome lightness of tone and touch.

In contrast to AGT, *Trace* does not attempt to smoothly blend fully scripted material with improvised exchange with audience members. The increasingly nuanced but inevitably distinct transitions in AGT between consistent, fully rehearsed text and spectator-specific improvisation are in *Trace* replaced with more extensive use of direct exchange with spectators, which is overtly punctuated with explicit sequences of prepared performance. At times, these prepared elements serve as *way stations* and provide opportunities for pause, reprieve, rest, and reflection. At others, they function as *landmarks*, declaring and staking out thematic territory for collective exploration. At others still, they provide *signposts*, marking the distance travelled, surveying accumulated experience, and proposing options for transition. These sections take multiple forms—games, songs, monologues, physical actions, dancing, and so on; all are conspicuously formal offerings, providing an explicit and overt, rather than implicit or elusive, infrastructure.

One example of these performance elements is the incorporation of *games*, which are played at specific junctures in the piece. These games serve multiple purposes: they introduce the idea of rules, a promise of the safety of roles and functions, the suggestion that effort (on the part of the audience) will be rewarded, and the promise of demonstrations of skill (at least on the part of the performers). The first game played, very early in the performance, is "hangman", a game of chance and deduction, but also a *dangerous* game, a game of life and death.

The context that is evoked within the piece is a primary school classroom—a place of remembered youth, of nostalgia, as well as a place of growth and connection amidst intense social vulnerability. In the original production, one of the four windows in the performance space overlooked a schoolyard playground and streamed (manufactured) rain throughout the entire performance, a visual allusion to both the ghost story genre and to the distorted perspective provided by memory. The first memories that are offered relate to children; befitting ghost stories, the children conjured are at risk, taking risks, going places they shouldn't, moving beyond supervision, "looking for trouble"—and likely to find it. The performers are playing and the performers are *playing*, inviting the audience to play with them even though—indeed, precisely *because*—the games are dangerous.

Underpinning all of these implicit strategies is the elusive narrative frame of "the lost child". Explicitly, a 1950s radio drama-style ghost story is introduced in multiple segments, recounting the fate of a schoolboy whose curiosity leads him to being first locked in a deserted schoolhouse and then lured by a phantom child onto the upper storey outer ledge, with disastrous consequences. Implicitly and pervasively, another narrative of another lost child provides the umbrella fictional framework of *Trace*, one that deviates from convention and focuses on the loss not of an actual child but rather of the individual will to bring a child onto a planet so utterly in the shadow of a looming environmental collapse. All of these elements, thus, playfully but persuasively foster a general anxiety about a world at risk, one haunted by the seductiveness of jeopardy, one outlined by the traces of its own vulnerability.

A dramaturgy of embrace is, in a sense, a response to this "background radiation saturating experience", and the elements that shift *Trace* most thoroughly in this direction are those that unfold *within* the framework established by the aforementioned signposts, way stations, and landmarks. The use of language departs from the hybrid nature of AGT and occupies a space that, drawing on the distinction that John Freeman has proposed between new performance writing and traditional dramatic text, "is neither blueprint nor act, somewhere between the ephemerality of performance and the permanence of print, between the fixed and the malleable ... like a map where nothing is ever quite to scale" (Freeman 2007, 28). These largely improvised sections are the aspects of the performance that consumed the vast majority of the company's creative and rehearsal resources and—more to the point—they are the processes that most explicitly gauge and facilitate the audience's readiness for risk. For while the genre-based framework remains constant across every performance of *Trace*, the specifics of the narratives that unfold within that framework are unique in each performance and are, essentially, *mined* by the performers in each iteration.

Trace may most accurately be envisioned as slowly revealing itself as a site of narrative construction through a process of memory extraction, exchange, and adaptation that we refer to as "memory weaving". The performers—co-creators Martin Julien and Michelle Polak—move through the performance in a linked series of one-on-one engagements with individual audience members, sharing and soliciting personal memories that then become single threads in the interwoven fabric of any individual performance's tapestry-like narrative. The nature of the memories offered and called forth is specific and strategic, targeted in a manner designed to foster individual investment while simultaneously steering participants away from the pull towards public therapy that may result in embarrassment or a sense of exploitation (whether in the moment or, more commonly, after the fact). This is accomplished through a focus on memories that are associated with a particular, deeply embodied, and *sensory-triggered* experience. The performers begin to construct a narrative on the basis of reminiscences of their own memories that are triggered by a distinct odour or taste or sound or texture—one's face against a cool brick wall, the sharp sounding of a recess bell, the humid chill of an autumn breeze on the back of one's neck. They then ask audience members, one by one (one performer interacting with one audience member in each instance), for corresponding or resonant memories and experiences. Precisely because of the heightened nature of such embodied memories, once one is shared by a participant the performer then selects a single element from the offering, which is then introduced into the emerging narrative, extracted from its original context and carried forward into the increasingly complex composite reminiscence being recounted within the performance.

This process was deeply influenced by the creative practice and practice-based research of Pil Hansen, both of which focus on the intersection between dramaturgy and cognitive science. Hansen is a founding member of Vertical City and its resident dramaturg, a role in which she also served on this production, and her work on what she calls "Performance Generating Systems" (see Hansen 2015; Hansen with Kaeja and Henderson 2015; Hansen with House 2016) offered effective tools for our navigation of risk.

Dramaturg's Notes: Pil Hansen

I was invited into this process at a stage when the team knew they were creating a ghost telling with some rehearsed and repeatable components and many instances of open-ended engagement with audience memories triggered by this material. I participated in practical discussions of how to avoid soliciting audience responses such as withdrawal, confession, or trauma recall, with reference to the risk such situations would entail for the actors and the audience alike. The idea of focusing on sensory details and returning to them when weaving the emergent dramaturgy of the performance provided a way to recalibrate strong responses with care and reduce the shared risk. When making this suggestion, however, my primary focus was on an underlying dynamic involving high stakes for the performance as a whole: the ability of improvised responses to self-organise and sustain a performance dramaturgy over time.

When we were developing the actors' task of engaging individual spectators, and determining rules and modes of interaction that could guide their improvisation, I was drawing upon a specific theoretical framework: Dynamical Systems Theory (Thelen and Smith 1994; Stevens and McKechnie 2005; Tribble 2017) as it is applied to systematic approaches to improvisation—what I elsewhere refer to as Performance Generating Systems. In short, this framework draws attention to how interactions between performers and spectators within a performance system self-organise in patterns around specific, but shifting, dominant parameters—such as empathy and a desire to be included socially, an element of competition, or even fatigue. Such systems depend on boundaries and constraints that reduce the number of possible actions to avoid falling into chaos. Without constraints the improvised interaction would not self-organise. At the same time, these systems also depend on new and unpredictable source materials for performers to engage with to continue to generate fresh performances. Without new sources, the improvisation would become predictable, repeat itself, and no longer produce shifting, self-organised patterns. In other words, for an improvisation system to work it needs to be semi-open. New sources of energy need to be restricted, but they also have to flow continuously. That takes me back to the underlying risk involved in the audience participation of *Trace*: without new memories from the audience, our performance would die out, but since spectators were neither informed of nor abiding by our tasks and rules, their influx of source memories was unrestricted and could easily pry the system open, thereby stopping it from self-organising.

Freshwater's mention of how spectators' choices in immersive performances are limited by the performance systems within which they make choices resonates when revisiting my response to this dramaturgical concern. By choosing to select only a few sensory details from each spectator-participant's shared memory as new improvisational source material, we were effectively restricting the spectators' agency in order to keep the performance system semi-open. That said, O'Grady's discussion of the negotiation of rules that takes place when one allows for both structure and fluidity (O'Grady 2011, 169) is equally relevant when reflecting on *Trace*. Audience members did gently negotiate the rules in that moment of direct touch and exchange of memories prior to the actors' selection of sensory information. Their agency in those moments became an accumulative aspect of everyone's experience. However, due to the improvisational constraints and the audience's developing anticipation of how the system "worked", this negotiation did not pry the system open—it affected the spectator-participants' co-production of the experience, but it did not affect the basic principles that allowed the improvisation to generate dramaturgical patterns.

There was a specific reason why I considered this dramaturgy important. In cognitive terms, it is understood that memory is constructive (Schacter and Addis 2007; Edelman and Tononi 2002). We perceive most of the present through memory, and memory is in turn adapted. When consciously recalling memory we construct it selectively and through the use of emotional and associative triggers that belong to a different moment and situation, but which are not differentiated in our experience. This ongoing adaptation of memory is not only how we learn; it is also how we adjust to each other socially. In *Trace*, audience members gradually "learn" memory weaving, so that by the time the actors have solicited a large collection of memory sources to work with, audience members are also less likely to try to negotiate the rules of interaction. More important, however, is the effect of an audience member recalling a memory triggered by the associations offered in *Trace*, experiencing sensory aspects of such a memory being transferred and reused by the actors, and listening to the memories of others with sensitivity to sensory detail. Through this process, individual memories are adapted, woven into collective memories, and charged with complex emotions drawn from multiple spectator-participants. If we had allowed the system to be pried wide open or become closed and repeatable, this embracing generation of collective memory through improvised performance would not have occurred. As I saw it, the interactive generation was the dramaturgy of the work and the underlying dynamic that our choices needed to facilitate.

*

As with any one person's memory, the memory of the room is a process of intersections, overlaps, and contamination, as each new sensory-triggered ingredient interacts with and alters all the others. As such, each audience member can trace a highly personal thread of their own experience within the performance's increasingly interlaced construction—unique within each performance and dependent on the courage and generosity of each audience—without the sense of having been manipulated or tricked into regrettable personal exposure.

It is in this dynamic that the authority of *Trace* exerts and defines itself; therein lies the line between the risk of failure and risk of success for both the performers and their audience in this "in-common" community of individuals. In practice, the intention is to provide audience members with an array of complementary yet distinct attentional registers or lenses that, combined, provide a set of checks and balances to maintain its fragile dynamic.

- Through the most conspicuous lens, the threat/promise of direct, one-to-one exchange with one of the performers in front of the rest of the audience shifts each spectator into a heightened sense of self-awareness and trepidation. As Alston has proposed, the encounter with such risk can result in a spectator-participant becoming "a 'hyperactively' creative subject ... [and] can provide a stimulus for the participant to alter the creative trajectory of a performance" (Alston 2013, 224).
- Through a separate lens, audience members relatively quickly recognise the workings of a composition process by which personal memories introduced into the performance environment are adapted and reattributed at the service of a collaboratively constructed tale. Curiosity piqued by this emergent process both mediates individual apprehension associated with participation and creates the perception/recognition of individual agency in an open system.
- Through a third lens, audience members become aware of the expertise of the performers, who balance a range of conventional performance tasks—singing, dancing, playing instruments, physical theatre, and traditional performance—with moment-to-moment improvisational exchange and the complex, ethically charged processes of memory weaving.
- And through yet another, perhaps the most significant, lens, audience members recognise and appreciate the highly uncommon state of vulnerability of the performers who, within these dynamics, must navigate this diverse and constantly shifting terrain without the protection of stable theatrical conventions or fixed narrative content—the tools that normally provide them access to facilitative authority.

Trace can thus be understood as an extension of both the operative dilemma of affect and interpretation first explored in *All Good Things* as well as the "poetics of failure" articulated by Bailes et al., in that its dramaturgy of embrace perpetually balances on an in-common edge between failure (of the process, of the connection between audience member and performer, of the collaborative storytelling system) and success (the efficient disavowal of difference and the seamless construction of a coherent narrative and performance event through the assertion of authoritative expertise). A dramaturgy of embrace must resist—and be seen and *experienced* as resisting—both of these gravitational pulls and must position itself at an intimate intersection—a meeting of performer and spectator out on a ledge: mutually vulnerable, mutually empowered, mutually present, mutually ready (but not too ready) … mutually at risk.

References

"About VCP." Vertical City. https://brucewbarton.com/about-2/.

"All Good Things." Vertical City. https://brucewbarton.com/all-good-things/.

Alston, Adam. 2013. Politics in the Dark: Risk Perception, Affect and Emotion in Lundahl & Seitl's *Rotating in a Room of Images*. In *Affective Performance and Cognitive Science: Body, Brain and Being*, ed. Nicola Shaughnessy, 217–228. London and New York: Bloomsbury Methuen Drama.

Alston, Adam. 2016. *Beyond Immersive Theatre*. London: Palgrave Macmillan.

Auslander, Philip. 1999/2008. *Liveness: Performance in a Mediatized Culture*. London: Routledge.

Bailes, Sara Jane. 2011. *Performance Theatre and the Poetics of Failure*. London and New York: Routledge.

Barton, Bruce. 2008. Subjectivity <>Culture <>Communications <>*Interm edia*: A Meditation on the 'Impure Interactions' of Performance and the 'In-between' Space of Intimacy in a Wired World. *Theatre Research in Canada* 29 (1): 51–92.

Barton, Bruce. 2009. Paradox as Process: Intermedial Anxiety and the Betrayals of Intimacy. *Theatre Journal* 61 (4): 575–601.

Barton, Bruce. 2010. Intimacy. In *Mapping Intermediality in Performance*, eds. Sarah Bay-Cheng, Chiel Kattenbelt, Andy Lavender, and Robin Nelson. Amsterdam: Amsterdam University Press.

Barton, Bruce. 2014. Performing the Paradox of Affect and Interpretation: Turbulence in Vertical City. *Performance Research* 19 (5): 59–66.

Claid, Emilyn. 2016. Messy Bits. In *Collaboration in Performance Practice: Premises, Workings and Failures*, eds. Noyale Colin and Stefanie Sachsenmaier, 259–79. Houndmills, Basingstoke, Hampshire: Palgrave Macmillan.

Edelman, Gerald M., and Giulio Tononi. 2002. Perception into Memory: The Remembered Present. In *A Universe of Consciousness: How Matter Becomes Imagination*, 102–10. New York: Basic.

Freeman, John. 2007. New Performance/New Writing. Houndmills, Basingstoke, Hampshire: Palgrave Macmillan.

Freshwater, Helen. 2009. *Theatre and Audience.* Houndmills, Basingstoke, Hampshire: Palgrave Macmillan.

Hansen, Pil. 2015. The Dramaturgy of Performance Generating Systems. In *Dance Dramaturgy: Modes of Agency, Awareness, and Engagement*, eds. Pil Hansen and Darcey Callison, 124–142. Basingstoke: Palgrave.

Hansen, Pil with Christopher House. 2015. Scoring performance Generating Systems. In*Performance Research* 20 (6): 65–73.

Hansen, Pil with Karen Kaeja and Ame Henderson. 2014. Self-organization and Transition in performance Generating Systems. In *Performance Research* 19 (5): 23–33.

Katzenstein, Inéz. A Leap Backwards into the Future: Paul Ramirez Jonas / 2004. In Failure. Documents of Contemporary Art, ed. Lisa Le Feuvre, 184–189. Cambridge: The MIT Press.

Lupton, Deborah. 2013. *Key Ideas: Risk*, 2nd ed. Florence, GB: Routledge.

Prager, Karen. 1995. *The Psychology of Intimacy.* New York: Guilford Press.

Prager, Karen. 2014. *The Dilemmas of Intimacy.* London: Routledge.

Prager, Karen and Linda J. Roberts. 2004. Deep Intimate Connection: Self and Intimacy in Couple Relationships. In *Handbook of Closeness and Intimacy*, eds. Debra J. Mashek and Arthur Aron, 43–60. New Jersey: Lawrence Erlbaum Associates

ProQuest ebrary. Accessed 20 August 2016.

Machon, Josephine. 2013a. *Immersive Theatres: Intimacy and Immediacy in Contemporary Performance.* Houndmills, Basingstoke, Hampshire: Palgrave Macmillan.

Machon, Josephine. 2013. (Syn)aesthetics and Immersive Theatre: Embodied Beholding in Lundahl & Seitl's *Rotating in a Room of Images*. In *Affective Performance and Cognitive Science: Body, Brain and Being*, ed. Nicola Shaughnessy, 199–216. London and New York: Bloomsbury Methuen Drama.

Massumi, Brian (ed.). 1993. *The Politics of Everyday Fear.* Minnesota: University of Minnesota Press.

Massumi, Brian. 2010. The Future Birth of the Affective Fact: The Political Ontology of Threat. In *The Affect Theory Reader*, eds. Melissa Gregg, and Gregory J. Seigworth, 52–70. Durham, NC: Duke University Press.

Nedelkopoulou, Eirini. 2015. The In-Common of Phenomenology. In *Performance and Phenomenology: Traditions and Transformations*, eds. Maaike Bleeker, Jon Foley Sherman, and Eirini Nedelkopoulou. New York and London: Routledge.

O'Grady, Alice. 2011. Interactivity: Functions and Risks. In *Performance Perspectives: A Critical Introduction*, eds. Jonathan Pitches, and Sita Popat, 165–174. Houndmills, Basingstoke, Hampshire: Palgrave Macmillan.

Radbourne, Jennifer, Hilary Glow, and Katya Johanson. 2013. Knowing and Measuring the Audience Experience. In *The Audience Experience: A Critical Analysis of Audiences in the Performing Arts*, eds. Jennifer Radbourne, Hilary Glow, and Katya Johanson, 1–14. Bristol: Intellect.

Read, Alan. 2013. *Theatre in the Expanded Field*. London and New York: Bloomsbury Methuen Drama.

Reddy, S. 1996. Claims to Expert Knowledge and the Subversion of Democracy: The Triumph of Risk over Uncertainty. *Economy and Society* 25 (2): 222–54.

Schacter, D. L., and D. R. Addis. 2007. The cognitive neuroscience of constructive memory: Remembering the past and imagining the future. In *Philosophical Transactions of the Royal Society B*, 362: 773–86.

Stevens, C. J., and S. McKechnie. 2005. Minds and motion: Dynamical systems in choreography, creativity, and dance. In *Tanz im Kopf: Yearbook 15 of the German Dance Research Society 2004*, eds. J. Birringer and J. Fenger, 241–52. Münster: LIT Verlag.

Thelen, Esther, and Linda B. Smith. 1994. *A Dynamic Systems Approach to the Development of Cognition and Action*. Cambridge, Mass.: MIT Press.

Tribble, Evelyn. 2017. Distributed Cognition, Memory and Performance. In *Performing the Remembered Present: The Cognition of Memory in Dance, Theatre and Music*, eds. Pil Hansen and Bettina Blaesing. London and New York: Bloomsbury Methuen.

White, Gareth. 2013. *Audience Participation in Theatre: Aesthetics of the Invitation*. Houndmills, Basingstoke, Hampshire: Palgrave Macmillan.

Collect Yourselves!: Risk, Intimacy, and Dissonance in Intermedial Performance

Jocelyn Spence, Stuart Andrews and David Frohlich

Introduction

The project discussed in this chapter did not set out to generate or investigate risk. Our intention was to explore whether a technological intervention could prompt people to interact with their personal digital photographs, and with each other, in ways that possessed the emotional and aesthetic impact of contemporary, professional autobiographical performance. Our interdisciplinary project aimed to extend the methods of human–computer interaction (HCI) and interaction design to address the subtle and slippery concepts of intensity, liminality, and transformation that are so critical to contemporary performance practice. Our premise was, and still is, that digital media technologies are so deeply entwined in many people's lives that they can be a fruitful point of departure for creating and understanding intermedial autobiographical performance.

This was a risky project in terms of the many ways in which it might have failed to achieve its goals, but we did not consider risk to be

J. Spence (✉) · S. Andrews · D. Frohlich
University of Surrey, Guildford, UK
e-mail: j.c.spence@surrey.ac.uk

© The Author(s) 2017

A. O'Grady (ed.), *Risk, Participation, and Performance Practice*,
DOI 10.1007/978-3-319-63242-1_7

relevant to the experience of interacting with our technological intervention. In fact, in our process of securing ethical approval to conduct this research, we argued emphatically that our participants would be in complete control of which photographs they chose to share and what they chose to say about those photographs, thereby eliminating the very idea of risk from their point of view. Our project succeeded in turning what might have been very ordinary, conversational photo-sharing sessions into performances that possessed critical properties of aesthetic, professional autobiographical performance. We came to see that this engagement with performance invited risk from its participants, which could contribute to discussions of risk as a perception of uncertainty (Slovic 2010), as a means of identity construction (Scott Jones and Raisborough 2007), and as an aspect of "edgework" (Lyng 1990) as applied to performance.

From the perspective of an audience member, the performances had many moments of deep engagement, emotional connection, entertainment, and beauty. The participants themselves described the speed and ease of making interpersonal connections and even the unexpected generation of intimacy. Analysis of the performances revealed that the power of their performances depended on the degree of risk that participants were willing to take, and that risk taking was closely tied to intimacy and dissonance. As discussed below, this does not imply an ontological struggle between digital media and live performance or limit the intimate to the purely live encounter. Rather, in line with the work of Maria Chatzichristodoulou and Rachel Zerihan (2009), we demonstrate that intimacy can be generated through a productive tension between media technology and live performance.

This chapter examines the pivotal role that risk, intimacy, and dissonance play in the transition from everyday conversation to a more aesthetic performance. Our references to the "aesthetic" refer to Erika Fischer-Lichte's (2008) notions of liminality and transformation, and map closely to points at which at least some audience members evidenced a particularly emotional or affective connection to the performer. To explain the workings of risk from both the performer's and the audience's point of view, the chapter first lays out the framework and methodology for our interdisciplinary approach to performance, rooting the discussion in existing work within both HCI and performance. We analyse our participants' engagement with risk and intimacy using theoretical frameworks from the perspective of both performer and audience member: Jess Dobkin's discussion of her own semi-autobiographical performance *The Lactation Station Breast Milk Bar*, and Adam Alston's experience of Lundahl & Seitl's one-on-one performance *Rotating in a Room of Images*. These texts offer detailed explanations of the felt experience of risk and intimacy from both the performer's and the spectator's viewpoint, both of which are important in the context of intimate performances with digital media. We then explore the connections among dissonance, intimacy, risk, and aesthetic moments of performance. In terms of our intermedial autobiographical performance, risk taking was the key link in a chain of events, including intimacy and dissonance, that created the opportunity for the aesthetics of performance to emerge. It is not only the case that an individual's decision to take a risk is a necessary component for the aesthetic experiences described here, but also that the experience of risk taking becomes an integral part of the performance situation as felt by both performers and audience members. Risk taking and vulnerability can therefore be understood as both potential points of entry into and pervasive aspects of rewarding and even transformational performance experiences.

Designing Performance, Performing Design

Five people sit in a semicircle around a table with a laptop controlling photographs projected on the wall in front of them (see Fig. 1). Together, they have forty minutes to create a performance from those photographs, even though none of them is trained in performance. They form their own audience; no one else is watching. Each participant has spent time over the previous week examining his or her photograph collections, in private, for images that respond to five different prompts written to guide them away from conventional media-sharing practices, towards a more reflective set of criteria. They will take turns telling each other the stories behind the photographs they have selected, aiming to share their time and attention so that everyone has the chance to tell all of their stories. Their curiosity is piqued, imagining what the others might reveal. They all log into the application together. They read the instructions for the performance—which does not take long, because there aren't many rules. Before they can worry too much about how to organise themselves, the timer begins to tick down, and the performance begins.

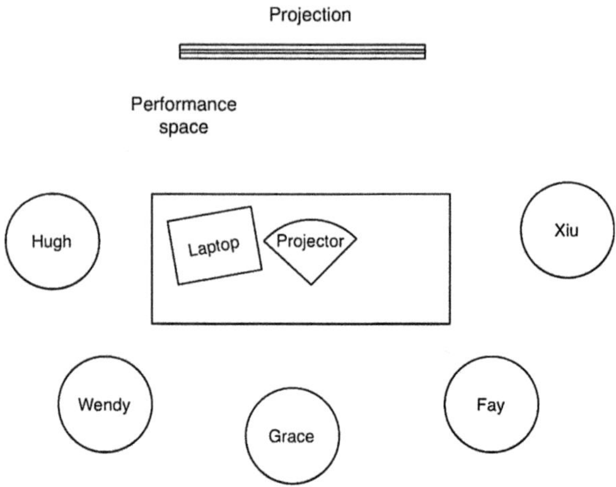

Fig. 1 The layout for a *Collect Yourselves!* performance

This is a description of a *Collect Yourselves!* performance. *Collect Yourselves!* is a browser-based application that guides non-performers through the experience of creating a performance around their own digital media.[1] Two performances were made by groups of friends and two by groups of strangers, with five to seven people per group. Each group was "closed" in that they performed only for each other, with no audience external to the five or seven participants (aside from the researchers monitoring the process). The data reported in this study come from the recorded performances, interviews, and questionnaires, which together were subjected to three forms of analysis: thematic, interaction, and coded performance analysis. *Collect Yourselves!* stands as an example of the emerging discipline of performative experience design (PED), a framework for setting technological, social, and artistic parameters to create opportunities for performative experiences with interactive technologies (see e.g. Spence et al. 2013; Spence 2016). The discipline draws equally from HCI, particularly interaction and experience design, and from performance studies, particularly the many traditions of presentational theatre (De Marinis 1993) and performance art (Goldberg 2011) or Live Art (Live Art Development Agency 2010). It is based on the observation that both experience design and much of the work in these strands of performance seek to create novel interactions among people and objects, sometimes including digital technologies, in order to explore intrapersonal, interpersonal, and/or sociocultural aspects of contemporary life. PED brings together the generative and analytic methods of these fields to better understand the contexts and implications of interacting with digital technologies.

If the participants had spent forty minutes chatting about their photographs following everyday practices of conversational media sharing, the design would have fitted squarely within the tradition of digital media-sharing research within HCI. Since roughly the turn of the millennium, researchers have created novel designs for the co-located sharing of personal digital photographs (e.g. Balabanović et al. 2000; Frohlich et al. 2004; Ah Kun and Marsden 2007; Clawson et al. 2008; Kirk et al. 2010; Lucero et al. 2011; Piper et al. 2013; Reitmaier et al. 2013) and developed theories of how people manage interpersonal interactions around the management and sharing of their digital photographs (e.g. Frohlich et al. 2002; Kirk et al. 2006; Stelmaszewska et al. 2008; Van House 2009; Sarvas and Frohlich 2011). Among the key findings are the observations that photographs are virtually always accompanied by "conversational storytelling" (Frohlich 2004, 137); that multimodal sharing involves negotiations around control (Crabtree et al. 2004; Lindley and Monk 2006); that people overestimate their ability to retrieve particular images (Whittaker et al. 2009); and that overexposure to digital images may result in a decrease in their perceived value (Petrelli and Whittaker 2010). Thus, even without considering the performative aspects of digital media sharing, these findings demonstrate that any new designs for co-located sharing should address forms of storytelling, negotiations of control, and the process of selecting images to share, all without imposing excessive exposure to an individual's photograph collection.

However, this project only drew half of its inspiration from HCI. The other half came from theories and practices in performance studies. This wide-ranging and contested field has influenced numerous disciplines throughout and beyond the humanities through the "performative turn". We agree with Richard Bauman, though, that at the most basic level, the underlying condition of almost every performance is the altered relationship between performer and spectator, which "calls forth special attention to and heightened awareness of the act of expression, and gives license to the audience to regard the act of expression and the performer with special intensity" (1975, 293). Bauman's definition opens up performance to include any number of deliberate interactions between a person who is calling attention to her actions and a person who acknowledges that performance with attention and (not necessarily deliberate) evaluation—in other words, an emergent exchange of attentions or energies among people that Fischer-Lichte might call the "autopoiesis" of an aesthetic event (2008, 162). This includes practices and traditions such as postdramatic theatre (Lehmann 2006), presentational performance (De Marinis 2007), autobiographical performance (Heddon 2008), storytelling (Wilson 2006), and devised performance (Govan et al. 2007).

In *Collect Yourselves!*, the aim was to explore the design space between ordinary, conversational digital media sharing and what Mike Wilson's "performance continuum" refers to as the more "cultural", "high intensity", "formal", "conscious", "high risk", and "high reward" conditions of professional, aesthetic performance (2006, 9). These terms indicate the qualities of storytelling performance that tend to mark it as different from everyday conversation. No clear-cut dividing line between the two exists: rather, as Bauman puts it, "personal narrative" is simply one type of "verbal art" that can be perceived as mundane or aesthetic to varying degrees (1975, 293). These perspectives on the relationship between ordinary conversation and aesthetic performance create a space for intervention into everyday practices of conversational media sharing. While it is impossible to claim a unified motivation or goal for all the work done within the diverse field of performance, many prominent theorists point to performance's potential to generate moments of empathy, emotion, insight, and transformation in its audiences (Phelan 2004; Dolan 2005; Fischer-Lichte 2008). Performance studies makes overt the attempt to understand these powerfully felt but somewhat nebulous affective states. If performance is not a rarefied experience accessible only to highly trained, talented, and intrinsically motivated individuals, then it should be possible to design parameters within which non-professionals may be guided towards a more "cultural", "high intensity", "formal", "conscious", "high risk", and/or "high reward" (Wilson 2006, 9) experience. The intended contribution of *Collect Yourselves!* was to use digital media technologies to nudge people towards these kinds of empathetic, emotional, insightful, and even transformative moments of performance. Although this project was framed in terms of HCI and experience design rather than practice-as-research, we have argued elsewhere that the two disciplines have a surprising number of overlapping methods and goals (Spence 2016). Thus the result of "using" our design would ideally be as much a performance to be experienced and analysed from the viewpoint

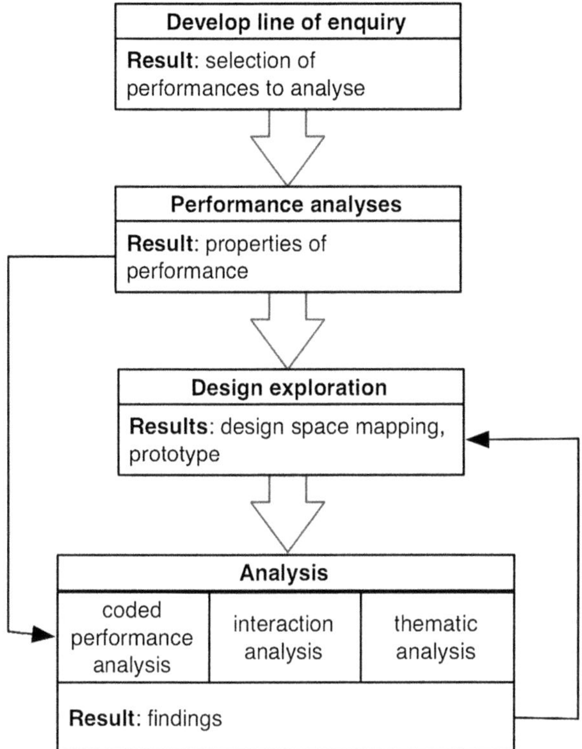

Fig. 2 The performative experience design methodology

of performance studies as it would be an instance of interaction or experience design.

In order to pursue the aesthetic aims of performance within the framework of experience design—and to explore the aims of digital media sharing within the framework of performance—we developed a methodology that entwines both perspectives, draws on methods from both fields, and analyses the results in terms of both experience design and performance (see Fig. 2). The methodology begins with the selection of a line of enquiry, in this case co-located digital media sharing, resulting in a number of performances to view in order to identify the perspectives they might offer. We chose to explore a wide range of autobiographical or quasi-autobiographical performances, from Robert Wilson's meticulously and spectacularly staged *The Life and Death of Marina Abramović* (2011) to Chris Thorpe and Hannah Jane Walker's immersive and participatory *The Oh F*ck Moment* (2012) to Daniel Gosling's evocative, non-linear, and fully mediated online piece *Transformer* (2003).

Ultimately, we selected for analysis four performances by UK artists that involved a single performer speaking directly to a relatively small audience about his or her life experiences, all in some way involving personal digital media: Third Angel's *Class of 76* (2000) and *Cape Wrath* (2011, 2012, 2013), Tom Marshman's *Legs 11* (2011), and Claire Murphy-Morgan's *Editor* (2012).[2] (The analysis of *Class of 76* was based on extensive documentation and discussion with the show's creator; while some theorists would argue that this is not a sound basis for a performance analysis, we found it adequate for our purposes in conjunction with the other analyses.) Our performance analyses aimed to identify properties that made them stand out in two ways: firstly, how they manifested themselves as autobiographical instead of fundamentally fictional; and secondly, how they asked for and earned their audiences' "special intensity" (Bauman 1975, 293).

Through our analyses we identified a set of shared properties. "Self-making" addresses the many ways in which the performer establishes a sense of self for an audience. "Situatedness" refers to the curious fact that all of these performances made explicit reference to the shared time and space of the performance itself. "Heightened attention" is a term used by Fischer-Lichte to describe the way in which audiences tend to pay attention to and assume significance in the objects and people involved in performance, and detect deviations from the patterns and repetitions that emerge (2008, 164–168). Finally, Fischer-Lichte's category of "liminality and transformation" (ibid., 174) differentiates mundane conversation from aesthetic events. Through these properties, performers invite spectators into a liminal state, a condition in which they experience both their own ordinary worldview and that of the performance taking place in front of them. This state of being between two worlds allows space for at least a temporary transformation of the spectator's perspective where new insights and empathies can arise.

These terms evoke the characteristics of "edgework" (Lyng 1990) in that professional autobiographical performers voluntarily expose themselves to situations that threaten their mental well-being (ibid., 857) by inviting intense evaluation of the selves they create through intermedial performance. They also exhibit special skills, prepare to control chaos (when a performance goes wrong), perceive their talents as "innate", and have been reported as experiencing at least some of the "self-determination", fear, and exhilaration described by edgeworkers (ibid., 859–860). Other researchers have connected edgework to performance: David Courtney sees "edgework" in the "competent viewers and listeners" who engage actively and critically with art in hopes of "transcendence" of aesthetic experience (2005), and Caroline Hellstrom and Irvine Lapsley (2015) identify edgework in the work of comedians who put their sense of self and their careers on the line to challenge and subvert the dominant neo-liberal expectations of society. Thus discussions in performance studies of risk and intense evaluation (Bauman 1975) seem to occupy much the same space as these compelling views on risk as a performative act of building perceptions and relations around the self. The next thing to do was to examine risky performance in action.

A Two-Phase Performance

At first glance, a *Collect Yourselves!* performance does not seem to be a risky or aesthetic event. The participants are not performing for any external audience (beyond the researchers, who disengage as much as possible from the performance event), and they are not forced to do anything outside the bounds of ordinary conversational media sharing. However, it is not what they are *forced* to do that matters. After all, if they were truly forced to do something, they might feel absolved of choice and therefore not perceive their actions as involving any personal risk. What matters is the combination of unusual, disorienting, and disconcerting ways that people are *prompted* to interact with their digital media, and with each other, before the performance event itself. The prompt creates both the expectation that all participants will respond in somewhat similar ways and the latitude for individual participants to negotiate those expectations.

As described above, the performance begins before the performers assemble. Each participant is sent a link to the first phase of the *Collect Yourselves!* application, where they find five written prompts to which they respond by uploading one or more photographs. The prompts are written to encourage a point of view towards personal photographs not commonly adopted in online or co-located photo sharing. One example is a prompt to find the photo closest in time to six months ago and tell the story behind it. This prompt may lead the participant to tell a banal story or a revealing one, depending on what she happened to be doing. A more challenging prompt is the one that asks participants to upload a photograph that is so embarrassing they have never shared it online. There is no function in the application that assesses the embarrassment quotient of the participants' photographs and forces them to choose something agonising. However, selecting a photo that is clearly not embarrassing at all would indicate that the participant is not "playing fair", that she is expecting to enjoy the spectacle of other people's embarrassment without embarrassing herself in return. This is not unlike the line that comedians walk in deciding how far they should push their audience with an establishment-challenging joke (Hellstrom and Lapsley 2015, 2). It is also worth remembering that according to Lyng, the preparations for an edgework experience "are integral parts of the total experience" (1990, 874) and not to be overlooked; this devising phase is similarly integral to *Collect Yourselves!*

Thus even in the first phase of the performance, where participants are left alone to select which photographs they want to share, they are beginning to negotiate with risk of the sort that Julie Scott Jones and Jayne Raisborough might identify as an "everyday" process within what will be a complex, emergent, discursive, and socially negotiated means of "identity construction and self-development" (2007, 6). For them, risk is an element of the everyday social contexts through which people create a sense of self and make choices to indicate that self to others, yet their choices are tightly bound within other discourses of identity and are therefore often perceived as constrained or foreordained (ibid., 6). In this sense, risk is not merely a decision to be made but a potentially meaningful experience that captures both a sense of self and a perception of how that self might interact with the world outside.

In the second phase, participants took turns projecting their selected photographs against the wall behind them and performing their stories about those photographs. Some of these were innocuous and forgettable, and audiences could simply indicate polite attention without engaging deeply. However, several of the photographs and stories made the performers vulnerable to disapproval by showing them in an unfavourable light, whether this was overtly embarrassing or merely banal. In many cases the performers reflected this vulnerability by violating the expectations of their audiences. By revealing their vocal mannerisms and body language of vulnerability, the performers fully embodied the risks they were taking in the act of performing the photo that they had committed to in the devising phase. By the same token, audience members in these small, closely arranged groups knew that the performers (and other audience members) could see and hear every indication of approval or disapproval, whether intentional or not. The moment that each individual audience member perceived the performer's vulnerability, and other audience members' reactions to it, she entered into a heightened ethical relationship with that performer (Heddon 2008, 124). She had to determine whether the performance would require active intervention—positive gestures of approval and reassurance, or even possibly an interruption of the performance—or whether she would reject the performer's story and indicate her disapproval, thereby risking injury to their relationship. At these points of vulnerability, "everyone experiences themselves as involved and responsible for a situation nobody single-handedly created" (Fischer-Lichte 2008, 165). The performers' displays of vulnerability created a "risky aesthetics" that ratcheted up the attention levels among the audience members and made the risks of performance palpable to everyone involved, therefore drawing them in by varying degrees. In other words, it was the willingness to take risks that transformed the experience from mundane conversation to aesthetic, charged performance event.

Vulnerability and Risk from Two Perspectives

Because the performers in *Collect Yourselves!* also formed the audience for each other's stories, it is helpful to look at vulnerability and risk in performance from the perspectives of both performer and audience member.[3] Jess Dobkin describes in vivid detail the anxieties underlying the development of her performance piece *The Lactation Station Breast Milk Bar*. As part of her overall "desire for meaningful, intimate exchange with an audience" (2012, 63), Dobkin performed the experience of trying to breastfeed her newborn daughter by offering her audiences samples of human breast milk to taste. Dobkin openly discussed her "disappointment and shame" (ibid., 70) at her failed attempts at breastfeeding and "encouraged" members of her audience "to share their thoughts and reflections at the bar" (ibid., 70). For Dobkin, a professional performer, there was significant risk involved in reviving her sense of defeat for an audience. "Even now when I discuss my experience of breastfeeding, the vulnerability and risk of imparting that information is present. Will I receive sympathy and understanding?" (ibid., 70). Some *Collect Yourselves!* participants described their own anxiety in similar terms, such as the written comment: "social pressure = was it funny? Did I make a good choice of picture?" (Anne,[4] Friend Group 2). In instances where participants made themselves vulnerable by admitting to failure or loss, the result was almost invariably an increase in interest and energy from their audience.

Dobkin also discusses vulnerability and risk in reference to personal photographs. The wall behind the milk bar sported a photograph of Dobkin "looking haggard and defeated" as she tried to feed her daughter (2012, 70). The dissonance between Dobkin's image there and her healthy, professional self behind the bar served as evidence of the difficulties in breastfeeding that she shared, in words, with her audiences, as well as a profound change in her physical and emotional state. In much the same way, several *Collect Yourselves!* participants took the risk of showing photographs of themselves looking very different or revealing something about themselves they would ordinarily hide from public view. As with the admissions of vulnerability, these dissonances led to spikes in audience attention and a corresponding intensity in the performance. Both Dobkin and these *Collect Yourselves!* participants performed not only in relation to their audiences but also in relation to their past selves, represented in photographs and contextualised through storytelling.

Many of Dobkin's audience members assumed the performance was motivated by her success in breastfeeding (ibid., 70), and Dobkin could have gone along with that fiction. However, her desire for intimacy with her audience motivated her to make herself vulnerable by revealing her failure. Had she played the role of successful breastfeeding champion, or only addressed issues faced by others, the risk would have centred on her audience's taboo-breaking acts of tasting human milk. But by engaging with her sense of shame and failure, she was not only holding up her "verbal art" of storytelling and soliciting stories for evaluation (Bauman 1975, 293); she was holding up her own real-life failure and the vulnerability that that entails. Dobkin engaged with risk in terms of "identity construction and self-development" (Scott Jones and Raisborough 2007, 6) as well as the "self-making" identified as a property of autobiographical performance, choosing to expose and frame herself through emergent processes of making herself vulnerable to others.

To complement Dobkin's exploration of risk and vulnerability on the part of the performer, we briefly discuss Adam Alston's (2013) analysis of risk and vulnerability as an audience member in a one-on-one performance, Lundahl & Seitl's *Rotating in a Room of Images*. This performance plunged Alston into a visceral sense of fear and discomfort. In *Rotating in a Room of Images*, the audience member enters a room full of white curtains, occluding any clear sense of what to expect. Then the room goes dark, and he is led by the hand through "a game of … stumbling and being guided through the pitch-black" (ibid., 219). Alston responded with "fear and trepidation" (ibid., 219), feeling himself at risk from unknown and irrational threats. Alston uses psychologist Paul Slovic's (2010) definition of risk as a subjective phenomenon based on the gap between what is and what might happen, freeing risk from its more common associations with the severity and likelihood of actual physical harm (e.g. Breakwell 2014, 3) and opening it up to any "perception relate[d] to an evaluation of future-oriented uncertainty" (Alston 2013, 223). Alston did not need to experience actual threats of harm in order for his feelings and behaviours to be shaped by the perceived risks in the performance space. As Alston was an "emotionally involved anticipating subject" (ibid., 226) who needed to physically negotiate an intentionally disorienting space, his sense of risk transformed him into "a 'hyperactively' creative subject" (ibid., 224) who perceived threats where there were none and consequently "trip[ped] and stumble[d] through the space" (ibid., 223).

Alston's analysis of the politics of participation extends beyond the remit of this discussion of risk, but he highlights the interconnections of affect, emotion, and risk as influences on participation. Using Slovic's approach, "risk" becomes an appropriate term to use for storytelling in the physically safe space of a small group of people telling stories about photographs that they themselves have selected to share, and of audience members having their physical and verbal reactions viewed at close quarters. Their perception of risk began in the devising phase, which prompted them to imagine the upcoming performance situation even though they had only the most basic understanding of what it might entail, and participants in the stranger groups also had no idea who their fellow performers would be. In fact, while many participants described how much they enjoyed any excuse to look through old photographs, several explained after the event that the pressure they felt to select appropriate photographs formed the dominant and sometimes negative impression of the entire devising phase. None of the participants anticipated physical harm, but they could imagine an unfavourable gap between their performances (or their reactions to another's performance) and the audience's evaluations of those performances (or reactions). However, simple stage fright is not sufficient to describe the emotions and aesthetics at play in the *Collect Yourselves!* performances. It was not the case that the most nervous performers produced the greatest (or least) aesthetic impact. The relationship between risk and aesthetics was more complex than that. *Collect Yourselves!* performances were at their most powerful when, like Dobkin, the participants chose to perform their own personal vulnerabilities and when, like Alston, the participants attended to each other's performances as "emotionally involved anticipating subject(s)" (ibid., 226) who negotiated their moment-by-moment responses to the self-disclosures issuing from their small and proximate groups. The risks taken by participants as they performed and as they formed the audience for each other involved the "self-making" or "identity construction and self-development" (2007, 6) of these autopoietic performance events (Fischer-Lichte 2008). Risk played a critical role in a chain of events leading from the individual decision to participate through to the collective creation of affectively and aesthetically potent moments of performance.

The Risky Chain

Collect Yourselves! prompted several instances of affectively powerful, emotionally gripping, aesthetically pleasing, liminal, and perhaps even transformational performance. These aesthetic high points were substantially different from the personally rewarding (Frohlich et al. 2002, 170) but conversational, low-intensity, informal, subconscious, and low-risk interactions (Wilson 2006, 9) that tend to occur in everyday media sharing. However, these high points did not appear *ex nihilo*. Each one occurred when the performer took a risk or made herself vulnerable. Each of these moments of risk was itself predicated on the establishment of intimacy between performer and audience members, and each moment of intimacy arose from a dissonance between the live performer and the photograph and story she performed. Again, no aesthetics occurred without risk or vulnerability, no risk or vulnerability occurred without intimacy, and no intimacy occurred without dissonance.

As the four *Collect Yourselves!* performances covered 101 individual stories over nearly three hours of performance time, this discussion focuses on responses to prompt three, the "embarrassing" prompt, because it dealt most explicitly with risk and led to several of the most compelling performances. The prompt read: "Find a picture of you or taken by you that isn't on any social networking site ... that you're maybe even a little bit embarrassed about." Participants were given full latitude to decide how embarrassing their photo should be and what they wanted to reveal about it (in fact, one participant borrowed a strategy from prompt five and uploaded nothing at all). Other prompts led to findings in line with those we present here.

Where dissonance was limited or non-existent, no intimacy emerged. For example, Leo in Stranger Group 1 spoke appreciatively of the street markets in Istanbul and displayed several gorgeous photographs of them. Only towards the end of his story did he admit the embarrassing part, which was that he and his wife had tried to run away from aggressive shopkeepers. There was no dissonance between the colourful images and the idea of not liking to haggle, and his performance led to no signs of intimacy or connection between himself and any of his audience members. However, storytelling can illuminate dissonance that is not immediately obvious to the audience. Wendy showed a photo of herself and her boyfriend pulling faces in their car, but the faces were not the embarrassing part for her. Neither was the slight red rash on her neck. Instead, what she found embarrassing was the fact that at the time the photo was taken, she was cripplingly embarrassed about the rash, nearly refusing to be seen in public. She was embarrassed about the fact that she had been so embarrassed in the past, and used her performance to poke fun at herself for having been so self-absorbed. Her audience realised that what they first thought was simply a photo of Wendy pulling a face was actually a sign of her genuine distress at being seen with a mild rash on her neck, and that the Wendy of today found her previous embarrassment to be embarrassing. This combination of dissonance—making an otherwise invisible change of attitude come to life—and a fresh self-discovery on Wendy's part made for a moment of intimacy between performer and audience members, who expressed their engagement by leaning forward and laughing sympathetically. What had seemed like a tiny cause for embarrassment in the photo of Wendy pulling a face was revealed to be a significant embarrassment about a crippling self-consciousness that no one in her audience seemed to have expected.

The most common way of creating dissonance was to display a photograph that clashed with the appearance or persona of the performer.

The handsome, adult Pablo in Friend Group 2 showed a picture of himself as a young child with a missing tooth, huge plastic glasses, and his pet rabbit in his arms, which drew instant attention and even verbal responses from his audience. He went on to reveal, offhandedly, that the next day his mother had cooked his pet rabbit for the family dinner, and that he had cried. His audience was now doubly drawn in, first by the intimacy of sharing an unflattering childhood photo and then by his revelation, which led to exclamations of sympathy and concern. Pablo deflected any potential criticism of his mother's conduct with the comment, "What you can expect, 200 people living in that town, you kill the rabbit, it's just the rabbit or you." This was met by gales of laughter and a sense of intimacy between Pablo and his audience, evidenced by tone of voice, body language, and verbal interjections. Intimacy in the context of performance practices, including the digital, can be defined as the sensation that prompts people who feel comfortable in their ability to communicate "to reveal something about themselves and connect in some form of meaningful exchange" (Chatzichristodoulou and Zerihan 2012, 1). The dissonance of Pablo's photograph, the revelation about his rabbit, his admission of tears, and his pragmatic attitude led to intimacy exactly as Chatzichristodoulou and Zerihan describe it. Because the *Collect Yourselves!* performances were shaped by prompts to which participants could respond in private at any convenient time and location using any format of photograph, even analogue, we argue that this digital system was a key component that allowed participants to create their own "meaningful exchange" of emotion and insight such as Pablo's, whose performance of a moment of vulnerability was met by an intense wave of acceptance by his audience. They in turn now had a slightly different perspective on Pablo and perhaps on life in small-town Spain.

While participants in stranger groups did not describe their experiences in terms of intimacy, they did explain how the performance created surprisingly strong and swift connections among them, and again this only happened in the wake of dissonance. In Stranger Group 1, Ebba showed a photograph of a piece of art she had made, a transparent glass sculpture of her own teeth. This image was dissonant on two levels. Firstly, it represented a hobby and a choice of topic that many people would find odd in someone whose appearance and manner were not particularly eccentric or artistic. As her story continued, though, Ebba revealed that one of her friends—another artist creating shocking glass sculptures of chickens being processed for the supermarket trade—reacted with utter horror and disgust to Ebba's teeth. Ebba's audience, some of whom had at first reacted with distaste at her photograph, were now invited to perceive the friend's reaction as Ebba did—in other words, as an overreaction. This put them in a position of having to re-evaluate their emerging perceptions of Ebba, her artwork, and her friend's reaction. The dissonances between Ebba's photo and her story forged an immediate sense of connection with her audience members, not necessarily through any identification with Ebba's experiences, but through the need to orient themselves to their shifting responses to Ebba's story. By creating this sense of connection, Ebba risked being rejected by some of her audience members, but she also created the space for them to transform their attitudes towards her choices, and she certainly used risk as a means of creating an identity (Scott Jones and Raisborough 2007) in relation to this room full of strangers.

The most compelling example of dissonance leading to risk through a type of intimacy was the photo taken by Hugh, in Friend Group 1, of a nearly naked man dancing on a pavement. Hugh and his friends are heterosexual and appeared to be socially conservative, and Hugh revealed a great deal of embarrassment through circuitous speech patterns peppered with phrases like "I guess" and "kind of" with corresponding body language. As Hugh described how much he appreciated watching this "really beautiful" man dance, his audience remained utterly impassive, with none of the smiles of recognition or sounds of encouragement that accompanied many of the other stories, including Hugh's. It would be easy to imagine Hugh beginning his story about the nearly naked man, then claiming his girlfriend had dared him to take the photo and disavowing any feelings of appreciation. However, Hugh continued, moving through multiple points at which he might easily have concluded this uncomfortable story. He finally broke his audience's stony silence when his comment that "his codpiece was quite scary" drew laughter. As his turn concluded, Hugh even said, "So it *should* be embarrassing ...", implying that for him it still was not. Hugh's decision to carry on making himself vulnerable was a very immediate and personal version of a performer's being "marked as subject to evaluation" for "competence" (Bauman 1975, 293). In Hugh's case, as in Jess Dobkin's, the "competence" that was being evaluated included not only the way he told his story but his choice of subject matter in the first place and his ability to convey his feelings to his audience. Hugh's tenacious performance and the muted positive response he eventually received created a bond of intimacy. It was not an apparently comfortable or welcome bond, as Hugh worked through a great deal of discomfort to achieve it. In either case, dissonance opened the door for vulnerability and an awkward intimacy, which led to a potentially transformational moment in these friends' relationships with each other and perhaps even their feelings about masculine sexuality.

Given the differentiation between conversational and aesthetic performance described by Wilson (2006, 9), we anticipated that friend groups might chat with each other instead of "perform", or that they would already have revealed whatever intimacies they were likely to wish to share, thereby precluding approaches to Wilson's "high intensity" or "high risk" performances (ibid.). In both cases, we were pleased to discover precisely the opposite. Groups of friends risked making themselves vulnerable to each other through sharing new intimacies, and any lapses into conversation actively supported the performance taking place. Friend groups spoke in terms of the "intimacy" of the performance experience without being prompted to think in those terms in any way: one, for example, reflected that "sharing our stories and the experience as a whole deepened the bond we have" (Barbara, Friend Group 2). Stranger groups behaved similarly to the friend groups in many ways, but their risk taking was often subtler and less frequent than in the friend groups. The connections described by stranger groups are experiences of the same type, if not quite the same intensity, as the intimacy described by friend groups.

Many participants revealed far deeper insights than the prompts required, and their audiences took in the import of these intimacies, whether delightedly or grudgingly. Hugh took a risk in making himself vulnerable in front of his audience, and that risk was rewarded in an emotionally and aesthetically compelling moment of performance. In the same way, everyone who created a sense of intimacy or connection with their audience members made themselves vulnerable to rejection. These risks created the emotional and aesthetic high points of each performance. Where dissonance or intimacy/connection were lacking, risk was lacking, and the performance felt flat. Where performers took risks, the performance came to life in a visible heightening of attention and exchange of energy among performers and audience members (Fischer-Lichte 2008). Small moments of liminality and the potential for transformation opened up, where for example both Hugh and his audience members might re-evaluate their attitudes towards the male body on public display. A rigorous analysis of all four performances revealed that no moments of liminality occurred without preceding or concurrent moments of risk.

Risky Aesthetics

Collect Yourselves! was an interdisciplinary experiment in digital media sharing and performance, seeking to expand the possibilities for non-professionals to tell stories from their own lives in ways that included the aesthetic properties of autobiographical performance. This shift from conversational to aesthetic performance hinged on our participants' willingness to take risks, a surprising result given the fact that only one or two of the five prompts suggested that participants should make themselves at all vulnerable, and participants had complete control at all times of what they wished to share. It was our intention from the outset of the design process to challenge our participants to choose photographs and stories that they would not ordinarily share. It seems possible that some element of personal risk is involved in meeting this challenge in a way that begins to approach the aesthetics of performance.

The situation of the performer is the most obviously risky. Many participants explained that the imperative to share what they had selected in the devising phase was the source of some strain but also contributed to the sense of connection and intimacy that all groups quickly formed. Participant comments parallel Dobkin's analysis of her experience of creating and performing *The Lactation Station Breast Milk Bar*. She, too, could have distanced herself from the distressing life experiences that she planned to share, but she remained committed to her artistic choices, including the display of a photo of herself looking miserable as she tried and failed to breastfeed her daughter. For Dobkin, the connection between intimacy and risk can hardly be overstated: "Any disclosure makes the performer vulnerable to being misunderstood; this is the risk that is required when intimate revelations are brought to an audience" (2012, 70). *Collect Yourselves!* demonstrates that this tight connection between risk and intimacy also holds true for non-professional participants in intermedial autobiographical performance, that both require some form of dissonance, and that both are essential for an aesthetic media-sharing event.

Alston's observations about the effects of affect and emotion on audience participation shed light on the subtly active role that audience members play. Alston sees a nuanced interplay of an audience member's affect, emotion, cognition, personal memory, unique life experiences, and perception of relevant sociocultural influences. Foremost among these are "affective memory and individuality" (2013, 226), both of which are called on to an extraordinary degree in these audience members who will at any moment stand up and take their place as performers, responding to the same creative prompts as their fellow performers. Audience members in *Collect Yourselves!* performances are not reacting to an unknown performer displaying her skills in a professional context: they are responding to peers sharing a common experience, each of whom is close enough to see every flicker of response, and each of whom will be just as close when the performance is over and the ordinary rules of conversation resume. Through PED, digital media technologies prompted the transformation of an ordinary conversational exchange into an aesthetic experience through the intertwining of dissonance, intimacy, and risk.

Notes

1. *Collect Yourselves!* was designed and built by Spence with contributions from Frohlich and Andrews.
2. These performers are well established creators of contemporary live performance, particularly autobiographical and/or digital performance, in the UK. While we are not at all insensitive to the lack of non-white performers or the preponderance of male performers, we have chosen to prioritise the diversity of relevant performance practices over a diversity of performer demographics.
3. Although *Collect Yourselves!* is participatory in many senses, it was not artist-led (Bishop 2012). We have found it more productive to view this project as made up of individuals who alternated roles of performer and audience member rather than as contributors to a participatory performance.
4. All participant names have been changed to preserve their anonymity.

References

Ah Kun, Leonard M., and Marsden, G. 2007. Co-present photo sharing on mobile devices. In *Proceedings of the 9th International Conference on Human Computer Interaction with Mobile Devices and Services*, 277–84. New York: ACM Press.

Alston, Adam. 2013. Politics in the Dark: Risk Perception, Affect and Emotion in Lundahl & Seitl's Rotating in a Room of Images. In *Affective Performance and Cognitive Science: Body, Brain and Being*, ed. Nicola Shaughnessy, 217–228. London and New York: Bloomsbury.

Balabanović, Marko, Chu, L., and Wolff, G. 2000. Storytelling with Digital Photographs. In *Proceedings of the SIGCHI Conference on Human Factors in Computing Systems*, 564–571. New York: ACM Press.

Bauman, Richard. 1975. Verbal Art as Performance. *American Anthropologist* 77 (2): 290–311.

Bishop, Claire. 2012. *Artificial Hells: Participatory Art and the Politics Of Spectatorship*. New York: Verso Books.

Breakwell, Glynis M. 2014. *The Psychology of Risk*, 2nd ed. Cambridge: Cambridge University Press.

Chatzichristodoulou, Maria, and Rachel Zerihan. 2009. Introduction. In *Interfaces of Rerformance*, ed. M. Chatzichristodoulou, et al., 1–5. Farnham, UK: Ashgate.

Chatzichristodoulou, Maria and Rachel Zerihan. 2012. Introduction. In *Intimacy Across Visceral and Digital Performance*, ed. Maria Chatzichristodoulou and Rachel Zerihan, 1–11. Basingstoke, UK and New York: Palgrave Macmillan.

Clawson, James, Amy Voida, Nirmal Patel, and Kent Lyons. 2008. Mobiphos: A Collocated-Synchronous Mobile Photo Sharing Application. In *Proceedings of the 10th International Conference on Human Computer Interaction with Mobile Devices and Services*, 187–95. New York: ACM Press.

Courtney, David. 2005. Edgework and the Aesthetic Paradigm: Resonances and High Hopes. In *EdgeWork: The Sociology of Risk-Taking*, ed. Stephen Lyng, 89–115. London: Routledge.

Crabtree, Andy, Tom Rodden, and John Mariani. 2004. Collaborating Around Collections: Informing the Continued Development of Photoware. In: *Proceedings of the 2004 ACM Conference on Computer Supported Cooperative Work*, 396–405. New York: ACM Press.

Dobkin, Jess. 2012. Performing with Mother's Milk: *The Lactation Station Breast Milk Bar*. In *Intimacy Across Visceral and Digital Performance*, ed. Maria Chatzichristodoulou, and Rachel Zerihan, 62–73. Basingstoke, UK and New York: Palgrave Macmillan.

Dolan, Jill. 2005. *Utopia in Performance: Finding Hope at the Theater*. Ann Arbor, MI: University of Michigan Press.

Fischer-Lichte, Erika. 2008. *The Transformative Power of Performance: A New Aesthetics*. London: Routledge.

Frohlich, David, Allan Kuchinsky, Celine Pering, Abbe Don, and Steven Ariss. 2002. Requirements for Photoware. In *Proceedings of the 2002 ACM Conference on Computer Supported Cooperative Work*, 166–75. New York: ACM Press.

Frohlich, David M. 2004. *Audiophotography: Bringing Photos To Life With Sounds*. Dordrecht, Boston and London: Springer and Kluwer Academic.

Frohlich, David M., Tony Clancy, John Robinson, and Enrico Costanza. 2004. The Audiophoto Desk. In *Proceedings of 2AD, Second International Conference on Appliance Design*. Bristol, UK: HP, np.

Goldberg, RoseLee. 2011. *Performance Art: From Futurism to the Present*, 3rd ed. New York: Thames and Hudson.

Govan, Emma, Helen Nicholson, and Katie Normington. 2007. *Making a Performance: Devising Histories and Contemporary Practices*. London: Routledge.

Heddon, Deirdre. 2008. *Autobiography and Performance*. Basingstoke: Palgrave Macmillan.

Hellstrom, Caroline and Irvine Lapsley. 2015. Humour and Happiness in an NPM World: Do They Speak in Jest? *Critical Perspectives on Accounting*, np.

Kirk, David, Abigail Sellen, Carsten Rother, and Kenneth R. Wood. 2006. Understanding Photowork. In *Proceedings of the SIGCHI Conference on Human Factors in Computing Systems*, 761–70. New York: ACM Press.

Kirk, David, Shahram Izadi, Abigail Sellen, Stuart Taylor, Richard Banks, and Otmar Hilliges. 2010. Opening Up the Family Archive. In *Proceedings of the 2010 ACM Conference on Computer Supported Cooperative Work*, 261–70. New York: ACM Press.

Lehmann, Hans-Thies. 2006. *Postdramatic Theatre*. Routledge.

Lindley, Siân, and Andrew Monk. 2006. Designing Appropriate Affordances for Electronic Photo Sharing Media. *CHI '06 Extended Abstracts on Human Factors in Computing Systems*, 1031–1036. New York: ACM Press.

Live Art Development Agency. 2010. *In time: A Collection of Live Art Case Studies*. Live Art Development Agency.

Lucero, Andrés, Jussi Holopainen, and Tero Jokela. 2011. Pass-Them-Around: Collaborative Use of Mobile Phones for Photo Sharing. In: *Proceedings of the 2011 Annual Conference on Human Factors in Computing Systems*, 1787–96. New York: ACM Press.

Lyng, Stephen. 1990. Edgework: A Social Psychological Analysis of Voluntary Risk Taking. *American Journal of Sociology* 95 (4): 851–886.

De Marinis, Marco. 1993. *The Semiotics of Performance*, trans. Áine O'Healy. Bloomington and Indianapolis: Indiana University Press.

De Marinis, Marco. 2007. The Performance Text. In *The Performance Studies Reader*, ed. Henry Bial, 280–99. Abingdon, Oxon and New York: Routledge.

Petrelli, Daniela, and Steve Whittaker. 2010. Family Memories in the Home: Contrasting Physical and Digital Mementos. *Personal and Ubiquitous Computing* 14 (2): 153–169.

Phelan, Peggy. 2004. Marina Abramović: Witnessing Shadows. *Theatre Journal* 56 (4): 569–577.

Piper, Anne Marie, Nadir Weibel, and James Hollan. 2013. Audio-Enhanced Paper Photos: Encouraging Social Interaction at Age 105. In *Proceedings of the 2013 Conference on Computer Supported Cooperative Work*, 215–24. New York: ACM Press.

Reitmaier, Thomas, Pierre Benz, and Gary Marsden. 2013. Designing and Theorizing Co-Located Interactions. In *Proceedings of the SIGCHI Conference on Human Factors in Computing Systems*, 381–90. New York: ACM Press.

Sarvas, Risto, and David M. Frohlich. 2011. *From Snapshots to Social Media: The Changing Picture of Domestic Photography*. New York: Springer-Verlag.

Scott Jones, Julie and Jayne Raisborough. 2007. Introduction: Situating Risk in the Everyday. In *Risks, Identities, and the Everyday*, ed. Julie Scott Jones and Jayne Raisborough, 1–8. Abingdon: Ashgate.

Slovic, Paul. 2010. *The Feeling of Risk: New Perspectives on Risk Perception*. London: Routledge.

Spence, Jocelyn. 2016. *Performative Experience Design*. Heidelberg, New York, Dordrecht and London: Springer.

Spence, Jocelyn, David Frohlich, and Stuart Andrews. 2013. Performative Experience Design: Where Autobiographical Performance and Human-Computer Interaction Meet. *Digital Creativity* 24 (2): 96–110.

Stelmaszewska, Hanna, Bob Fields, and Ann Blandford. 2008. The Roles of Time, Place, Value and Relationships in Collocated Photo Sharing with Camera Phones. In *Proceedings of the 22nd British HCI Group Annual Conference on People and Computers: Culture, Creativity, Interaction*, 141–50. Swinton, UK: British Computer Society.

House, Van, and A. Nancy. 2009. Collocated Photo Sharing, Story-telling, and the Performance of Self. *International Journal of Human-Computer Studies* 67 (12): 1073–1086.

Whittaker, Steve, Ofer Bergman, and Paul Clough. 2009. Easy on that Trigger Dad: A Study of Long Term Family Photo Retrieval. *Personal and Ubiquitous Computing* 14: 31–43.

Wilson, Michael. 2006. *Storytelling and Theatre: Contemporary Storytellers and Their Art*. Basingstoke: Palgrave Macmillan.

PART III

Risking the Self: Identities, Playing with Risk, and Encountering the Edge

At the Risk of Being Sincere: Participation and Delegation in South African Contemporary Live Art

Rat Western

Cultural practice in the South African post-apartheid age has long grappled with the politics and aesthetics of representation. During the apartheid era, the aesthetics of resistance predominated and was "deployed in a largely polarised political terrain, with artists … focusing on the brutality of the larger 'common enemy', the apartheid state" (Atkinson 1999, 15). There was very real risk to the artist inherent in these aesthetics of resistance, not merely in terms of professional success or failure. Cultural practitioners who created such aesthetics might be arrested, interrogated, and tortured. Their works could be censored and they themselves banned and exiled. But the position taken by resistance art "often considered [it] more strategic to disseminate oppositional images than to be critical of the assumptions underlying artistic production, or the conditions of its reception" (ibid.). In post-apartheid South Africa, artistic representations of racial or gendered "others" have incurred a complex set

R. Western (✉)
Rhodes University, Grahamstown, South Africa
e-mail: rat.western@gmail.com

© The Author(s) 2017

A. O'Grady (ed.), *Risk, Participation, and Performance Practice*,
DOI 10.1007/978-3-319-63242-1_8

of political risks due to what Craig Owens terms "the indignity of speaking for others" (1994, 262).

In this chapter I discuss three South African case studies of participatory and/or delegated performance art: Brett Bailey's *Exhibit A* (2012), Gavin Krastin's *#omnomnom* (2014), and Igshaan Adams's *Bismillah* (2014).[1] These works make implicit references to racial identity, yet their inclusion of delegated performers and/or participatory audiences carries more multifaceted risks and complicates the political power dynamics of binarised racial classification. In contrast to ideas of authenticity, as they relate to the presence of the artist's own physical body or to that of the delegated performer, I compare facets of sincerity. Sincerity, I argue, is of paramount importance for the participatory work because it explores "the zone of contact" (Taylor 2001, 23) between the viewer and the viewed. It is through this *zone of contact* that issues raised by the "ethical turn in art criticism" (Bishop 2006, 180), concerns around audience agency, and allegories of inequality between both audiences and artists and artists and delegated performers are explored. Sincerity as a strategy carries a personal risk because it asks the participant (either performer or audience) to consider a parity between feeling and its declaration and to manifest this through a profound consideration of intent. Sincerity implies an interaction with an other (a speaking *with* or *to*, rather than *for*, an other)—something that goes further than a flattened aesthetic of identity representation.[2]

On Binaries: Authenticity, Sincerity, the Real, and Risk

Authenticity and sincerity are concepts, often conflated, that are intrinsically linked to notions of truth, honesty, and something which is in some way "real". The debate around what is constituted as "real" in performance was reignited by Marina Abramović in an interview in the wake of her retrospective at the Museum of Modern Art. "To be a performance artist, you have to hate theatre", she is quoted as saying. "Theatre is fake … The knife is not real, the blood is not real, and the emotions are not real. Performance is just the opposite: the knife is real, the blood is real, and the emotions are real" (quoted in Ayers 2010). But "real" and "fake" are unnecessarily formalist binaries. In participatory performance, what is crucial is the nature of an experience and its potential to bleed into understandings of everyday life, whether their impetus is "real" interaction or a *real* emotional exchange in a "fake" environment.

Often used as synonyms, authenticity and sincerity differ in a crucial philosophical subtlety, as tourism theorist John P. Taylor illuminates: “sincerity is significantly different from authenticity in that it occurs in the zone of contact among participating groups or individuals, rather than appearing as an internal quality of a thing, self, or Other” (2001, 23). Taylor, writing on tourism experiences of Maori culture, argues that the search for authenticity is essentially linked to a Western quest for origins—a sentimentality about pre-contact aboriginal culture and a nostalgia which imagines this culture to be in a kind of time-warp stasis prior to European contact. Social anthropologist Richard Handler also describes authenticity as something linked to both the West and to its favouring of individuality, whilst he represents Trilling’s observations of sincerity as “privileg[ing] social relationships rather than individual selfhood” (1986, 3).

Walter Benjamin’s theories on authenticity clearly have salience for both theorists:

> Even the most perfect reproduction of a work of art is lacking in one element: its presence in time and place … The presence of the original is the prerequisite to the concept of authenticity. (2008, 21)

Here, authenticity is linked to the theory of an original, and to a temporal frame to which the “original” has borne witness. Authenticity carries a kind of nostalgia, as its history always takes place at a distance from those who view an “original”. Benjamin defines this historical resonance of the art object as its “auratic mode” (ibid., 23–24), but this “aura” is something linked to the lifespan of the art object and although a viewer may stand in the presence of that “aura”, its authenticity remains a part of the artwork. Whilst such a reading of authenticity is inherently Modernist, in a post-colonial context these readings are, like much of the history of former colonies, “ghosts [which] continue to haunt” (Taylor 2001, 25). Artists from such contexts are thus frequently encouraged to work within a presentation of self under a kind of “branded authentic identity”. Authenticity, thus represented as a fixed interior state rather than an individual personality in exchange with others, often results in a flattening of identity based primarily on an oversimplified conception of race, gender, sexual preference, or some combination of these.

Divergences between what is meant by “authenticity” and “sincerity”, however, should not be read as conclusive binaries. The use of authenticity can be beneficial in participatory performance and the "aura" of an object or individual can be conferred, albeit momentary, like a light fleetingly shared. As Bishop writes, "the [delegated] performers also delegate something to the artist: a guarantee of authenticity, through their proximity to everyday social reality, conventionally denied to the artist who deals merely in representations" (2012, 237). The delegated performer is thus both a representation and a real-life referent who, through an "aura" of experience, brings things closer to reality. The converse of this is that the delegated performer may be out of context, so whilst their everyday role may be authentic (and their selection as a performer may be based on this), their context in a performance is not. Here we begin to see how things that may be set up as binaries (real and fake) represent instead a more complex sliding greyscale.

Lionel Trilling, in his book *Authenticity and Sincerity*, suggests another distinction between the terms—a question of taste or fashionable usage in common parlance:

> To praise a work ... by calling it sincere is now at best a way of saying that although it need be given no aesthetic or intellectual admiration, it was at least conceived in innocence of heart. (1972, 6)

The word sincerity tends to evoke a muzzy sensibility which is earnest, yet lacking in sophistication. As Trilling demonstrates, to describe something as sincere is at best a backhanded compliment. The ardent exposure of deeply held sentiments through a sincere act is uncomfortable or possibly embarrassing. As Gareth White elaborates, "[t]o expose unconsidered thoughts or emotions in a semi-public space is risky, just as it is to display incompetence, inappropriate enthusiasm, neediness, distress or loss of poise" (2013, 76). The awkwardness associated with sincerity is exactly what makes it risky and therefore interesting. It places something at stake, something deeply personal and therefore something very *real* in the space of experience and emotion.

Swiss curator Aoife Rosenmeyer (2010) questions this contemporary discomfiture among artists to express sincerity:

> [Sincerity] is most definitely not fashionable; instead artists and critics hide behind strategies of, at best, self-referential or self-depreciatory glibness, or, at worst, irony and cynicism. The straightforward attempt to be sincere, honest and open whilst leaving something at stake is rare indeed ...

> Accepting the compromises entailed in living in the modern world, is sincerity possible in art without the artist having to cover their embarrassment through any of the contemporary strategies of dissembling?

Artists, theorists, and critics seem to prefer a form of taxonomy when it comes to explaining works through text. The reasoning here might be pragmatic—binaries are neater than conceptual bleeds. Given the history of our country, as South Africans we should be wary of delineations which seek to create hierarchies. Considering the risks practitioners were once prepared to take for their art in this country, surely the risk of potentially losing an air of sophistication should be relatively minor? When it comes to participatory work, however, binaries seem to be the order of the day: Is it performance art or contemporary theatre, live art or social practice, is it "real" or "fake", and most importantly is the audience active or passive? Bishop has this to say on the danger of binarising active and passive audiences:

> The binary of active/passive always ends up in a deadlock: either a disparagement of the spectator because he does nothing, while the performers on stage do something—or the converse claim that those who act are inferior to those who are able to look, contemplate ideas, and have critical distance on the world. [This] binary ... is reductive and unproductive, because it serves only as an allegory of inequality. (2012, 37–38)

The same "allegory of inequality" can be seen in any binary which seeks to create power structures between audiences and artworks, audiences and performers, or creative practitioners of varying persuasions. Because of the implied lack of sophistication sincerity carries, an appeal towards "authenticity" in lieu of (or as a distraction to) the much debated "reality" of performance is often reiterated when it comes to participative art. The inclusion of either the artist's own physical body, delegated non-professional performers, or a mixture of the two would seem to lend a "realness" and therefore authenticity to a work. If a work focuses on this construction of "authenticity", it places emphasis on the side of the performers and their "realness" or "legitimacy". This weighting sidelines the participatory *zone of contact* between audiences and artworks or between the real and the spectacle. A core element of participatory art is the importance of *immediacy* in a shared moment *between* individuals which cannot be rehearsed if audiences are given agency in their participation.

As a part of this preoccupation with authenticity, participatory art is also particularly concerned with codes of ethical behaviour, especially when utilising non-professional performers to re-enact themselves or when adopting a form of performance which replicates or quotes from real-life events not originally framed as artistic events. This focus on ethics once again sidelines the *zone of contact* between artist and audience because an additional concern arises for the participatory audience: To what degree is the audience complicit in the ethical (or unethical) practice of the artist? Concerns over correct ethical behaviour often supersede aesthetic or conceptual merit in art critique. As Bishop points out:

> The social turn in contemporary art has prompted an ethical turn in art criticism. This is manifest in a heightened attention to *how* a given collaboration is undertaken ... artists are increasingly judged by their working process ... and criticized for any hint of potential exploitation that fails to "fully" represent their subjects, as if such a thing were possible. (2006, 181)

While it is important not to be casually exploitative of participants (performers or audiences), this ethical preoccupation equates socially orientated art practice with actual social work. It presumes that such art work should be therapeutic in its intent, employing approaches which are comforting and comfortable for its participants. As Bishop describes, "a socially collaborative art project could be deemed a success if it works on the level of social intervention even though it founders on the level of art ... it also constitutes a rejection of any art that might offend or trouble its audience" (ibid., 183). This focus on ethics over aesthetics makes for an interesting parallel to South African resistance art of the apartheid era, which emphasised activism over artistic value. As a reactive rather than an active approach to art making, the potential for such art to reimagine its social circumstances through social work also means that it runs the risk of remaining embedded in the narratives of the social ills it seeks to transcend. As Jamal points out, "[t]he very reactive nature of resistance culture, therefore, ensured that it remained implicated in the very specular and juridical economy that it sought to undo" (2005, 3).

There is a potential problem in criticising a participatory work for being undemocratic towards its participants. This critique may deny the fact that intentionally disconcerting or discomforting participants, and playing on social or political inequalities, can be a means for drawing attention to such discriminations as they exist in everyday life. Such work may risk reiterating the social inequalities it seeks to critique, but is this any more of a risk than presenting a neatly delineated, communally considered work in a bubble? The latter may offer its participants such a sense of safe social cohesion in an artificially controlled environment, that they do not consider where such behaviours may be taken further in everyday life. They may leave feeling comforted by their involvement in a particular project and that they have "done their bit".

This ethical turn in art criticism leads to a stultification in participatory practice because it seeks to polemicise any work whose aim is not to please or to present an agreeable experience for those involved. But as curator Frie Leysen stated in her keynote address to the 2015 Australian Theatre Forum: "Art should not please. On the contrary. Art has to show where it hurts in our societies, in our world. We urgently need the courage back to pick up this role of disturbers again" (quoted in Watts 2015). One approach to taking up this "role of disturbers" may be to employ strategies of risky aesthetics. However, risk should not remain merely a "role" or a "costume" that can be put on or taken off. The nature of risk is contextual and the use of it as an aesthetic may lead to a reading contrary to an artist's intentions. As Dror Harari notes:

> [G]iven the contextual nature of risk as a concept fed on cultural beliefs and world views, what, then, is the purpose and effect of risk-taking in performance in times when risk is being obsessively analysed and assessed in order to be tamed? (2009, 174)

Context is significant, because to publicise a work as "risky" potentially carries a converse kind of risk in that the audience may not consider the work "risky" at all. This marketing may be considered merely a kind of sensationalism, meant to garner response, but not to disturb any comfort zones or make anyone think more deeply about their realities. Producing an artwork which creates awareness, or shifts ways of looking, is no easy feat and an ambition to do so is a risk in and of itself. To be aware of the contextual nature of risk, one must have a continually shifting awareness of one's audience, which means being aware of the sincerity one presents or encounters at a *zone of contact*. Interaction is itself a risk whose reward is "a performance ... that is even more ephemeral and unique than most live performance, and that is demonstratively a product of the people who are present at the event" (White 2013, 74).

The sense of immediacy that is made possible through sincerity is the basis for the kind of risk, which Harari describes as "strategies that accentuate and problematize the fundamental actional/performative notion of the 'here and now', which, especially when put in inverted commas, refers both to itself and to its deliberate representation" (2009, 175). Risk in this sense is both the real and its representation, and is more descriptive of the slippage between various categorised binaries and between the island-like authentic individuals who may participate in any given performance. Ethical concerns put at risk what kinds of risk may or may not be permissible, especially when there is this underlying expectation of participatory work: that it must to some small degree "repair the social bond" (Bishop 2012, 11). But does this repair need to be a grand solution? Or is it possible that an artist may risk approaching his audience with a call to sincerity, through a demonstration of his own sincerity, and ask that a social bond be healed in the smallest yet most sincere way—in the "here and now"?

Exhibit A/B: Brett Bailey

I am willing to see you the individual, but I can't because another has cast you as a character in history and he has told you that I, your audience, am synonymous with countless others who look like me. We may share a line of sight, but there is a blindness enforced by this other. I can't see you and you can't see me. I can see your island, but I cannot swim across to feel what the weather is like there and you cannot swim to me. So we stare across that ocean of history between us. Neither of us are more enabled to cross that breach.[3]

Drawing on the tradition of nineteenth-century human zoos, *Exhibit A/B* is a work which Bailey prefers to call an exhibition rather than a dramatic performance.[4] Mirroring the colonial "freak shows" which took people from the colonies to serve as exhibits in European touring exhibitions, this display presents twelve different scenes in the style of an ethnographic museum. Each of these scenes is starkly lit in a darkened space complete with museological trappings: historical artefacts, glass boxes, and contextualising information cards. These cards tell of an atrocity meted out by a colonial force to a particular racial group or to specific individuals. For the most part these scenes are historical, depicting people in period dress, but interspersed among them are characters from more recent history: a Sudanese refugee who suffocated on a deportation flight, a woman of mixed racial heritage whose family was split over government racial "reclassification" of her parentage which rendered her parents' marriage illegal in apartheid South Africa. The details of each are grotesque. The most important feature of these displays is their subjects—live performers dressed for the part. The performers' gaze is the crux of the work. You, the viewer, may look at the scenes, but they look back at you (Fig. 1).

A century on, one can hope that racial and ethical norms have progressed at least to the degree that the majority of audiences would find something abhorrent in using human subjects as if they were objects. This is what the exhibition trades on—the shock factor of using people in this way and thus in revisiting both this and the contextualising history presented on the information cards. The core of the work lies in the gaze of the performers who determinedly stare at the viewer. The expectation is that audiences will feel shame—shame in looking, shame in the histories—and thus, feeling humiliation and horror, be unable to return the gaze of the exhibited performers glaring so defiantly back. Bailey talks specifically about this tactic of "shame" in several interviews, but to feel shame as an audience presupposes several things about the audience—that his audience is white, that they accept some complicit part, that the shock and weight of this history is something that the audience are unfamiliar with and, therefore, that they have no familiar coping mechanisms when confronted with the awfulness of it all.

The performers are local, non-professional residents of the areas in which the production took place (with the exception of a four-person Namibian choir who travelled with the production). Bailey spent much time in researching his histories and in workshopping with his participants. This forms the major part of his response to the boycott petition started by journalist Sara Myers, which accused the work of being racist and subsequently resulted in the closure of the Barbican (London) version of the show. "The rehearsals include exercises in endurance, self-awareness and meditation", Bailey said in a press release (2014) following the decision to close the show. "There is a lot of care, coaching and compassion." When the petition was launched, some of the performers were the first to attempt to bridge the divide in reading this work. "We find this piece to be a powerful tool in the fight against racism. Individually, we chose to do this piece because art impacts people on a deeper emotional level that can spark change" (*Guardian* 2014).

Fig. 1 "A Place in the Sun", from Brett Bailey's *Exhibit A/B*, 2014. *Photo* Murdo Macleod

How is it that some could view this work as a racist reiteration, and therefore as the fetishisation of a colonial past, and others could view it as an emancipatory experience which sought to redress persistent issues of racism in present society? The key comes in an area of experience which many practitioners do not even consider when it comes to participatory experience—the virtual realm of participatory public media. The increasing onslaught of social media allows everyone with a keyboard the opportunity to speak, and this becomes a supplementary experience in itself. Mary Corrigall observed this nature of a work's consumption via the internet, in particular remarking on the online reiteration of a specific image from the production—that of a half-naked woman chained to a bed. "In this way Bailey's *Exhibit B* has been distilled via the web ... to this single image—making it the veritable final product" (2014).

Many of those who protested against the Barbican showing of *Exhibit B* had not experienced the work live. Bailey made much of this fact in his defence: the work needs to be experienced in the flesh.

> The listed components of each installation includes spectators—it is only complete with an audience. The installation is not about the cultural or anatomical difference between the colonial subject and the spectator; it is about the relationship between the two. It is about looking and being looked at. Both performer and spectator are contained within the frame. (2014)

It is the relationship between the artist and his viewer that needs further ethical contemplation and is the *zone of contact* which is not discussed either by those who protested the work, or by Bailey in his defence of his ethical treatment of his performers. The moral dilemma here is not whether Bailey has collaborated ethically with his performers or not, but that he does not collaborate ethically with his audience, whom he explicitly denotes as part of the work. The audience are mere functionaries fulfilling his expectations of a colonial gaze, but what if those are not the eyes with which they look? He thus runs the risk of failing in what he insists is the purpose of the work: to provoke discomfiture in the act of looking and in othering. This reminder of a hateful history (and its contemporary manifestations) does little to heal it. The performers describe a cathartic experience in being able to confront the viewer, but, further than catharsis, what does this gaze generate as a healing tool? Anger can be a powerful tool in restoring self-confidence, but once that is repaired what does one do with that anger? Shame, too, can be cathartic initially in recognising a problem and resolving to rectify a circumstance or being mindful of such pitfalls in the future, but neither anger nor shame is a healthy state of consciousness to be continually perpetuated. Both can render subjects impotent, or lead to their withdrawal from the *zone of contact* which evokes these feelings in order to isolate themselves from the traumas of others. The performers are silenced in the guise of statistical figures rather than contemporary individuals with complex personal stories. Likewise, the audience are presented for the performers as amorphous manifestations of ethnic presuppositions. This work does not allow either side to embrace the complexity of the individual—either their own or that of another—and share in those complexities which make us human.

This work is problematic not because of a simple binary of race, which its protesters decry as its failing, but because it fails to see any of those involved, regardless of race, as individuals who should be afforded more nuanced agency in negotiating such risky territories. Ironically, the petition and the protest followed something of the same pattern. Labelling Bailey as "the white South African" comes with its own racial presumptions. The protest's main focus was the problematic reiteration of images of black people as victims, yet at the same time these protesters reinforced the stereotype of black victimhood in the assumption that the performers were being exploited. In insisting that the show be banned, they were also assuming that no one could make up their own mind on these issues by viewing the work. This defence of individualism and basic human rights conversely ends up trampling all over such concerns. The best form of protest against any contentious artwork may be to "break the rules" of the performance—not through random acts, but with calculated thought and a refusal of the constraints of the work (in this case, not talking). When something offends us, instead of resorting to petitioning and protesting, sincere individual acts of refusal may be more powerful. Why leap straight into civil disobedience when rejecting bourgeois politeness may do the trick?

The failure of artistic sincerity in this work is evident in how the artist himself remains, throughout the process, a very distant figure. Artists may make use of delegated performers in order to appeal to authenticity, but it is impossible to use this strategy to present one's own sincerity. Deborah Seddon points to this absence of the artist as a possible solution to the problematics of the work: "Bailey does not include himself in this work. It would have been easy enough. Bailey could have appeared in a final exhibit room, providing statistics on his own body and origin as is done for the other performers, turning the gaze on himself, on the South African of European descent" (2012, 45). But perhaps this is not so easy, any more than it would have been easy for those who protested *Exhibit B* to have rather taken a more personalised approach to intervention. In both cases this would have required sincere, individualised action, and neither side was willing to risk exposing their individualism through an act of sincerity. Wishing to avoid the shaming response of ridicule, putting anything as heavy as personal sincerity on the scale is risky in case there is nothing other than rejection, derision, and disgust to balance it.

This is why risk *is* important. As Seddon continues, "if South Africans are to move beyond the history of colonialism, apartheid and race that has traumatised us all, it is necessary especially for those in a position of privilege, to take risks, to move beyond an easy comfort zone" (ibid.). Risk, if it is to have any true or lasting resonance, needs to be shared risk. Artists and audiences need to partake of that risk equally in order for there to be any meeting of collective sincerity. The risk of sincerity is the risk of embarrassment, vulnerability, and shame. These themes are the core of *Exhibit A/B* and this is exactly why including the artist's own physical presence would shift the work from a finger-pointing exercise or a nostalgic fetishising of history into a work that meditates on the painful histories and contemporary dangers of ethnographically categorising people.

#*Omnomnom*: Gavin Krastin

How do you feed? On what do you feed? We don't talk about feeding. We talk about consumption—a more polite form where we chew with our mouths shut, but we devour just the same. Do you lick your lips? Do you lick your fingers? Do you slurp to show satisfaction or honour the chef? Do you know which fork and knife to use? Do you finish your plate regardless of taste or do you waste and spit out regardless of manners? What do you find hardest to chew, what gives you sustenance and do you swallow it because you are watched or do you cough it up because it sticks in your craw?

In 2010, South African businessman Kenny Kunene caused a media controversy at his nightclub birthday party when he served up sushi displayed on the bodies of naked black women. The African National

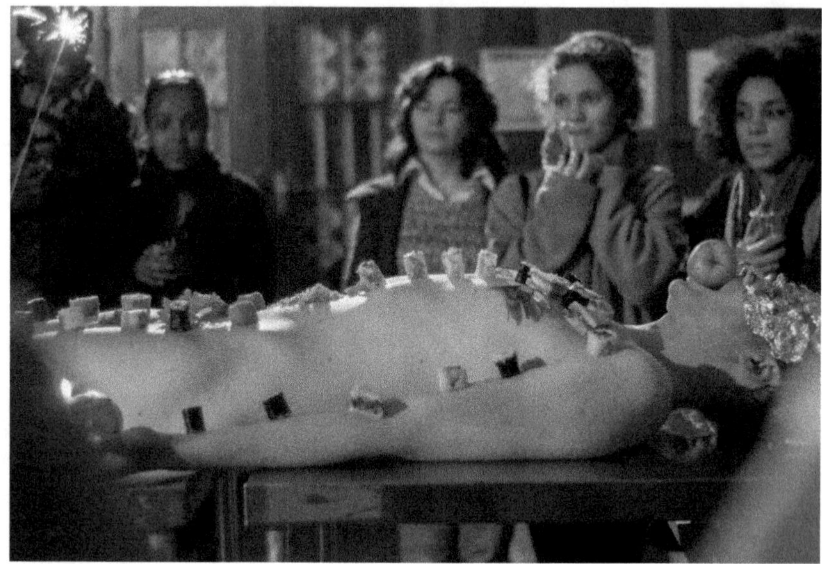

Fig. 2 Gavin Krastin and participating audience members in *#omnomnom*, 2014. *Photo* Sarah Schäfer

Congress (ANC) Woman's league issued a statement deploring "this practice as an attack on the bodily integrity and dignity of all women" (Subramany 2011). Taking this event as a starting point for his *National Arts Festival* work *#omnomnom*, Gavin Krastin set out to look at the ways in which South Africans celebrate and commemorate. The work took place in 2014, the twentieth anniversary of South Africa's democracy and the fortieth anniversary of the National Arts Festival, which inspired this meditation on the rituals of birthday parties, anniversaries, celebratory customs, and gluttonous festivities. Choosing to subvert the role of female and black bodies as sites of possession, control, and submission, Krastin presented his own white male body as a platter, but also as a metaphor for "meat and land for participating spectators to mark, exploit, colonise and devour" (Krastin 2014) (Fig. 2).

In *#omnomnom*, a title referencing social media hashtags for sharing what might broadly be described as tasty offerings, Krastin lay naked on a steel gurney with a halved grapefruit covering his genitals. Appearing both as a corpse and as a sacrificial offering, his head was surrounded by a halo of pizza slices and his face was decorated with gold leaf that evoked more the tinfoil of takeaway restaurant remainders than the embellishments of church ornament. The space was a Victorian university dining hall, complete with stained-glass windows, built to commemorate a sisterhood of nuns. Audiences were invited to eat a variety of foods that were tenderly laid out by another performer on the artist's naked body. A display of neatly arranged sushi soon gave way to more messy morsels: sticky ribs placed over Krastin's ribs, pumpkin, samp, fast food. Burgers were placed over his nipples and a giant bucket of KFC chicken was finally placed in his crotch. Krastin invited his audience to take part in this ritual and display their cultural eating preferences and habits in a process which became richly layered in terms of what and how we celebrate.

The National Arts Festival takes place in Grahamstown in winter, when temperatures often dip below freezing at night. The dining hall had no heating and at 6.00 pm the space was very cold. Most audience members were bundled up in scarves and jackets and their festive conviviality was in stark contrast to the naked shivering body lying exposed as a platter. Krastin speaks about the cold and how the food and the audience became a comfort:

> I had no idea how comforting the food placed on my body, or the touch of the audience would be. When that was removed, it felt like a bullet going through my body. It felt like someone was pulling something off me. You are so cold, so vulnerable that, when that little piece of sushi or that hand on your foot are gone it's so incredibly painful. (Krastin, pers. comm.)

But not all the audience were oblivious to the artist's discomfort. Some tried to cover him with the food or place hands on him to try to warm him—one woman wrapped her scarf around his feet. One reviewer speaks about her discomfort and confusion over his physical distress: "My basic life support medic (and simple human) instincts wanted to cover him with a blanket. My audience and intellectual training told me that he was suffering for his art and that the best thing I could do was to leave him be" (De Swardt 2014).

This split impulse between accepted rules of engagement with an artwork and personal volition to "do something" to ease one's own conscience is very different in this case from *Exhibit A/B*, which was explicit in its programme note about the rules of participation. Krastin's invitation was to see his body as "meat or land". The reticence to take this invitation too literally may be the result of a combination of social politeness and the awareness of what colonial history and its remainders have done in treating bodies and land with a conquering possessiveness. There is risk, however, in presenting this open invitation, because reliance on conservative behaviours cannot be guaranteed. Krastin presents his work and invitation with sincerity, paying careful attention to the finer aesthetic details of a ritual. The rest he leaves to the impulses of his audience in the hope they will be equally thoughtful in their actions. Krastin, contemplating the idea of honesty in an audience, says, "I think it's very complex. There can be a lot of lies and it's almost become 'trendy' to deliberately not enjoy a work or to be stand-offish" (Krastin, pers. comm.). But he also thinks that audiences can be conservative and at times confused about the experience they "ought" to be having:

> I would much rather have you walk out of my show than stay and feel trapped. This is your experience, do whatever you feel is fitting. This is where authenticity and sincerity come in. You are not bound by this bourgeois politeness. Do whatever you feel like you need to do in that moment to have your experience. (Ibid.)

This is exactly what one audience member did in one showing, taking literally Krastin's call to "colonise and devour" his body. In a series of actions best described as an enactment of foreplay, the audience member pawed, licked, and ate Krastin's grapefruit in a lascivious way. The act was offensive, not because of its sexual crudity, but because it did not seem to come from a sincere place of desire. It was rather an act of upstaging in a work that is designed to be a conversation. The action by no means broke the work, as Krastin was quite willing to accept whatever the audience chose to do, yet it was an interesting occurrence in that it shows that being sincere as an artist does not necessarily elicit a similar response in the audience. Perhaps this was exactly what provoked this audience member's behaviour: that he felt uncomfortable with the work being a sincere meditation on celebratory rituals and therefore attempted to disassemble this sensibility with what amounted to a schoolboy prank. For all the sexual gratuity of the action, in some senses this display was then also a conservative response. Employing gestures clearly designed for spectacle as opposed to subtle communication or exchange, his actions completely disregarded the *zone of contact* that made this work a communal ritual.

Breaking with social constructs of "reality" in order to see things differently may be part of participatory art, but even if the social order is shifted within a performance, there needs to be a sense of continuum with everyday reality in order for the work to make an impact outside of itself. For all the artifice and theatricality a work may entail, it is still a *real* thing in the world if it is capable of producing an emotive response and not a Mardi Gras playroom. Mutual respect is a concrete part of being sincere, as Krastin explains: "I'm not saying please test ALL the boundaries and go balls to the wall, there needs to be a basic respect because at the same time I could do whatever I want to you as my audience, but I am not going to" (ibid.).

Bismillah: Igshaan Adams

We don't see death. Not anymore. We don't spend a night's vigil with a corpse to make sure the spirit has really flown. We don't wail beside an empty cage, rock it to see that it is indeed vacant or sit beside it in the small hours where we may be silent enough to listen to all the words that were not said in life. Now we see corpses as abject, a pollutant, so much waste we put aside from those who remain living. The dead walk uncomfortably among us because we do not get the right moment to say good bye.

There is not much written about Igshaan Adams's *Bismillah* (2014), a work which has been performed at three different locations and has had its documentation screened once internationally.[5] There are no opinion pieces which critically discuss this work, yet it is repeatedly reported in constant reiterations of the work's press release that:

> Exploring anticipated ways of seeing and being seen, Adams draws from tensions and complexities within his own Islamic background. In *Bismillah*, Adams performs with his father, who prepares his body for burial in the Islamic cleansing and wrapping ritual as if he had died. (ArtSMART 2014)

Part of the absence of critical review may be due to the fact that in locations other than the National Arts Festival it was performed under the title *Please Remember II*. But even under this title, there is little or no commentary. Given that the work is about death, this might not be

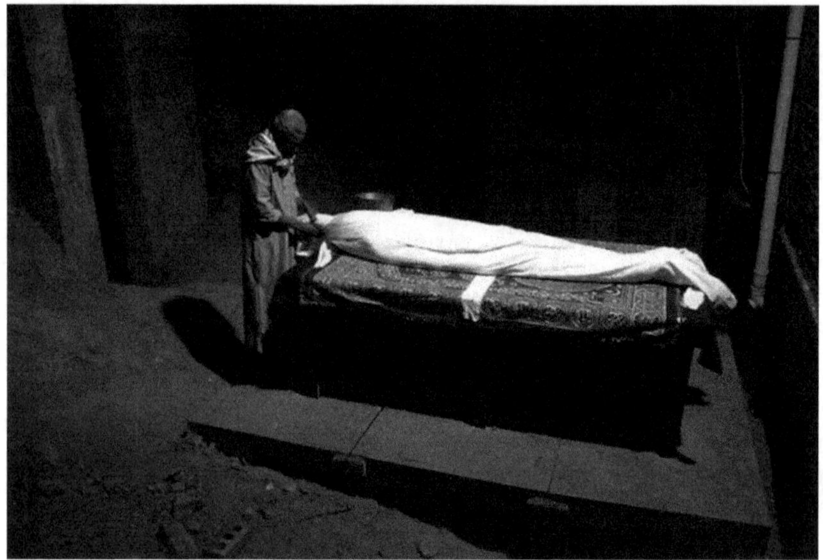

Fig. 3 Bismillah at National Arts Festival: Igshaan Adams being wrapped by his father, Amien Adams, 2014. *Photo* Ruth Simbao

surprising. Death is a difficult subject to broach with critical analysis. Is this a good death or a bad death? We are taught not to speak ill of the dead and perhaps that translates even when the death is a fictitious one. It may be the appropriation of a culturally specific ritual process—the Islamic funerary rite—that makes analysis overly sensitised (Fig. 3).

The contextual nature of risk is demonstrated here both in the absence of discussion of the work's central theme of death and in the emphasis placed on the artist's cultural identity as being "authentically" liminal. Cultural understandings of the social taboo of death certainly do come into play with this work. One of the few thoughtful examinations of the topic is offered by Melvin Minaar (2014) in an Afrikaans review of *Between Subject and Object*, a curated exhibition on representations of death at which the work was performed. In this review Minaar demonstrates how, in another language (Adams's own first language), certain nuances in talking about death and its representations are sometimes untranslatable. Minaar's review speaks more generally of how this particular exhibition deals with the topic of death in an unsentimental way, and how each of the works provokes the viewer to turn this contemplation inwards. He does not specifically discuss Adams's work, but his take on the exhibition as a whole can be used as a reading for exactly what this work calls the viewer to witness—the objecthood of a subjective experience.

Ironically, a redoubling of this objecthood (rather than subjecthood of the artist) is the direct result of how Adams and his work are marketed. The press release begins with a statement which delineates the identity of the artist rather than the work on show: "Igshaan Adams is an installation, mixed-media and performance artist whose works speak to his experiences of racial, religious and sexual liminality in South Africa" (ArtSMART 2014). This particular kind of quantifying, an appeal to the identity politics of the artist, is an appeal to authenticity. The artist is described as complex in his hybrid identity as a "coloured", or mixed-race, homosexual Muslim in various sources. Phrases describing his work repeatedly state that he "investigates racial, cultural, and sexual identity" (O'Toole 2015) or "investigates hybrid identity, particularly in relation to race and sexuality" (Kinsman 2014), or that "his work speaks to his experiences of racial, religious and sexual liminality" (Blank Projects 2015). This constant appeal to the hybrid identity of the artist is thus packaged as a kind of "authentic" legitimacy, yet this closes down the possibility of outside readings of the complex work he makes rather than illuminating it. We are left with no *zone of contact*, no mirror in which to see ourselves unless we directly share the finite attributes with which he is accredited. As viewers, we are denied a personalised and potentially diverse interpretation of Adams's social comment (on liminality), as this has become solidified into presuming an "authentic" construction of both the artist's identity and his voice, a voice that speaks *to* that authentic identity rather than *with* it. "Authenticity", in this regard, presents an argument as a fait accompli and identity as a fixed interior state—to critique the work is thus to critique the authority of an artist's identity rather than the work as a separate expression, which makes for tricky terrain.

It is, however, important to separate the voices. Which are those of the artist, and which are those of people who have a stake in how his artistic intent is read? Those who brand and market artistic output may not have any controlling or nefarious intent, merely a canny sense of what is most easily marketable in a world so oversaturated with "Is" having an individual opinion on the world around them. Perhaps if market forces did not pull so strongly in favour of those whose sales pitch is the "authentic" product and instead gave more attention to those practices which offer a sincere experience, gallerists and curators might be less inclined to dress up the packaging.

True to an authentic identity of a more complex kind is Adams's own voice and intent in direct interview. Far from performing a direct correlation to the divisions so neatly ascribed to his identity, he at times seems a little mystified that such aspects of his identity should seem to be contradictory. In an interview with curator Clare Butcher, she asks him to comment on the coexistence of these seemingly contradictory aspects, in particular his sexuality, his faith, and his career as an artist. At first he hesitates and fumbles, unsure where to start, which is understandable when he does express his point: "Artist … Muslim, I don't know what to say to that … It's just all part of the experience of being me, being an artist, being a Muslim, it all just comes together … I can't separate the two" (quoted in Butcher 2013, 7:10).

In my own interview with him, Adams talks about overcoming a process of denying certain aspects of his identity and making his peace with this, but says that he still quests for a deeper understanding of knowing the authentic self. He says:

> The search for the authentic self … [has become] a looking at the self beyond these stupid labels …. Is it possible to behave in the same way all the time with everyone that you meet? I was struck by this idea: why am I responding to the Imaam differently to my best friend and my grandmother and is it possible to be "the self" all the time and be authentic in every moment of every day? How possible is that? I think I got to a point where I realised that, that authentic self, it remains a mystery it's out of reach, it's somewhere inside. (Adams 2015, pers. comm.)

Much of Adams's work includes representations of Rorschach tests, which, as a symbol, speaks plainly about an understanding of viewer projection and what can be denoted from the psychology of that projection. In *Bismillah* Adams presents the ultimate Rorschach test—a dead body. The fact that it is not a real dead body does not actually matter. Adams's body becomes a site of projection and therefore a *zone of contact* for the audience. It is a site in which to contemplate death and other dead bodies—ones they have seen and ones they have not been permitted to see because modern culture, in general, spends less time with its dead.

It would seem from the press release categorising Adams's work within a particular cultural frame, rather than as a rite of passage in a particularised voice, that what is being presented is a cultural "other". Being Muslim in the present age is fraught with political risks, but is it not possible to view Islam as a philosophical spiritualism, like any other, rather than as a political dogma which includes and excludes?

Adams speaks about what prompted this work in a radio interview:

> Firstly, I think this artwork will be extremely personal because of the fact that this is my biological father so the history of our relationship will come into play and strangely he is really excited about all of this. I was really ready to blackmail him to be part of it. (quoted in Morton 2013, 12:40)

This brings us back to Rosenmeyer's (2010) question: "is sincerity possible in art without the artist having to cover their embarrassment through ... strategies of dissembling?" Perhaps the answer here is that it is hard to communicate coherently about that which is so deeply personal. A kind of coyness or bravado seeps into make light of weighty subjects, because there is always a lurking fear that an expression of sincerity may come across as clichéd. There is a huge risk in presenting personal feelings in the public realm, yet conversely there is a worse kind of risk in undermining the self: appearing to lack personal depth. Adams has a troubled history with his father and discussing this in public may seem to be an airing of dirty laundry. This work is both a private ritual between two people who do not have a strong history of intimacy and something broader about death and loss. Adams's explanation continues:

> The inspiration for the work comes from someone in my own family who is heavily addicted to drugs, someone who I loved very much and had a very close relationship with at one point. But unfortunately she is completely destroyed by the drugs and I realised that I had gone through this process of mourning her death despite the fact that she is still alive and I think this is a common story. (quoted in Morton 2013, 13:30)

In the artist's own voice, the intent of this work has very little to do with the categorised labels of his particular identity. It does not even have much to do with Islam beyond the fact that this is the most immediately familiar framework for the artist within which to represent rituals of death. The change of title from *Please Remember II* to *Bismillah* seems to underline the Islamic theme, so I asked the curator of the National Arts Festival version, Ruth Simbao, what prompted it:

> From my perspective it changed partly to register the fact that it became a very different performance in the monument basement ... The site had a very different feel. The one in Cape Town was quite clinical and white and surrounded by other artworks and this was like walking down into a grave and being under the earth. (2015, pers. comm.)

Simbao suggested a title change and *Bismillah* was Adams's suggestion. Despite the Islamic resonance, this titling has another reading: a holy title to separate this rendition, as more sacred, from a more secular version. *Bismillah* seems in that light very apposite. "In the name of God" may be the only space where we can find a one true self, or in the reflection of death, the death of another, which makes us contemplate our own doings and inevitable death where we can no longer atone. In death, all that we have done is now irrevocable. It can never be tempered or contradicted by another action. As a theme one could not evoke a more sincere and therefore socially unifying experience. The authenticity or realness of the artist's death is irrelevant in this representation's ability to function as a mirror. Death, as with identity, cannot be branded because, as an experience, it is infinite and therefore cannot be categorised in the language of the finite.

Some Conclusions

There is not always a clear separation between what constitutes authenticity, sincerity, and realness. As concepts these three have the capacity to slip and bleed into one another. We can be sure that authenticity, as it stands alone, is not a dialogue, merely a fact unto itself. Conversely, sincerity cannot exist in isolation, but is always an exchange with another. Realness is almost the residue of the two—that which is a genuine article and that which is a genuine exchange both collide in our daily experience.

From *Exhibit A/B* we may see the risk in failing to acknowledge the individual, whether this be the artist, the delegated performer, or the audience. The rigid structures of a performance that might have an appeal to authenticity, but no suggestion of sincerity, prevent a *zone of contact*. Rather than a conversation, we are left with a silence in which we can hear and feel nothing. In *#omnomnom* we see that sincerity on the part of the artist does not necessarily evoke the same kind of response from an audience, but that maintaining a sincere position makes a nonsense of an insincere reaction. This gives us pause to think about what we do as audiences when we are given agency. Adams's work demonstrates that labels of "authenticity" run the risk of obscuring an artist's sincere intent. Fixed representations of "authentic" identity are prohibitive for participatory work as they function like an inflexible script, rather than opening up possibilities for conversation. As gallerists or theatre directors we should be mindful of how we package ideas so as to not present them as theoretical illustrations, contradict an artist's own voice, or close down the *zone of contact* which allows for a diversity of readings.

So what is risk? The capacity to stand out, to be different? To proclaim your right to a momentary limelight because of your difference which makes you unique at the same time as it ought to give that right to anyone else? Or do we take the plunge to swim across that archipelago and reach out to someone else's island, to arrive on that shore bedraggled and half drowned, less than well presented, but sincere in the attempt, to meet another on their own terms? We are each islands, one each amongst millions, but there are ways of perceiving a mainland by taking a moment to step out into the sea between—a blurred messy meaty soup of humanity in which various blobs take but a moment to bubble to the surface. Would any of us dare risk that?

Notes

1. Claire Bishop describes this as "hiring non-professionals or specialists in other fields to undertake the job of being present and performing … on behalf of the artist" (2012, 219).
2. In the Sartrean sense of a person not one's self, rather than the post-colonial term denoting a racial or cultural "other" as advocated by Edward Said.
3. Following the advice of Stoller (1989, 139) that "one cannot perceive, conceive, speak or write in a cultural vacuum", and of Ndebele (1986, 65) that "break[ing] down the closed epistemological structures of South African oppression … free[ing] the entire social imagination of the oppressed from the laws of perception that have characterised apartheid society … means extending the writer's perceptions of what can be written about, and the means and methods of writing", paragraphs in *italics* are my own meditations on the experience of these works. They represent a personalised vision of the work under discussion which might be

represented more theoretically, but would thus suffer the distance ascribed to authenticity rather than the immediacy of exchange present in sincerity. In its form my text would thus seem to contradict my thesis.

4. Various iterations of this work have taken place, each focusing on different colonial powers. *Exhibit A* showed in Austria, Germany, Belgium, South Africa, and the Netherlands. *Exhibit B* showed in Scotland, England, Moscow, and France.
5. 2014 *Between Subject and Object*. Michaelis Galleries, Cape Town; 2014 *Blind Spot*. National Arts Festival, Grahamstown; 2014 *Paul Klee Center's Summer Academy*. Bern, Switzerland (film screening); 2013 *Three Abdullahs*. Centre for African Studies, UCT.

References

Adams, Igshaan. 2015. *Interview with Rat Western*, 2 April.

ArtSMART. 2014. National Arts Festival Performance Art Press Release. http://www.news.artsmart.co.za/2014/06/naf-performance-art.html. Accessed 23 June 2015.

Atkinson, Brenda. 1999. Introduction. In *Grey Areas: Representation, Identity, and Politics in Contemporary South African Art*, ed. Brenda Atkinson, and Candace Breitz. Johannesburg: Chalkham Hill Press.

Ayers, Robert. 2010. 'The Knife is Real, the Blood is Real, and the Emotions are Real.'—Robert Ayers in conversation with Marina Abramović. http://www.askyfilledwithshootingstars.com/wordpress/?p=1197. Accessed 23 June 2015.

Bailey, Brett. 2014. Yes, Exhibit B is Challenging—But I Never Sought to Alienate or Offend. *The Guardian Online*. http://www.theguardian.com/commentisfree/2014/sep/24/exhibit-b-challenging-work-never-sought-alienate-offend-brett-bailey. Accessed 23 June 2015.

Benjamin, Walter. 2008. *The Work of Art in the Age of Its Technological Reproducibility, and Other Writings on Media*, ed. Michael W. Jennings et al. Cambridge, MA: Harvard University Press.

Bishop, C. 2006. The Social Turn: Collaboration and Its Discontents. *ARTFORUM* (February 2006), 179–185. New York: Artforum.

Bishop, Claire. 2012. *Artificial Hells: Participatory Art and the Politics of Spectatorship*. London and New York: Verso Books.

Blank Projects. Igshaan Adams: CV | Bio. *BlankProjects.com*. http://www.blank-projects.com/cv-and-bio/igshaan-adams. Accessed 23 June 2015.

Butcher, Clare. 2013. Special Event—Igshaan Adams and Clare Butcher (part II). *Vimeo*. http://www.vimeo.com/65713486. Accessed 20 Apr 2015.

Corrigall, Mary. 2014. The Virtual Exhibit. *Incorrigible Corrigall Blogspot*. http://www.corrigall.blogspot.com/2014/10/the-virtual-exhibit.html. Accessed 23 June 2015.

De Swardt, Moira. 2014. A Talked About Piece #Omnomnom. Looking at Arts, Culture and Entertainment in Gauteng. http://www.artscomments.wordpress.com/2014/07/13/a-talked-about-piece-omnomnom/. Accessed 23 June 2015.

Gaiman, Neil. 2001. *American Gods*. New York: HarperCollins.

Guardian. 2014. Exhibit B: is the 'human zoo' Racist? The Performers Respond. *The Guardian Online*. http://www.theguardian.com/culture/2014/sep/05/exhibit-b-is-the-human-zoo-racist-the-performers-respond. Accessed 23 June 2015.

Handler, Richard. 1986. Authenticity. *Anthropology Today* 2 (1): 2–4.

Harari, Dror. 2009. Risk in Performance: Facing the Future. *Theatre Research International* 34 (2): 173–179.

Jamal, Ashraf. 2005. *Predicaments of Culture in South Africa*. Pretoria: University of South Africa Press.

Kinsman, Houghton. 2014. Tracing Emerging Artistic Practice in South Africa. *Another Africa*. http://www.anotherafrica.net/art-culture/tracing-emerging-artistic-practice-in-south-african. Accessed 23 June 2015.

Krastin, Gavin. 2014. Press Release #Omnomnom. *GavinKrastin.com*. http://www.gavinkrastin.com/2014/08/omnomnom-2014.html. Accessed 23 June 2015.

Minaar, Melvin. 2014. KunswerkOorDoodKeer Die Blik Inwaarts. *Die Burger Wes-Kaap*. http://www.netwerk24.com/vermaak/2014-08-23-kunswerk-oor-dood-keer-die-blik-inwaarts?redirect_from=dieburger. Accessed 23 June 2015.

Morton, Shafiq. 2013. Interview About the Three Abdullahs Exhibition with Justin Davy (Curator), Weaam Williams (Filmmaker), Igshaan Adams (Artist) and Haroon Gunn-Salie (Artist). *Voice of the Cape Radio Station*. http://www.3abdullahs.tumblr.com/post/117515291260/a-voice-of-the-cape-radio-station-interview-about. Accessed 23 June 2015.

Ndebele, Njabulo. 1986. "Redefining Relevance" in *Rediscovery of the Ordinary*. 2006. UKZN Press. pp. 55–72. This speech was originally delivered at a Writer's conference in Sweden in 1986.

Ndebele, Njabulo. 2012. *Love and Politics: Sister Quinlan and the Future We Have Desired*. http://www.njabulondebele.co.za/blog/entry/love_and_politics_sister_quinlan_and_the_future_we_have_desired/. Accessed 23 June 2015.

O'Toole, Sean. 2015. Igshaan Adams: BLANK PROJECTS. *ArtForum.com*. http://www.artforum.com/index.php?pn=picks&id=50094&view=print. Accessed 23 June 2015.

Owens, Craig. 1994. *Beyond Recognition: Representation, Power, and Culture*. Oakland, CA: University of California Press.

Rosenmeyer, Aoife. 2010. Curator's Statement. Ueli Alder, David Raymond Conroy, Lilly McElroy, Cecile Weibel. http://www.dienstgebaeude.ch/13b_Rosenmeyer_text.pdf. Accessed 23 June 2015.

Simbao, Ruth. 2015. *Email to Rat Western*, 6 May.
Seddon, Deborah. 2012. As if Things Weren't Hot Enough. *Art South Africa* 11 (1): 44–45.
Stoller, Paul. 1989. *The Taste of Ethnographic Things: The Senses in Anthropology*. Philadelphia, PA: Penn Press.
Subramany, Deshnee. 2011. ANCWL Unimpressed with Kunene's Sushi Bash. *Mail and Guardian*. http://www.mg.co.za/article/2011-02-02-ancwl-unimpressed-with-kunenes-sushi-bash. Accessed 23 June 2015.
Taylor, John P. 2001. Authenticity and Sincerity in Tourism. *Annals of Tourism Research* 28 (1): 7–26.
Trilling, Lionel. 1972. *Sincerity and Authenticity*. Cambridge, MA: Harvard University Press.
Watts, Richard. 2015. Disturbing, Not Pleasing, Should be Art's Role. *Performing Arts Hub*. http://www.performing.artshub.com.au/news-article/news/performing-arts/richard-watts/disturbing-not-pleasing-should-be-arts-role-246981. Accessed 23 June 2015.
White, Gareth. 2013. *Audience Participation in Theatre: Aesthetics of the Invitation*. London: Palgrave.

Upon Awakening: Addiction, Performance, and Aesthetics of Authenticity

Zoe Zontou

This chapter explores aspects of the complex relationship between addiction, performance, and aesthetics. In particular, it attempts to conceptualise what we might call "risky aesthetics" in participatory theatre practices by way of an exploration of particular facets of the philosophy of Deleuze and Guattari—namely, notions of "becoming" and practices of "experimentation" as set out in *Mille Plateaux* (1987). This will be developed in conjunction with addiction theories (Alexander 2008; Seddon 2010) and the aesthetics of autobiographical performance (Briginshaw 2001; Maguire 2015; White 2015). It explores the many and complex ways in which the identities of people in recovery from addiction are manifested through dance performance, not just as fixed identity markers (although these are also crucial), but also as engagements in becomings (in the Deleuzian sense). Risk is examined in relation to drug-taking behaviours in this instance, but also by drawing on Deleuzian notions of experimentation alongside neuroscientific research on cognitive experience and performance (Arnold 2014; Lewis 2015; Shaughnessy 2013). In other words, this chapter argues that there is a

Z. Zontou (✉)
Liverpool Hope University, Liverpool, UK
e-mail: zontouz@hope.ac.uk

© The Author(s) 2017

A. O'Grady (ed.), *Risk, Participation, and Performance Practice*,
DOI 10.1007/978-3-319-63242-1_9

strong affiliation between risk taking in drug addiction and risk taking in performance making. To this end, it proposes that participation in performance can provide a platform from which to encourage an affirmative yet creatively challenging form of risk taking, and in so doing produce a generative aesthetic praxis for performers. In an endeavour to further deploy this argument, this chapter poses the following questions: What happens when drug addicts dance their stories on stage? Do we create a "politically risky metaphor"? Do their collective bodies have the power to make an affirmative political claim and create challenging juxtapositions between the stigmatised/artistic body dyad? For example, what happens when a professional dancer's body performs next to an addicted/stigmatised body?

To evidence the arguments and relate them to applied performance, the work of Fallen Angels Dance Theatre Company is examined as a case study. Fallen Angels is a professional dance theatre company working with addicts, people in recovery, and the wider community. In 2014, it received funding from Arts Council England to produce the performance *Upon Awakening*. The project brought together for the first time professional dancers and non-professional dancers, working together in a collaboration to choreograph personal stories of addiction and recovery. The performance was shown at the Royal Opera House in London, among other venues, and at festivals. The methodological frameworks of this chapter are a synthesis of reflective ethnography, practice-led research, and quantitative modes of enquiry. I have worked with the group since 2012 as principal researcher and creative consultant. In addition, the arguments presented in this chapter are drawn from my body of research in the field of addiction and performance (Reynolds and Zontou 2014; Zontou 2012, 2013).

Risky Aesthetics in Applied Performance

Frost and Yarrow state that "we are in an area when it has become fashionable to examine the 'aesthetics of risk'" (Frost and Yarrow 2016, 242), but aesthetics in applied performance have always been risky.[1] Since the late 1980s and 1990s, applied performance (also known as socially engaged theatre, applied and social theatre, or community theatre) has been largely connected with discourses around impact and instrumentalism, where the ethics and impact or "usefulness" were prioritised over the aesthetic value of the work. Authors such as Claire

Bishop (2011), Michael Balfour (2009), and James Thompson (2009), among others, have scrutinised this tendency, arguing that it contributes to what Eleonora Belfiore (2009) calls "bullshit rhetoric". This is due to the fact that these practices have been mainly perceived to serve certain political agendas. Particularly in the UK, in the early 1990s the ideological and economic shifts in government policies introduced a neo-liberal model of practice that fostered a new relationship between socially engaged arts and policymaking. Theatre as a social intervention was perceived as a powerful tool to promote personal or behavioural change (Balfour 2009; Thompson 2009) and education (Winston 2010). Funding from external or public bodies was widely available in support of these practices. Alongside this, there was a growing interest in measuring the social impact of the arts, which resulted in a "donor agenda" (Balfour 2009) relationship between art organisations and funding bodies. Evaluating and monitoring the social and economic value of these practices was prioritised over their aesthetic value. As Shannon Jackson (2011) reminds us, the "social turn" of the arts to place stronger emphasis on social practice was a necessity for the development, validity, and security of funding of these practices. Despite this, it should not be dismissed that, at the same time, these practices generated a different form of aesthetic, a type of aesthetic that derives directly from vulnerable and disadvantaged communities and is opposed to any discourse on dominant understandings of institutionalised aesthetics. This "aesthetic heterogeneity" (Jackson 2011, 14) has been informed by the narratives and embodied experiences of individuals who engage in the creative process. The multiplicity and diversity of their life experiences are the basis of this type of aesthetic. It is grounded in stories of risk, vulnerability, memory, and resistance. Hence, it seems deeply problematic to examine aesthetics in isolation from the social context of the work, and without considering the specific risks that are associated with the artistic choices made in each case. Fundamental to our understanding of these aesthetics is a consideration of the backdrop of the social and political context in which the artistic work takes place. Working with vulnerable and marginalised communities requires a deeper understanding of the characteristics and social and cultural values that are specific to each social group. It therefore entails an awareness of the cultural or political constructions faced by certain social groups. Having a greater awareness of these issues prior to initiating the creative process is crucial in order to fully comprehend how to work artistically and socially with vulnerable groups. It is necessary for practitioners working in participatory arts to be clear about their own approach to the role of aesthetics in vulnerable contexts. In turn, this will determine which types of risky aesthetics are appropriate in each case.

In recent years, there has been a growing interest in bridging the gap between the social, instrumental, and aesthetic parameters of applied performance. James Thompson in his renowned book *Performance Affects: Applied Theatre and the End of Effect* (2009) reiterated the role of beauty in applied performance. Drawing on his experience of working in places of war, conflict, and environmental disaster, Thompson called for a turn to the notion of affective practice. He asserted that applied theatre should be better regarded for its ability to restore beauty to the lives of those affected by war and conflict. For Thompson, the notion of beauty in performance refers to and manifests the need to centralise an individual's potential to create and enact moments and stories that they regard as beautiful. With this argument he attempted to change the direction of the debate regarding theatre's efficacy to support behavioural or societal change (effect), advocating the need to place further emphasis on the importance of engaging participants and communities in the creation of moments that they regard as beautiful, and in doing so generate positive feelings (affect). He states:

> The sheer physical enjoyment and energy that these projects can elicit, make them potential examples of the enactment of beauty—a performance of beauty—moments that make the heart beat faster, and people start a search for "something of the same scale". (Thompson 2009, 56)

He connects affective practice with the aesthetics that emerge from moments that make the heart beat faster, in situations where the aftermath of war, the risk of national security, or environmental disaster are the only reality. The participants' experiences of risky lives become the modus operandi of the creative practice and define performance making in these contexts. Thompson's emphasis on affective practice has been supported by other scholars such as Joe Winston (2010), who explores the role of beauty in educational theatre. Comparable to Thompson's arguments, Winston concludes that awakening aesthetic value in educational settings is an essential part of developing cultural citizens. By exploring the role of aesthetics through the lenses of educational and developmental theories, he argues that learning how to relate to aesthetics is an important asset for developing learners' cultural and social identity. More recently, Gareth White (2015) in his volume *Applied Theatre: Aesthetics* gathered academics and practitioners to respond to questions about the relevance of aesthetics in applied performance. Contributors to this volume addressed a number of issues relating to the complex relationships between applied theatre practice, aesthetic theory, and efficacy, uncovering further the complexities of participation and its relation to aesthetics. For instance, Kirsten Sadeghi-Yekta's chapter (2015) discusses her experiences of conducting research on applied theatre's international aesthetics in an arts centre in Cambodia. She draws our attention to the competing aesthetic criteria often shared by artists, participants, government bodies, and international non-governmental organisations involved in applied theatre projects. As she maintains, contesting understandings of aesthetics can lead to tensions, forcing artists to produce the same type of work in order to match the aesthetics of the funding bodies or dominant Western understandings of art aesthetics, resulting in aesthetic homogeneity. Risky aesthetics, therefore, become a form of protection, ensuring the preservation of the unique work that is being produced by applied theatre practitioners. It is a way of maintaining aesthetic heterogeneity and adding value to the artistic work that has been produced through, or as a result of, the participants' vulnerable and risky lives. Furthermore, risky aesthetics become a platform within which to pose crucial questions about artistic autonomy, inclusivity, and representation. Addressing these questions is important for the context of this chapter, and more broadly for applied theatre practice as a whole, as it brings to the surface the many and complex ways in which risky lives are negotiated to create an aesthetic but also introduces a radical understanding to our enquiry. It is important for artists working in participatory settings to embrace this aesthetic and situate it within the larger picture of performing arts. This is a radical approach as it sets out to contradict the dominant institutionalised aesthetics. Instead, it places the aesthetics that emerge from risky lives at the epicentre of the creative process. I return to this argument later in the chapter when I discuss in detail the work of Fallen Angels, where I propose the genesis of a form of aesthetic that moves beyond dominant institutionalised aesthetics. This links with Augusto Boal's notion that democratisation of the creative practice sits at the heart of applied theatre:

> We seek the Beauty hidden in the heart of each and every citizen, since every citizen is an artist—each in his or her own way: even though some

> may not be capable of creating an *Aesthetic Product* which enlightens all of us, all are capable of developing an *Aesthetic Process* which enriches themselves. (2006, 39, italics in original)

Boal's remark regarding a participant's incapacity to create an aesthetic product can be misleading. In my view, his argument does not imply that they are unable to create an aesthetic product per se, but that they are unable to go against the accepted/dominant aesthetics that have been manifested in the art world. Hence, he turns our attention to aesthetics as a cognitive notion of self-expression and identity formation, liberated from any pre-established conceptions of beauty in the arts. However, this is equally problematic as it enlarges the gap between participatory theatre and artistic excellence. It excludes the possibility of generating a different aesthetic capable of embracing artistic work that is generated by the experiences of every citizen, and is equally able to "enlighten all of us".

Concerns about the aesthetics of applied performance practices have been raised throughout my research and my artistic work with people in recovery from addiction. Aside from the issues of stigmatisation and exclusion, the biggest challenges that I have to face are related to discovering means of representing personal experience in ways that go against sentimental aesthetics or promote the exploitation of human experience. In previous work I have problematised the complexity of working with personal stories of addiction recovery (Zontou 2014). While exploring examples of popular culture representations of addiction, I highlighted the limitations of language and text to challenge the stereotypes and stigmas of addiction. I argued that an additional emphasis on safeguarding the participants' personal experiences is needed. For this I suggested that a different form of representation is required, one that moves away from victimising the performers. I recommended that bringing the stigmatised body into performance, and engaging audiences with the performers' personal journeys, is a potentially powerful strategy to challenge social perceptions. It is my contention that any discussion about aesthetics in applied performance ultimately becomes a discussion about authenticity and ethics. For people in recovery from addiction, exposing their past experiences of vulnerability can be risky, unethical, and problematic yet equally beautiful and empowering. The dichotomy between vulnerable lives of addiction recovery and risky aesthetics produces a strong juxtaposition between the stigmatised/artistic dyad versus the ethics/politics of representation. Problematising the complex tension between vulnerable lives and risky aesthetics is fundamental, particularly when we work artistically with autobiographical experiences. My argument echoes Tom Maguire, who maintains,

> offering one's life story involves a risk to the teller in exposing herself to the judgments of other people; the teller makes herself vulnerable to their incomprehension, ridicule or rejection. The risk may be intensified where these is no pre-existing relationship and the teller can not rely on shared assumption and values. (Maguire 2015, 60)

To add to this argument, the risk of exposing vulnerabilities can be magnified when the performers are stigmatised through their past experiences of addiction dependency. As Clark Baim, in Chap. 4 of this volume, points out, "staging pain and suffering is not an answer in itself and runs the serious risk of voyeurism, collusion with oppression, and even reabuse and retraumatisation of victims" (Baim 000). Hence, working towards an autobiographical performance requires a disintegration of previous conceptions about one's self in order to allow space for the reshaping of identity, and subsequently generating an alternative aesthetic. This aesthetic derives from the process of recollection of past embodied experiences of shame, guilt, and trauma and is informed by the multiplicity of identities and conceptions of pre-stigma and post-stigma self. The role of vulnerability in autobiographical performance is to initiate the process of deconstructing personal experience. Vulnerability is not perceived as a weakness but rather as the starting point to understand one's life narrative and by doing so to maintain worthiness and authenticity. Narratives of addiction and recovery are not always coherent and are difficult to pin down. This slipperiness is the result of addiction recovery being a circular ongoing process that is often slowly constructed through language and repetition in the privacy of counselling rooms and group therapy meetings. These stories are in flux and exist as unending performances of becoming and identity formation (Lewis 2015; White 1996). Working with personal narratives in dance theatre means that these stories, however incoherent, incomplete, or fractured, are finding a way to be constructed as meaning-making entities in front of an audience, who in turn acknowledge them as signs of identity formation. Paul Bayes Kitcher, artistic director of Fallen Angels, asserts:

> When addicts come into group settings and recovery they become used to expressing themselves verbally so it becomes easier for them to articulate what they have been through and how they feel. This becomes very useful when we start to develop movement material through improvisational tasks as they have emotional intelligence. What I experience when I see this is something very transformative and powerful, as the movement they create becomes beautifully broken, but whole at the same time, making the quality authentic and honest. (Bayes Kitcher 2016, pers. comm.)

Bayes Kitcher underlines the choreographer's ability to incorporate and translate personal experience into an artistic product that should be equally regarded for its artistic excellence. By acknowledging the challenges presented when working with communities, in terms of balancing institutional aesthetics as well as encompassing the aesthetics of the experience, he calls for the aesthetics of authenticity. This echoes Christine Lomas, who suggests that "to empower implies a challenge to prevailing systems, with emphasis on the authentic, on non-traditional aesthetics, and on a way of working predominantly concerned with facilitation" (1998, 159). Applying this understanding to applied performance practice, and the context of this chapter, it could be argued it is crucial to move away from pre-established conceptions of aesthetics, so as to allow the aesthetics of authenticity to become equivalent to aesthetics of artistic excellence. The aesthetics of authenticity in turn produce moments of post-authenticity, when performing embodied experiences of addiction moves beyond the truthful representation of "real" experiences and instead places emphasis on a phenomenological and semiotic understanding of bodies on stage. The authenticity of vulnerable narratives and the many ways that they are presented on the theatrical stage offer new possibilities for reimagining and conveying meaning to these experiences. These representations overreach "real" story representation to provide a deeper exploration of how personal experiences of risk can be manifested through movement. Rat Western's (Chap. 8, this volume) analysis of the connections between authenticity, sincerity, and risk are useful to my argument. Drawing on Walter Benjamin's theories on authenticity, she suggests that risk is "contextual" and thus capable of challenging both the "real" and representations of the real. Western's approach to risk as contextual, liberated from any preconceptions about real and its representation, illuminates my argument as it opens up new possibilities for exploring how personal stories can be presented on stage. To develop this, I assert that risky aesthetics are an invitation to renegotiate the different dynamics involved in making theatre in social contexts. The aesthetics that emerge directly from the personal experiences of marginalised communities and run contrary to the institutionalised aesthetics that dominate cultural production are crucial here. Risky aesthetics as a concept provides an explanatory framework to reshape the way that institutionalised aesthetics inform the construction of our subjectivity in terms of what we perceive as artistic value. Hence, risky aesthetics is a platform for the critical vulnerabilities of the participants to be reconfigured into aesthetic products capable of enlightening all of us. The power of vulnerability opens up space for a post-authentic exploration of the multiple and risky dynamics of putting a group of recovering addicts on stage to dance their stories. To build on this argument, I turn now to conceptualising the connection between risk, addiction, and performance.

Connections Between Drugs, Performance, and Risk

So far in this chapter I have broadly situated aesthetics within the field of applied performance. This section moves the discussion forward in order to draw connections between risky aesthetics in performance making and drug addiction. In doing so, I draw on evidence from my previous body of research in the field of addiction and performance (2007–2015) and from a series of practice-based projects, participant observations, and interviews that I conducted in the UK and Greece.[2] The participatory research methods that I utilised, in conjunction with the artistry and improvisatory nature of the creative practices that I investigated, provided successive points of encounter between autobiographical experience, performance, and risk. The research findings indicate that, regardless of the context of the project, the participants, especially those who did not have any previous experience of participating in performing arts, drew connections between their experiences of drug taking and those of creating theatre and/or performing. They made references to feelings of the buzz or “high”, euphoria, and a sense of belonging. In a first attempt to theorise these responses I coined the term “alternative substance” (Zontou 2012, 304). This refers to the possibilities of using applied performance as a medium to make an affirmative impact on the participants' lives and help them on their journeys to recovery. This echoes the work of Nicholas Arnold (2014), who has identified significant parallels between the effects of psychoactive chemicals and performance on the body. Drawing on neuroscientific studies, Arnold maintains that, similar to psychoactive drugs, performing can activate our reward system, also known as the "dopamine system". Dopamine is one of the many important neurotransmitters that are associated with the "pleasure system" of the brain. When released it provides pleasure and a sense of euphoria and belonging. Various triggers such as food, sex, and physical activities such as performing can activate it naturally, but drugs such as psychedelics, cocaine, and ecstasy have been widely used to reinforce dopamine release.[3] Shamanistic rituals of performing the body (Winkelman 2002, 2011), together with contemporary cultural trends such as rave and club dancing (Joe-Laidler and Hunt 2013; Papadimitropoulos 2009), have been considered as paradigmatic of the way performance, alerted states of consciousness,[4] and cognition are interconnected. In recent years, neuroscientists and theatre scholars have begun to explore these connections (McConachie and Hart 2007; Blair and Cook 2016). For instance, contributors to the volume *Affective Performance and Cognitive Science: Body, Brain and Being* (Shaughnessy 2013) bring new insights to the way brains and bodies engage with performance, and the particular risks that are associated with this process. By bringing together cognitive science and performance studies, they explore new understandings of perception, emotion, imagination, and empathy. Drawing on cognitive science research on the embodiment of human perception and interaction has created new possibilities for theatre scholars and artists alike to deepen their explorations of how embodied risky experiences can be presented on stage. Hood's (2013) chapter on the representation of physical pain through performance is particularly relevant to my argument. She offers an in-depth account of how the representations of pain, as an objective embodied experience, can offer themselves as a vehicle to understand risky aesthetics. This relates directly to my analysis of how vulnerability in performance is a process within which to situate risk taking as a form of aesthetic.

Notwithstanding these studies, historically there has been a strong affiliation between alerted states of consciousness, performance, and drug taking, to the point that the cultural and social connotations linking drug misuse and aesthetic experience have become a paradigm of drug subcultures (Boothroyd 2006; Brodie and Redfield 2002). The representations of drugs in popular culture, or what Klein (1993) refers to as the "sublime" aesthetics of the drug experience, have been intertextually depicted in myriad examples of film, art, music, and theatre. In contemporary performance practice, drugs have been widely used to stimulate the artist's creative impulse or to enhance audiences' aesthetic experiences and perceptions. Professional performance artists have experimented with extensive drug and alcohol use as a way to enhance their performance aesthetics. The Wooster Group, for example, in its piece *L.S.D. (... Just the high points...)* (1985) tried to re-enact the first part of its performance after taking LSD. More recently, Bryony Kimming's piece *7 day drunk* (2011) was the result of a week of creative experimentation conducted at a medically maintained level of drunkenness. The outcomes of Kimming's creative experiment were put together and performed by her sober. In both cases, the artists did not "act" being high or drunk; they actually experienced it. The audience bore witness to the performers' highs and were also able to watch the creative product of the performers' drunkenness. Aside from the drug or alcohol consumption, another commonality of the above examples is the level of risk that was taken by the performers in their excessive use of substances. Both examples pose important questions about creativity, drugs, and performance aesthetics. An important aspect of the above examples lies in the artists' emphasis on the authentication of the experience. The "real" experience of intoxication operated as a signifier of the "real" experience of performing being high or drunk. Nevertheless, it should be acknowledged that the deliberate act of making themselves vulnerable risk takers is deeply problematic for two main reasons. Firstly, the level of risk taking was maintained at a controlled level. For instance, Kimming's alcohol consumption was monitored by a team of medical doctors, which minimised the risk of overdose or other health implications. Secondly, the social status of the performers as artists played a significant role in the way their performances were received by the audience. In contrast, when it comes to people in recovery from addiction, the level of risk involved in performing their vulnerability is significantly higher and more complex. Their vulnerability is the result of stigma, discrimination, and prolonged feelings of social disconnection. In this regard, they are not deliberately *becoming* vulnerable; they *are* vulnerable. Risk taking in this instance is considerably intricate. It requires a deeper understanding of the affirmation between risk taking in performance making and risk taking in drug consumption.

Similarly to drug consumption, voluntary risk taking is another factor that has become normalised in contemporary cultural practice, particularly when it is being discussed in association with health and body and its implications for drug subcultures. A considerable amount of literature has been published on the connection between risk taking, club dancing, and drugs (Milhet et al. 2011; Hunt and Evans 2003; Wibberley 2003). For instance, in a study entitled *Dancing on Drugs*, Fiona Measham et al. (2000) explore the complex relationship between drug misuse, risk taking, and club dancing. According to their findings, club goers, although they were aware of the health and legal risks associated with drug use, perceived drug consumption as an essential part of the dancing experience and therefore a risk worth taking. Despite the fact that the Measham et al. study involved informants who consider themselves recreational users, it is my contention that their findings are relevant to people in recovery from addiction. This is because, similarly to clubbers, for addicts risk taking expresses a resistance to conforming to the dominant risk culture. They prefer to consider themselves "risk-takers instead of 'at-risk' victims" (Peretti-Watel and Moatti 2006, 678). The distinction between risk takers and at-risk victims is of paramount significance for my argument. It highlights an underlying complexity between risk and vulnerability that is relevant to addiction recovery and risky aesthetics in participatory arts. It reverses the meaning of risk so that it becomes an empowering concept capable of challenging pre-established identities. Risk, in these instances, contributes to the proliferation of drug taking as an identity marker. It provides a platform to convey a sense of self-determination, individuality, and self-discovery, a quest for meaning making and even freedom (Seddon 2010). In a society where risk is something to be continuously avoided, based on mainstream health promotion models of behaviour or anti-drug campaigns, risk has become an instrument of social control that reinforces the mediatisation of deviance and contributes to the stigmatisation of drug addiction. Therefore, voluntary risk taking can be read as a symbol of resistance and an attempt to contest the dominant risk culture. This resonates with the perspective of Bruce Alexander (2008), who has claimed drug addiction is a sign of social dislocation and meaninglessness. It is not just about the direct effects that drugs such as heroin have on the brain per se, but rather the whole risk-taking lifestyle of searching for the next fix, funding habits, engaging in deviancy and escaping police. Hence, risk taking is an essential part of this process. Drug users become social actors as they have to lie/perform to social services, police, and family to decrease suspicion about their habits. As their relationship with the drug changes and escalates, risk becomes a tool for survival. Both drugs and risk replace their sense of belonging and identity and become the vehicle to escape social reality. Aside from the legal, social, and psychological risks, the biggest implications of drug taking are connected with risking their bodies. Kemps illustrates that drug addicts "live a disturbed relationship to their bodies" (2009, 120), whether this is because of injecting, snorting, smoking, neglecting to eat or sleep, or the physical pain of withdrawal syndrome. As addiction escalates, the risks of withdrawal syndrome and extreme bodily pain overcome the risks of prosecution, overdose, or potential death. Addicts develop a cellular relationship with their drug and subsequently with their bodies. Hence, the process of recovery from addiction has been regarded as a reconfiguration of the complex relationship between the individual and their body. Recovery from addiction requires a complete restoration of the sense of self. To this end, many people in recovery from addiction refer to their journey as a rebirth (McIntosh and McKeganey 2000; White 1996). The process of becoming recovered is a continuum that facilitates the process of framing and reframing past experiences as well as constructing a new sense of self relevant to those in the transition phrase of recostructing their idenities, as for example of the people in recovery from addiction that are in transit through discontinuing drug misuse and reconstructing their identity. Therefore, past experiences and the many ways in which they are remembered and revisited are an essential aspect of becoming recovered. As social psychologist Oksanen denotes, becoming is "a creative flow, that makes things change and opens up new ways of seeing, feeling and perceiving" (2013, 59). Oksanen is arguing this from the point of view of social psychology, in which creative flow is a developmental process. He utilises the Deleuzian concept of becoming as a conceptual framework to understand the relationship between recovery, the body, and the production of desire. Nevertheless, his definition of becoming is relevant here as it indicates that there is a strong connection between becoming, recovery from addiction, and the aesthetics of participatory arts. When working artistically with people in recovery from addiction, the creative process is an invitation to revisit their past experiences as a means of both reconciling their past with the present and finding ways to move forward. However, as Deleuze and Guattari (1987) point out,

> Drug addicts continually fall back into what they wanted to escape: a segmentarity all the more rigid for being marginal, a territorialization all the more artificial for being based on chemical substances, hallucinatory forms, and fantasy subjectifications. Drug addicts may be considered as precursors or experimenters who tirelessly blaze new paths of life, but their cautiousness lacks the foundation for caution. (1987, 285)

In order to explore further this concept of drug addicts "as precursors or experimenters who tirelessly blaze new paths of life" and to connect it with participatory theatre practices, I consider risk taking in the arts as a form of creative experimentation that embraces embodied experience. The implementation of dance and movement can be an effective way to introduce participants to experimentation and positive risk taking, especially in terms of translating past embodied experiences of addiction, stigma, and deviancy into an aesthetically challenging dance theatre piece. However, the danger with addiction is that addicts "continually fall back into what they wanted to escape". I see "alternative risky aesthetics" as the passage between and betwixt two cultures: the culture of addiction and the culture of recovery. Risky aesthetics in this context can be understood as a reconfiguration of past experience. It is a dynamic medium to help addicts get out of (Deleuze and Guattari 1987) the embodied, identitarian, and self-expressive personal performance making. Instead, it moves them into a mode of critical enquiry along the lines of Deleuze and Guattari's notion of becoming. By the same token, this supports the development of a sense of critical agency by inviting the participant and audience alike to understand the performance piece as a becoming, not only a marker of identity. This is because the performance is presented as a process of becoming rather than as a final identity marker event. Achieving this is not always easy and presents some crucial challenges for practitioners. It requires a deeper understanding of the nexus between risky aesthetics and performing risk and vulnerability. In the next section, I shift my analysis in order to explore the possibilities and challenges of creating a dance theatre piece based on the participants' risky lives of addiction and recovery.

Fallen Angels Dance Theatre: In the Making of *Upon Awakening*

Upon Awakening is the latest production by Fallen Angels. It premiered at the Lowry Theatre in Manchester and was then performed at the Royal Opera House in 2014. Since then it has been performed in different venues and at events such as the UK Recovery Walk.[5] This project was a particularly significant moment for the development of Fallen Angels as it was part of a series of events launching its charity status. The aim of the final performance was to enhance the organisation's profile as a charity devoted to challenging stereotypes placed on people in recovery from addiction through live performance. This was an opportunity to demonstrate its vision of ensuring artistic excellence whilst raising awareness that art has the potential to change lives with its rehabilitative power. The performance at the Royal Opera House's Clore Studio Upstairs was a particularly important step toward achieving this goal. Aside from the performance, the project itself was a pivotal moment for Fallen Angels as it brought together for the first time five community dancers who were in recovery from addiction and three professional dancers. In August 2014, the team engaged in a one-week intensive workshop. The creative process was framed around the participants' personal experiences of recovering from addiction. It aimed to creatively reflect on and consider wider philosophical themes around the concept of "awakening" and its associations with recovery and dance theatre. By using the theme of awakening as a starting point, participants were asked to offer their responses by sharing their personal experiences of moments of awakening or stepping stones. These responses were then transformed into an exchange of movements and sequences between community dancers and professionals. Throughout this process the participants were given an opportunity to revisit and reshape their stories using artistic forms. Using the concept of awakening as a metaphor for recovery allowed them to add a symbolic affirmative dimension to their life experiences (Fig. 1).

In the secondary phase the professional dancers developed selected movements and routines that were further refined into exploratory sequences. This collaboration produced several benefits for both the professional and the community dancers. The community dancers had an opportunity to reconsider their journeys by revisiting their personal experiences through artistic means and translating them into dance

Fig. 1 Fallen Angels Dance Theatre, *Letting Go* directed by Paul Bayes Kitcher Royal Opera House London 2014. Photo Brian Slater

routines. The dancers were able to interpret these stories through movement and gain insight into the complexities of addiction, understanding each individual member's journey to recovery as different and diverse. In this way the community dancers became co-performers, leading the devising process and choreographing their own stories. Their verbal and embodied personal accounts operated as self-referential trajectories and formed a valuable part of the creative process. Furthermore, throughout these experimentations they were constantly engaging with "becomings" that allowed them to frame their embodied subjectivity and recognise their identity as an entity that is not fixed but inherently in flux. It provided an opportunity to create links between their past, present, and future, and to see their own lives progressing, moving to meaningfulness, from painful past to viable future. By working with movement, symbolism, and personal storytelling the participants deepened the physical and emotional aspects of addiction recovery. This echoes the views of Sonia,[6] one of the community dancers, who said, "sometimes in addiction emotions are lost along the way, dancing brings it all back" (Sonia 2014).

In this context aesthetics can be understood as a theory of experimentation with real experiences. This process facilitated their transformation of themselves but also the transformation of their understanding of the world. It encouraged them to find creative ways to communicate their experiences to a wider audience and in so doing to explore where they positioned themselves socially, as citizens and as members of the community. Moreover, the embodied encounters with the professional dancers opened up the possibility for critical enquiry, challenging the juxtaposition of the trained/stigmatised body and the "real"/fictional experiences. These exchanges between the drug-using body and the trained body formulated a critical framework within which to consider questions about stigmatisation and exclusion.

This process is not simple. It can lead to complex dilemmas, particularly when the experimentation needs to produce material for a public performance. Notwithstanding the mutual creative benefits for both groups, this process presented challenges relevant to the questions about aesthetic heterogeneity and risk that I discussed earlier. Specifically, it raised one significant question: How feasible is it to ensure artistic excellence and aesthetic quality when working with vulnerable communities? Throughout the evaluation process, the directors concluded that the intensity of the rehearsal process, combined with the lack of professional training for community dancers, created barriers for the true integration of both groups. They assert: "We felt that there was still development needed until we could integrate the professionals with community members to create a high quality artistic production, particularly in terms of improvisation and somatic frameworks" (Bayes Kitcher and Morris 2014, pers. comm.). Driven by their commitment to implement a person-centred approach, they made the decision to actively include everyone and to give to all the opportunity to tell their story and work alongside the professionals. Aside from the pressure to provide a participant-centred approach, I would argue that this ambivalence arose because of a higher demand to meet the pre-existing standards of institutionalised aesthetics such as those of the Royal Opera House. The tension between artistic excellence and the social values of participatory performance created a dichotomy and cast doubt on Bayes Kitcher's artistic autonomy. This became apparent in an email correspondence between us in August 2014:

> The project is going really well here ... My thoughts are being constantly evaluated as I sometimes struggle with decision making surrounding

> artistic excellence and the notion of integrating recovery dancers into this! Bringing vulnerable adults into a professional process can be problematic, in terms of discipline and ability to cope and sustain at such a high level. Retaining information, steps, choreography can be very challenging. There is always an issue when trying to firm down and retaining material … Questions appearing … Should they be put into this environment? How can this be a good experience for both recovery artists and professional dancers? Does our want to care, hinder the artistic process and the ability of the dancers? As a director how can I choose between a person's innate and unique gift of performance verses their inability to retain direction. There can be beauty in the moment but can this be reliable? Or guaranteed in each performance? What is professionally acceptable? What are the expectations of the audience/programmers/funders? (Bayes Kitcher 2014)

It is evident that Bayes Kitcher is divided between the ethics of participation and giving greater emphasis to achieving artistic excellence. Safeguarding the participants was prioritised over the aesthetic quality of the piece. In doing so, he questions the idea of participatory arts versus inclusivity versus artistic excellence and returns to the argument that I presented earlier on regarding risky aesthetics as a paradox that reveals the limitations of pre-established conceptions of aesthetics. For the final performance, he decided to divide the groups. In the first part community dancers performed their own introductory piece, *Letting Go*, which was followed by the professional dancers performing *Upon Awakening*. This decision to separate the performance created some interesting symbolical references that reveal further the dichotomy between the addicted/stigmatised bodies versus the trained bodies of the professional dancers. It raises questions about the politics of representing vulnerability on stage and the role of risky aesthetics in it. In the next section I discuss these issues in relation to the performance at the Royal Opera House. Drawing on the Deleuzian concept of "becoming", I offer an account of how the dynamics between the vulnerable bodies and the trained bodies can be reversed through performance.

Becomings at Royal Opera House

The Royal Opera House is one of the world's leading opera companies and also houses the Royal Opera Ballet. It is renowned both for its outstanding performances of traditional opera and for commissioning new works. On Tuesday, 18 November 2014, while opera goers were arriving in the main auditorium to watch *L'Elisir d'Amore*, directed by Laurent Pelly, Fallen Angels' audience were settling down at the Clore Studio Upstairs for a very different performance. The event was opened and introduced by Fallen Angels' directors. Following this the community dancers had the opportunity to talk about their stories from addiction to recovery and their involvement with Fallen Angels. These introductory speeches achieved the goal of setting a personal and interactive tone for the two performances that were due to be presented, highlighting and enforcing the charity's mission to play a role in promoting dance theatre and its transformative power. In the first performance, *Letting Go*, the community dancers offered an honest and emotional account of their stories of recovery. A synthesis of swaying movements of falling and getting up, accompanied by recorded voice-overs such as "are we dancing, dreaming, or awake?" and "our bodies are moving, our minds are open" and a blue wash stage lighting, all collided to create a dark, dream-like atmosphere. The authentication of their experiences was evidenced in their sharp, imperfect movements, and in the different shapes of their bodies, which signified their past experiences of years of substance misuse and living on the edge of addiction. This analogy was further enriched through dance phrases and isolated movements such as falls and tumbling, which were carefully shaped to symbolise the failures, despair, and complexities of addiction, as well as the merits of recovery. The finale of the first performance concluded with the five performers standing on stage with their arms wide open, in a symbolic gesture of embracing the audience and passing the message on that addicts do recover. Following this, the professional dancers who offered their own response to the issues of addiction with *Upon Awakening* developed the concepts that the first piece introduced. Their piece gave emphasis to the concept of awakening after the darkness of addiction. As Claire Cohen points out in her review in *London Dance*:

> Filling the vast dark void of the Clore Studio with a handful of performers who were giving out a strong silent message: recovering from addiction propels you to the depths, but you can win through. After the raw authenticity of the first group it was evident [that the professional dancers] were *acting*. But they'd absorbed their lessons well, for their dancing was utterly compelling. (Cohen 2014, n.p., my emphasis)

Fig. 2 Fallen Angels Dance Theatre, *Letting Go* directed by Paul Bayes Kitcher Royal Opera House London 2014. Photo Brian Slater

The juxtaposition between "a handful of performers who were giving out a strong silent message" and the other group's "obvious acting" provides us with a useful framework to conceptualise the paradox of risky aesthetics (Fig. 2). Risky aesthetics blur the boundaries between the subjectivity of the personal experience in antithesis to a trained body. It is precisely the subjectivity of the collective embodied experience of the community dancers that creates the basis for a generative form of aesthetic. A generative form of aesthetic means a type of aesthetic that derives directly from past embodied experiences of shame, guilt, and trauma and is informed by the multiplicity of the community dancers' identities. This is a useful context in which to articulate how a dance theatre piece performed by a group of recovering addicts can draw attention to the dynamics of participatory theatre. The contrast between the recovering body and the trained body of the professional dancer creates a powerful dialogical interplay and raises questions about body politics and post-authenticity. At the basis of risky aesthetics is the invitation from performer to audience and to fellow performer to move beyond the normative processes of judgement, both aesthetically and socially. This is possible by inviting performers and audiences to approach the performance as a becoming instead of as a fixed identity marker. Risky aesthetics is the platform within which this transition becomes possible. Drawing on Antonin Artaud's "To be done with the judgment of god", Deleuzian becomings insinuate an end of judgement (Scheer 2009). Judgement in this instance relates to the societal stigmatisation and exclusion of people in recovery from addiction and, by the same token, judgement of their performance in terms of its aesthetic value. One way to deconstruct society and its preconceptions about addicts and aesthetics is to start with the body. Aesthetics play a fundamental role in deconstructing the body in what Artaud refers to as the "body without organs (BoW)" (Scheer 2009, 40–44), a concept that Deleuze and Guattari develop in *Anti-Oedipus* (1983) and *A Thousand Plateaus* (1987). Risky aesthetics depend upon a process of becoming vulnerable, not only for the recovering-from-addiction performer but also in relation to the normative aesthetic values of, for example, the Royal Opera House. In an interesting analysis of Deleuzian ethico-aesthetics and drug addiction, Petra Malins maintains,

> [A] body should, ultimately, be valued for what it can do (rather than what it essentially "is"), and ... assemblages should be assessed in relation to their enabling, or blocking, of a body's potential to become other. (2004, 84)

This was clearly evident in the case of the first piece for two main reasons: firstly, because for the first time in the history of the Royal Opera House a group of recovering addicts was given the opportunity to perform their stories. This allowed them to transition from being addicts to being artists whose experiences are valued within the cultural canon and the setting of the Royal Opera House. Secondly, their embodied experience of addiction was immersive and gathered into a single context, an assemblage (Fig. 3).

The aesthetics of their collective post-authenticity and the power of their bodies "to become other" in front of their audiences deconstructed the dominant, institutionalised aesthetics. This process of engaging in becomings constructs the genesis of risky aesthetics. This was made possible by the multiple symbolic exchanges between performers and

Fig. 3 Fallen Angels Dance Theatre, *Letting Go* directed by Paul Bayes Kitcher Royal Opera House London 2014. Photo Brian Slater

audiences. The presence of a group of recovering addicts on stage runs contrary to the institutionalised aesthetics that dominate cultural production. It reinforces a consideration of the role of vulnerability in performance making. The becoming of aesthetics emerges from participants' experiences and is associated with the repositioning of the participants' embodied subjectivity at the centre of the audience's attention. Malins argues that

> Bodies—even those which are as rigidly and abjectly stratified as the "junkie"—can always change their territories and relations and form new assemblages. The idea of a stable identity (once a junkie, always a junkie) must be destabilized and abolished. (Malins 2004, 101)

The community dancers' performance opened up the possibility for the creation of new becomings. Their narratives suggested that the performers' identities are dependent upon their bodies; however, while they perform and re-perform, their vulnerabilities are constantly changing. This, in conjunction with the nonverbal semiotic positioning of their bodies on stage, allows them to overcome the limitations of language in order to create a direct metaphor, a political symbolism. The presence of their bodies on stage as vulnerable subjects recaptured the power of performance to create multiple transitions between stigmatised bodies and artistic bodies, which is a powerful metaphor. In particular, the anonymity of their bodies relates to the social anonymity and noiselessness of drug addicts (Alexander 2008). However, when their story is told through a body, it focuses the audience's attention on that body and its ability to become other, co-constituting its identity. As Samantha, a community dancer, maintains, "the body has its own intelligence and wants to express that and sometimes where words won't come, movement expresses what words can't" (Samantha 2014).[7] The experience of performing vulnerability has the capacity to agitate and exceed the limitations of identity and representation. It brings attention to the complex possibilities that critical vulnerabilities are conceived on the theatrical stage. At the end of the performance at the Royal Opera House the vulnerable bodies of the recovering addicts had become powerful engagements in becoming, casting doubt on societal perceptions of stigma and exclusion.

Conclusion

In summary, this chapter argued that there is a strong affiliation between risk taking in drug addiction and performance. By exploring the connection between risk taking in drug consumption and its associations with performance making, it asserted that risk taking in arts is a form of creative experimentation. This experimentation places the vulnerable risky stories of addiction recovery at the centre of the creative process and in so doing facilitates the genesis of an alternative aesthetic. This type of aesthetic encompasses past and present experiences of vulnerability and risk. It is grounded in the authentic and real experiences of vulnerable lives and operates in opposition to the dominant institutionalised aesthetics that dominate the arts world. The work of Fallen Angels Dance Theatre was discussed as a case study, particularly in reference to how autobiographical experiences can be translated into a dance theatre piece. Vulnerability was presented as a process that opens up space for a post-authentic exploration of the multiple and risky identities of the community dancers to be expressed. Drawing on the theories of Deleuze and Guattari (1987), this chapter claimed that throughout creative experimentations and engagements in becomings, the community dancers framed and reframed their embodied subjectivity. Risky aesthetics offered a platform for their critical vulnerabilities to be presented and reconfigured as an entity that is not fixed but inherently in transit. The process of becoming vulnerable on the theatrical stage created a political symbolism in ways that challenged the social stereotypes of addiction recovery and aesthetic excellence, respectively. Risk aesthetics was presented as a powerful concept within which to critically interrogate the many and complex possibilities of using socially engaged theatre with vulnerable adults.

Notes

1. In order to avoid terminological confusion, I use the term applied performance (as opposed to applied theatre), which reflects on the range of practices that Fallen Angels implements (dance, theatre, film, personal storytelling, and creative writing). In addition, I approach performance with its broader meaning.
2. Since 2007, I have conducted a series of projects and ethnographic research working in partnership with the following organisations and theatre companies: 18ANO (2007–2010) and KETHEA (2008–2010) in Greece, and Addiction Dependency Solutions (2007–2011), Drug Advice and Sexual Health (2008–2009), Breaking Image (2007), Outside the Edge Theatre Company (2012), and Fallen Angels (2012–2016) in the UK.
3. Ecstasy, also known as MDMA or Molly, is a synthetic drug that affects mood and perception. It was particularly popular in the 1980s and early 1990s and is closely associated with the dance club culture (FRANK 2016).
4. Altered states of consciousness (ASCs) is a concept first introduced by Tart (1969) in order to describe the way in which mental states such as hypnosis, dreaming, meditation, and drug-induced condition reveal "a qualitative shift in the pattern of mental functioning" (Tart cited in Hughes 1999, 7).
5. The UK Recovery Walk takes place every year in a different city. For further information see http://www.facesandvoicesofrecoveryuk.org.
6. All participants' names have been changed to protect their identities.
7. I thank Gary Anderson for helping me to work this out.

References

Alexander, Bruce. 2008. *The Globalisation of Addiction: A Study in Poverty of the Spirit*. New York: Oxford University Press.

Arnold, Nicholas. 2014. 'The Roar of the Grease-paint, the Smell of the Crowd': Performance as an Addictive Process. In *Performance and Addiction*, ed. James Reynolds, and Zoe Zontou, 264–283. Newcastle: Cambridge Scholars.

Balfour, Michael. 2009. The Politics of Intention: Looking for a Theatre of Little Changes. *Research in Drama Education: The Journal of Applied Theatre and Performance* 14 (3): 347–359. doi:10.1080/13569780903072125.

Bayes Kitcher Paul email message to author, 20 August 2014. The following references are interviews with the author: Bayes Kitcher Paul in discussion with the author, March 2016. Samantha (Fallen angels community dancer) in discussion with the author, July 2014. Sonia (Fallen angels community dancer) in discussion with the author, July 2014.

Belfiore, Eleanora. 2009. On Bullshit in Cultural Policy Practice and Research: Notes from the British Case. *International Journal of Cultural Policy* 15 (3): 343–359. doi:10.1080/10286630902806080.

Bishop, Claire. 2011. *Artificial Hells: Participatory Art and the Politics of Spectatorship*. London: Verso Books.

Blair, Rhonda, and Amy Cook (eds.). 2016. *Theatre, Performance and Cognition: Languages, Bodies and Ecologies*. London: Bloomsbury Methuen Drama.

Boal, Augusto. 2006. *The Aesthetics of the Oppressed*. New York and London: Routledge.

Boothroyd, Dave. 2006. *Culture on Drugs: Narco-cultural Studies of High Modernity*. Manchester: Manchester University Press.

Briginshaw, Valerie A. 2001. *Dance, Space and Subjectivity*. Basingstoke: Palgrave Macmillan.

Brodie, Janet Farrell, and Marc Redfield (eds.). 2002. *High Anxieties: Cultural Studies in Addiction*. Berkeley, CA: University of California Press.

Cohen, Claire. 2014. Review: Fallen Angels Dance Theatre—Letting Go/Upon Awakening—Clore studio, Royal Opera House. Londondance.com. Accessed 25 Nov 2014. http://londondance.com/articles/reviews/fallen-angels-dance-theatre-letting-go-upon-awaken/. Accessed 1 Sept 2016.

Deleuze, Gilles, and Félix Guattari. 1983. *Anti-Oedipus: Capitalism and Schizophrenia*, 6th ed. Minneapolis, MN: University of Minnesota Press.

Deleuze, Gilles, and Félix Guattari. 1987. *A Thousand Plateaus: Capitalism and Schizophrenia*. Minneapolis, MN: University of Minnesota Press.

FRANK. 2016. Ecstasy. http://www.talktofrank.com/drug/ecstasy. Accessed 11 July 2016.

Frost, Anthony, and Ralph Yarrow. 2016. *Improvisation in Drama*, 3rd ed. Basingstoke: Palgrave Macmillan.

Hood, Erin. 2013. Uncertain Knowledge: Representing Physical Pain Through Performance. In *Affective Performance and Cognitive Science: Body, Brain, and Being*, ed. Nicola Shaughnessy, 69–82. London: Methuen Drama.
Hughes, Jim. 1999. *Altered States: Creativity Under the Influence*. New York: Watson-Guptill Publications.
Hunt, Geoffrey, and Kristin Evans. 2003. Dancing and Drugs: A Cross-National Exploration. *Journal of Contemporary Drug Problems* 30: 779–814.
Jackson, Shannon. 2011. *Social Works: Performing Art, Supporting Publics*. New York and London: Routledge.
Joe-Laidler, Karen, and Geoffrey Hunt. 2013. Unlocking the Spiritual with Club Drugs: A Case Study of Two Youth Cultures. *Substance Use and Misuse* 48 (12): 1099–1108. doi:10.3109/10826084.2013.808067.
Kemp, Ryan. 2009. The Lived-Body of Drug Addiction. *Existential Analysis* 20 (1): 120–132.
Klein, Richard. 1993. *Cigarettes Are Sublime*. Durham, NC: Duke University Press Books.
Lewis, Marc. 2015. *The Biology of Desire: Why Addiction Is Not a Disease*. New York: Public Affairs, U.S.
Lomas, C.M. 1998. Art and the Community: Breaking the Aesthetic of Disempowerment. In *Dance, Power, and Difference*, ed. Sherry B. Shapiro. Champaign, IL: Human Kinetics.
Maguire, Tom. 2015. *Performing Story on the Contemporary Stage*. Basingstoke: Palgrave.
Malins, Peta. 2004. Machinic Assemblages: Deleuze, Guattari and an Ethico-Aesthetics of Drug Use. *Janus Head* 7 (1): 84–104.
McConachie, Bruce, and F. Elizabeth Hart (eds.). 2007. *Performance and Cognition: Theatre Studies and the Cognitive Turn*. London: Routledge.
McIntosh, James, and Neil McKeganey. 2000. Addicts' Narratives of Recovery from Drug Use: Constructing a Non-Addict Identity. *Social Science and Medicine* 50 (10): 1501–1510. doi:10.1016/s0277-9536(99)00409-8.
Measham, Fiona, Judith Aldridge, and Howard Parker. 2000. *Dancing on Drugs: Risk, Health and Hedonism in the British Club Scene*. London: Free Association Books.
Milhet, Maitena, Henri Bergeron, and Geoffrey Hunt (eds.). 2011. *Drugs and Culture: Knowledge, Consumption and Policy*. Farnham: Ashgate.
Oksanen, Atte. 2013. Deleuze and the Theory of Addiction. *Journal of Psychoactive Drugs* 45 (1): 57–67. doi:10.1080/02791072.2013.763563.
Papadimitropoulos, Panagiotis. 2009. Psychedelic Trance: Ritual, Belief and Transcendental Experience in Modern Raves. *Durham Anthropology Journal* 16 (2): 67–74.
Peretti-Watel, Patrick, and Jean-Paul Moatti. 2006. Understanding Risk Behaviours: How the Sociology of Deviance May Contribute? The Case of

Drug-Taking. *Social Science & Medicine*, 63 (3): 675–679. doi:10.1016/j.socscimed.2006.01.029.

Reynolds, James, and Zoe Zontou (eds.). 2014. *Addiction and Performance.* Newcastle: Cambridge Scholars.

Sadeghi-Yekta, Kirsten. 2015. Competing International Players and Their Aesthetic Imperatives. In *Applied Theatre: Aesthetics*, ed. Gareth White. United Kingdom: Methuen Drama.

Scheer, Edward. 2009. I Artaud BwO: The Uses of Artaud's *To Have Done with the Judgement of God.* In *Deleuze and Performance*, ed. Laura Cull, 37–53. Edinburgh: Edinburgh University Press.

Seddon, Toby. 2010. *A History of Drugs: Drugs and Freedom in the Liberal Age.* New York, NY: Routledge Cavendish.

Shaughnessy, Nicola (ed.). 2013. *Affective Performance and Cognitive Science: Body, Brain and Being.* London: Bloomsbury Methuen Drama.

Thompson, James. 2009. *Performance Affects: Applied Theatre and the End of Effect.* Basingstoke: Palgrave Macmillan.

White, Gareth. 2015. *Applied Theatre: Aesthetics.* London: Bloomsbury Methuen Drama.

White, William L. 1996. *Pathways: From the Culture of Addiction to the Culture of Recovery.* Center City, MN: Hazelden Publishing.

Wibberley, Christopher. 2003. Drugs for Dancing? *Addiction Research & Theory* 11 (3): 207–208. doi:10.1080/1606635031000123300.

Winkelman, Michael. 2002. Shamanism, Neurotheology and Contemporary Healing. *Anthropology News* 43 (4): 18–19. doi:10.1111/j.1556-3502.2002.tb00014.x.

Winkelman, Michael. 2011. Shamanism and the Evolutionary Origins of Spirituality and Healing. *NeuroQuantology* 9 (1): 54–71. doi:10.14704/nq.2011.9.1.390.

Winston, Joe. 2010. *Beauty and Education.* New York: Routledge.

Zontou, Zoe. 2012. Applied Theatre as an 'Alternative Substance': Reflections from an Applied Theatre Project with People in Recovery from Alcohol and Drug Dependency. *Journal Of Applied Arts and Health* 2 (3): 303–315. doi:10.1386/jaah.2.3.303_7.

Zontou, Zoe. 2013. An Allegory of Addiction Recovery: Exploring the Performance of *Eumenides* by Aeschylus, as Adapted by 18 ANO Theatre Group. *Research in Drama Education: The Journal of Applied Theatre and Performance* 18 (3): 261–275. doi:10.1080/13569783.2013.810931.

Zontou, Zoe. 2014. Staging Recovery from Addiction. In *Addiction and Performance*, ed. James Reynolds, and Zoe Zontou. Newcastle: Cambridge Scholars.

Risk in Theatrical Performances in the City: Creating Impact and Identities

André Carreira

This chapter focuses on participatory theatrical performances in the city. It aims to discuss the relationship between theatrical performances in urban space and risk taking by performers and the audience which, in turn, can create new experiences for both parties. My goal is to examine the city as dramaturgy and risk as an element of performers' work. The chapter's central objective is to explore the use of risk as an instrument of experimentation in urban theatrical performances. To do this, I examine my own artistic productions in public spaces as a theatre director, creating relationships through a new concept of street theatre. I have worked with the idea of street theatre as the occupation of urban spaces, which is related to civic participation and different forms of public engagement. This is why I discuss participation *as* risk.

The reflections that I present in this chapter are based on my experience making dramatic productions for non-theatrical spaces, which I call here *theatre in the city*. These experiences are the result of my work with different artistic groups over the past twenty years and took place in tandem with the courses I taught in both undergraduate and graduate

---

A. Carreira (✉)
Santa Catarina State University, Florianópolis, Brazil
e-mail: carreira@udesc.br

© The Author(s) 2017

A. O'Grady (ed.), *Risk, Participation, and Performance Practice*,
DOI 10.1007/978-3-319-63242-1_10

programmes. These studies were related both to the creation of theatre that appropriates urban spaces—particularly spaces where there is an intense circulation of citizens—and to the exploration of the limits of the work of actors.

These experiments with drama aim to disrupt the attention of passers-by and create a rupture in the daily life of common users of the streets. At the same time I, and the groups with whom I have worked, have sought to investigate extreme opportunities for creation by actors. These studies also discussed possibilities for taking radical artistic actions that could include different forms of participation by city residents. Therefore, I also discuss risk in the context of actors' work in contemporary street theatre. Risk is both physical and mental. This theatrical approach seeks to expand performers' abilities to take risks and to explore urban boundaries.

It is necessary to consider the city as dramaturgy in order to investigate the possibilities for theatre that invades the city's public spaces. By positioning the performers to take risks, we can amplify the opportunities to break citizens' routines and discuss the city as a theatrical space. Through these procedures we can increase the physical and symbolic interactions between people in the city and performers as part of social experience. Using fiction as a starting point, we can incorporate a proposition that considers the creation of theatre in the city as a real, lived experience.

Working with risk leads actors to take their own risks, assuming a radical position that enables them to seek opportunities for new ways to inhabit the city, transforming it into a space for theatrical interplay that invites political discussion. We were able to experiment more as we became more comfortable in pushing our own and others' boundaries. This is a complex reality because the audience reads both the physical body of the person and the character they portray. By taking real risks, the actors make the action more compelling, which can open an audience up to a kind of intimacy with the performers. The actors feel more vulnerable as they perform, which is important, because this vulnerability can be used as the focus of all street performances.

This chapter starts with the concept of city as dramaturgy, an idea that I have developed in my artistic practices. I then present different points of view from urban studies about public space as a territory of conflict. After that, to discuss participation, I refer to the work of Rosalyn Deutsche, Claire Bishop, and Erika Fischer-Lichte. Finally, I propose the idea of risk as material for a "theatre of invasion", a kind of performance that is made by occupying public spaces with the objective of breaking up daily routine, through the use of ludic materials.

The Theatre of Invasion and the City as Dramaturgy

The objective of my artistic practice in the city is to construct performances that take the most mobilising elements possible from the spatial realm to create dramatic sequences that engage the public as they develop.

Working with this premise, I propose that the performers experiment with conditions for creativity. They begin with exercises that imply being in the city in a situation of fictional interplay to create a dialogue with the context of the street. Using this idea as a starting point, I experiment with actors trying out different forms of breaking the daily flow in different public spaces to create situations in which the theatrical scene and real life are related and in which the participation of passers-by is fundamental. These exercises seek to both give voice to the passers-by and allow the performers to try to understand the life of the city from within the performance, that is, to connect with the passers-by in the everyday scene to create new scenes (Fig. 1).

The idea of the city as dramaturgy implies the participation of people who use the city as an element of the composition, given that these users and their habits shape the structure of the city's environment. Thus, to study urban dramaturgy it is important to construct scenic-based exercises through which the performers engage passers-by.

Participation is thus understood as an action that establishes closer ties between artistic language and political fact, that is, between the poetic field and the social field. To participate is thus to intervene in the construction of a work in which individuals go beyond their condition as spectators who interpret the work. It is necessary to remember that Italian historian Marco De Marinis observed that to be part of an artistic work one can be in the place of the artist-creator as well as in that of the spectator and of the critic. Nevertheless, this perspective is directly related to the type of participation that is based on the production of meaning in the context of the work.

Meanwhile, theatre that invades urban space works with a logic opposite to that of Relational Art as suggested by Bourriaud (2002). Relational Art appears to produce experiences that are said to be

Fig. 1 *Das Saborosas Aventuras de Dom Quixote de La Mancha*—Grupo Teatro que Roda. *Photo* Lev Rebostein

subordinate to social and cultural contexts without, in fact, questioning their ties to these contexts and certainly without considering the aesthetic and linguistic dimensions. There is thus an acceptance of the relational structures, whereas the participation sought by the Theatre of Invasion attempts to break with the established rules of conviviality in order to open up new horizons of relationships in urban spaces that are clearly supported by the production of the poetic objects that envelop the city. In this case, passers-by produce their own participation, aware that they are facing an artistic object, and they can thus experience aesthetic pleasure as a material of their active transformation of the event.

In my experience, this is done through the realisation of small scenes in which the performers invade public spaces using their bodies in a manner that is out of the ordinary. Thus, we experiment with performers lying on the ground in a bus station while speaking with people who pass by; performers seated in chairs that are on billboards or in trees who engage in dialogue with passers-by; and groups of performers moving through public transportation, such as buses or subway cars, while enacting a precisely choreographed scene, such as a group of people reading a newspaper synchronically.

All of these modes of occupation were used to produce materials for the creation of invasive theatrical performances. Discovering ways of dialoguing with the users of the city, using artistic experiments, enables these users to fulfil more than the role of simple informants who provide us with the material for our creation. The fact that the performers are in the city and are doing research within a performance process radically changes their perception of the city. It involves their conducting a reading of the city through the lens of a performance condition that shifts them, as artists, out of a zone of security because the exchange with the passers-by is mediated by fiction.

Artistic interventions have a powerful capacity to provoke shifts of perception about how we can behave in situations that deviate from the daily or normal routine. This is due to the fact that they visit playful territories that facilitate the inversion of order, as French anthropologist Jean Duvignaud affirms in his book *Le jeu du jeu* (1980).

From the time of the Dadaists to the Situationist's Theory of the Dérive (Debord 1999) and the productions of the Living Theater (Tytell 1995) through to today, we can consider different approaches that take the relational spaces of the city as a realm for artistic experiences that converse with the effective participation of citizens. The city is a living space constructed by a multiplicity of forces, among which are the users who directly or indirectly intervene in all events that take place in the public space.

When considering artistic actions that invade the urban space to create an experience of participation, another element that is worth considering is affect. Brazilian cities can be hostile environments in which passers-by often feel threatened in some way. Therefore, producing moments in which strangers can overcome these situations of anxiety and submit themselves to a form of interplay with the performers is a strong way of generating a discussion about the rules of urban space and public participation.

In addition to these elements, we also experimented with scenes that included actors running through streets, through subway corridors, and on bus platforms, as well as crawling along building facades and walking on roofs and marquees. In these different situations the risk for the performers was real. It was within these risky experiments that we sought to create forms of connection with the "accidental" public in the streets. The fear the performers faced and the sensation the spectators felt mediated the relationship between them. This constituted a fundamental element for the interplay between the actors and the passers-by.

In the process of this theatrical approach and appropriation of the urban silhouette, the transformation of the use of urban space is inevitable, and this allows new connections to form between the spectacle and the public. These ties are built through a re-assignment of the use of urban space, a transformation of the condition of passers-by, and a communion in the act of sharing a situation of risk, and consequently, the state of readiness that both the performers and the passers-by should experience.

The City as Disputed Territory

Streets, squares, and pavements are areas of permanent dispute as different forces struggle to establish uses and identities that define the fragments of the city. On the one hand, institutional actions construct a regulated image of the city—the functional and touristic city—while on the other hand, social forces occupy and contemplate the city, based on each of their own daily uses and, particularly, their immediate needs. Thus, the territorial dispute in the city takes place between the order of security and the chaotic and irreverent occupations of citizens. It impedes the strict control of space, even if control is a goal that is well defined by governmental norms. There is also a private occupation of public spaces in the city, and consequently there are movements of resistance that insist on the preservation of the city as a space for everyone. In this context, theatrical performances in the city can produce moments in which the identities in dispute are questioned by means of participation. As the Mexican scholar Mario Cesaroli argues, "the contemporary city is losing the 'relationship element' and space is not necessarily public any more; it is turning into an essential accessory solely for individual mobility" (2014, 239). This is why street theatre performers need to discuss the sense of public spaces from their own practical experiences of them. The performance must be created through practices that oppose mass culture and consumerism if it looks for a social interaction to establish new patterns of artistry on the streets.

All of this can be summarised in the contemporary confrontation between the uses of the city of consumption and the city of politics, and all the intermediary actions that take place in this zone of conflict.

The daily lives of cities turbulently express the tensions that traverse our societies.

The Brazilian geographer Milton Santos has written that in our time we can see a symbiosis between the city and techniques that reverberate in the power that ebbs and flows in social and economic contexts (2004, 17). This happens because the process can be understood as an economy of thought adapted to an instrumental logic, which has the function of reorganising our behaviour in the city as part of a complex system of production and consumerism. It means that we are losing public spaces where communities could confront social conflicts. For this reason, the ethics of citizen occupation of the city requires the construction of practices that create spaces of sociability that go beyond the flows of consumption and that stimulate the possibilities of participation to politicise the space of sociability. It is on this terrain that different artistic projects that seek to recover an urban utopia as a site of conviviality are built. To say this is not to affirm that these projects can erase the conflict through artistic practices, but rather it is to recognise that the city's spaces are realms for processing these conflicts. We must understand participation—even participation that is part of an artistic event—as a voluntary intervention in the development of conflict.

The space that invites citizens' participation must be recognised as an arena in which the citizenry can contemplate various points of view and, based on their collective interests, consider various alternative policies. We consider the occupying public squares as the creation of forums where a wide variety of political and ideological forces, directly or indirectly, debate the future of their respective countries or collectives. A recent example of this was seen at Tahrir Square in Cairo, which for weeks was the centre of political life in the city. All of the living forces that could coexist were represented there, expressing their differences and engaging in political argument, and this is what produced a violent and authoritarian response from the reigning powers, an expression of fear.

This is a fundamental perspective for considering the hypothesis that artistic actions invade the city, even when considering the different levels of impact that exist between an artistic initiative and the decision making effected by broader layers of society. Only by considering this space as disputed territory can artistic action be projected beyond a form of immediate entertainment, constructing an interplay that diverts and simultaneously constructs spaces of discussion about the meaning of the city. The spaces of participation, or the lack thereof, are placed in evidence.

If we consider artistic creation as a fundamental practice of social interplay, it is necessary to politicise this type of artistic action, less by the thematic aspects of the projects and more through experimentation with the way space is occupied and the manner in which (physical) bodies are used by the actors. It is the bodily practice of using space that can produce in individuals an opening up toward shared experience. Through the experience of occupation, the passers-by animate and transform the theme of the project.

Exploring this territory of conflict is a key task for the production of performances that seek dialogue with the city. This already implies a shift from a place of pure (theatrical) presentation to one in which performers cannot abandon their role as citizens. Instead, they approach other citizens so that together they can undertake transformative actions. In this case, we need to recognise the potential that artistic performance has for transformative action when it is able to effectively incorporate the participation of passers-by.

To shift the passers-by from the position of mere spectators to that of active participants is an important element of the process of constructing the performance. To produce this change is to expand the possibilities from which new perspectives emerge about the uses of the city, and about the place of people in public space. For this reason, it is essential that passers-by be able to discover new forms of being in the public space.

It is impossible to consider artistic creation in urban space without supposing the possibility of a central role for city residents, who represent the most unstable element we can consider in relation to government planning, business actions, and the legal order that disrupts daily urban life. This requires us to think of risk as an element in the process of creation: performers and spectators conduct actions that place them in situations of instability that stem from their occupation of the space. The passers-by are part of the creative process, which includes the incorporation of the ingredient of unpredictability. The street brings to the artist the risk of error, of unexpected variation, of a rupture that disorganises what was planned and causes the city to penetrate the artistic action. At the same time, it puts passers-by in an unexpected territory that is caused by the alteration of order, making them participate and not be simply users of the city streets.

Despite considering participation as something inherent to the context of the city, it is important to note that the very idea of participation has acquired growing importance in contemporary artistic projects through the valorisation of new forms of democratic administration. Participation, as a sign of the valorisation of any institutional or governmental action, permeates the discourse of a wide variety of social organisations, as well as that of artists, even when the very notion of participation is not fully explored.

To reflect on public spaces as places for artistic experiences that incorporate participation, it is first necessary to understand that it is most common to identify as public spaces those that remain after a process of accelerated occupation due to real estate expansion and government actions of urban modernisation. These remnants of public space constitute what is currently administered as public space. Therefore, art in public spaces is an art of resistance to privatisation, which swallows the public.

Even if authors such as Víctor Neves affirm that "public space is a space of action, a locus for the living experiences of the individual with his immediate surroundings and with other (people), making identity a factor of agglutination, of mobilization for collective action" (2014, 252), it can increasingly be perceived that city spaces are less public, or they are appropriated for commerce or are administered to benefit corporate marketing. For this reason, the occupation of public spaces with artistic actions is a necessary gesture of resistance in large cities.

The image of the city as a major support for advertising has intensified. Large corporations are no longer satisfied with billboards; they seek to place their names on public streets. We can see this in the case of a cellular telephone company that acquired the rights to place its name on the most important square in Madrid and on its metro station so that for over a year these places were no longer known only as the Puerta del Sol. Artists can play an important role in the discussion of the appropriation of public spaces by creating experiences that discuss this logic and that propose to passers-by the development of new forms of being in the streets. They can perceive that the possibilities for public participation are related to a project of reconquering the city.

This echoes with the view that, as Pau Pedragosa affirms, currently a "city is defined only by the perception of an image that refuses to consider the relationship between identity and space, and for this reason can only provide a 'fluctuating' identity without its own space" (2014, 226).

Fig. 2 *Antigona Cidade*. *Photo* Léo Macário

The culture of images and of hyperconsumption also corrodes the notion of public space as convivial space. Certainly, this does not mean that citizens have completely lost their capacity for occupying and using public space as a forum for political life. The different movements that have occupied squares and the permanence of the tactic of holding street demonstrations indicate that not all perceptions of public space have succumbed to the sphere of virtual social networks. Nevertheless, the substitution of the occupation of public space by virtual encounters is evident.

Are we losing a sense of space? Pedragosa also posits the question: "are we not failing to understand space as a carrier of meaning linked to our practices and uses of space?" (ibid., 226). Considering this question, it is necessary to remember that living in a city is a corporeal experience: We are destined to move through it, and for this reason we inscribe it on our bodies. Thus, we continue every day to resist, despite the depletion of meanings in interactions triggered by the practices of the image (Fig. 2).

The experience of invading zones of the city through performance actions requires that we confront questions related to the two elements that are the focus of this text: experimentation with situations of risk and participation as prime material for the impact of theatrical performance; and experimentation's link to ethics when committed to disputing the processes for constructing the identities of urban spaces. It is also necessary to affirm that the very notion of participation is controversial and the related need to reflect on the possibility that participation is not an instrumental experience, but rather a sign of collective and individual autonomy for those who decide to break with the logic of repetition.

These processes take place in dialogue with the materiality of the urban space, that is, amid the flows and variations in its repertoire of uses and in relation to the appropriation of physical structures. These materials shape the dramatic plane of any creative process that takes place within the city, and they are the elements that determine what makes the spectacle, or watching the spectacle, into a redefinition of the city, even if in an ephemeral way.

It is precisely for this reason that it is important to discuss how the conditions of public spaces and the social experience of identities perforate the theatrical scene, making it porous and transparent. Urban performances can construct spaces of fleeting conviviality that stimulate exchange and participation. This can be seen in a more complex way through the experiences of neighbourhood theatres, the occupation of neighbourhoods, and professional artistic practices that question the place of the citizen in public spaces.

Because of its adverse and conflictive environment, the city offers creators an enormous quantity of material for the construction of performances that encourage participatory experiences. The theatrical performances create new unstable zones in a naturally unstable territory. I see performance in the city as an exercise for intensifying the experience of inhabiting urban spaces. This type of artistic proposal requires that both performers and spectators experience different ways of adapting to events, and this, in turn, requires reflection on the conditions of effective participation.

It is these conditions that open up possibilities for the creation of intense, although provisional, ties, because they take place in situations characterised by their ephemerality. Both performers and passers-by interact with elements of the unexpected with great intensity, given that the city is a living organism that does not shirk from being invaded by a performance; to the contrary, it incorporates it and intensifies it with its own dynamics.

The streets have repertories of uses that are articulated by their inhabitants and these are related to the processes of constructing identities that define the imagery of cities. For this reason, the invasion of the theatrical performance creates dialogue with the identities of the citizens who consider the city to be theirs. The construction of images that are a key element for the production of urban identities is related to what the anthropologist Néstor García Canclini considers to be the multiple cities fabricated by the uses of their inhabitants, and by the overlapping of territories identified by the citizens (2005). Kevin Lynch observed in the 1950s that flows and landmarks are elements that organise our image of the city (1960). The relationship between this image and the practice of inhabiting spaces produces the process for identifying the material for constructing artistic projects that seek participation. In these circumstances, the identity of the space (in the city) is the starting point that stimulates passers-by to become spectators of an artistic moment.

Theatrical Performances and Participation

In reflecting upon participation and artistic initiatives, I considered the research of Claire Bishop, whose book *Artificial Hells* points to relevant elements when discussing artistic projects that seek participation. Bishop concludes that:

> Activation of the audience in participatory art is positioned against its mystic counterpart, passive spectatorial consumption. Participation thus forms part of a larger narrative that traverses modernity. Art must be directed against contemplations, against spectatorship, against the passivity of the masses paralyzed by the spectacle of modern life. This desire to activate the audience in participatory art is at the same time a drive to emancipate it from a state of alienation induced by the dominant ideological order—be it consumer capitalism, totalitarian socialism, or military dictatorship. Beginning from this premise, participatory art aims to restore and realise a communal, collective space of shared social engagement. (2012, 275)

Bishop also affirms that study of these questions requires observing the tensions between quality and equality, singular and collective authorship, and the "ongoing struggle to find artistic equivalents for political positions" (ibid., 3). Bishop also delimits the experiences of participatory art, considering three key moments: the historic avant-garde in Europe in the twentieth century; the 1960s and 1970s; and the revival of the 1990s, just after the fall of communism. She affirms that:

> Each phase has been accompanied by utopian rethinking of art's relationship to the social and of its political potential—manifested in a reconsideration of the ways in which art is produced, consumed and debated. (Ibid., 3)

In her book *Evictions: Art and Spatial Politics* (1996), Rosalyn Deutsche compares works that ask spectators to decipher relationships and contents already inscribed in images, without invoking them to examine their own role and participation in the production of the images. On the other hand, there is an entire generation of artists who think of images as a social relationship, and who consider the spectator as a subject constructed by the object, from which it thus would apparently be separate. In addition, Deutsche affirms that:

> The artworks of Louise Lawler and Hans Haacke present politicized ways of engaging urban contexts. Unlike the new public art, these works do not collaborate in the design of the redeveloped city. Unlike neoexpressionist city painting, they do not seek to transcend urban social conditions. On the contrary, they draw attention to those conditions. But they do not reduce art's social meaning to a simple reflection of "external" social reality, a model that leaves art per se politically neutral. Instead, they employ spatial tactics developed in postmodern art-site-specificity, institutional critique, critiques of representation to reveal the social relations that constitute both aesthetic and urban spaces. (Ibid., xvii)

From this point of view, a perception emerges that takes the direct effectiveness of participation in an event that transcends art as it is happening as they key element of the repercussions it has in the social sphere. In this case, in particular, that element would be the capacity to activate participation based on artistic projects that intend to go beyond criticism of the condition of urban spaces.

Considering that the city is a space of conflict, it can also be perceived that different tensions shape the space of the streets each day. This is precisely what makes this space particularly sensitive to artistic experience. It also stimulates thinking about the potential of artistic forms that invoke participation by experimenting with risk. Because it is an environment of conflict, it has all the elements that shape the basis of social relationships, which are present in the streets. There are echoes and discourses that are directly tied to the projects of society and to practices of resistance. This determines the existence of conflict, even if various repressive means are used to keep the streets calm and functioning most of the time. Nevertheless, in the street there is always a fuse ready to be lit. Explosions are always imminent, even if much time passes without hearing their blasts.

Passers-by do not rehearse with the artists. They do not know the objectives proposed by those who initiate the creative process, and, finally, they do not have a reason to completely respect what was previously planned. The passers-by have the liberty to incorporate their own desires and ideas into the artistic object, which is basically a provocation for opening a new creative process. This is a key element when we consider the idea of participation, given that if participation does not include the ability to decide the outcome of the event, it is nothing more than a mere representation of the act of participation.

A decisive question is therefore: Can participatory artistic practices be proposed that do more than produce provocative moments over which the artistic team does not have any influence at the time of contact with the passers-by? To escape from the mere role of agents provocateurs, it is necessary to think of the intensity of the practices proposed and to create mechanisms for interplay that allow the performers to take advantage of all of the interferences of the passers-by as material for deepening the experience. For the participation to be more than a reflection of an instant of liberty—even if this is also important from the perspective of an artistic intervention—it is necessary to think of instruments of connection that project themselves beyond the moment of the performance. At the same time, it should be considered that the intensity of the experience must suppose the production of residues among the spectators that stimulate later comments and narratives as a consequence of having participated in the artistic event. I call "residues" those images or memories from the performance that hours afterward make the spectators still feel the need to comment on their experience with others. It creates the possibility for the ephemeral to last longer than the performance itself.

It is important to work with a structure of interplay that is based on risk for both parties because this allows for the establishment of commitment to passing spectators. This structure should be supported by creating the greatest possible proximity between performers and spectators, so that both must run some risk during the presentation process.

Nevertheless, despite all the strategies that can be adopted to open spaces for participation and to construct ties that stimulate a participation that is not immediately depleted, it is necessary to reflect on the importance of participation for the political aspect of the artistic statement as well as for its own development as a language in the city.

Understood abstractly, "participation" can mean very little, especially in times when institutional norms demand collaboration and participation in official projects. It is necessary to think of the idea of participation in the context of projects and initiatives that break with the logic of domination, and even more so in cases where participation can camouflage the biased instrumentalisation of power. To think of participation as an initiative that chooses to intervene in the collective in order to transform shared and social living conditions demarcates a territory that allows us to think of its very role across a wide variety of artistic actions.

Based on this perspective, I propose we consider participation based on need. I do this by considering my own questions as an artist and researcher in relation to the possibilities for achieving effective participation in creative processes and presentations.

I thus begin by recognising that this image and the practice of inhabiting spaces produce the processes for identifying material for constructing artistic projects that seek participation. The identity associated with the space of the city is the starting point for stimulating the passers-by to become spectators. The term "participation", which is so important to the artistic movements of today, runs the risk of having its meaning diminished by an insistence on its use through tireless repetition and the association of participation with an enormous diversity of artistic practices. Some of these practices, for example, are too closely associated with the international market of dramatic arts festivals.

Given the difficulties of finding meaning and strength in the idea of participation, an inevitable sense of anguish arises among artists who see in their projects the opportunity for transformation. What can be said of the sincere militants who place their faith in the transformation of society as a result of collective conscious action? The action of performance itself can open spaces of participation. As the Spanish author José Antonio Sánchez says:

> When theatre leaves the theatre building and performers feel free of an artistic tension, it is possible to discover the efficacy of transformation and the masking. This efficacy comes from the possibility to do effective the

> strength of theatrical convention out of its own space. The transformation could be effective when the actor appears in front of its collectivity as an incarnation of what it represents, as a real or fictional character. (2014, 29)

The poverty of encounters and distrust of the possibility for people's effective participation seems to turn political and artistic initiatives into events that are not truly participatory, but only representations of participation; that is, they become mere reality shows in our society of spectacles. Persistent distrust corrodes the possibility for effective participation that has a potentially transformative role.

In this context, it should be considered whether effective participation is only possible when a need or a threat that mobilises individuals and collectives is perceived. It is unlikely that participation will be born as part of a rational project that results from goodwill, that is, from a mobilisation driven by the very need to participate in constructing a better world. It is interesting, for example, to think about Erika Fischer-Lichte's analyses of Marina Abramović's experiences with her audience:

> Abramovic created a situation wherein the audience was suspended between the norms and rules of art and everyday life, between aesthetic and ethical imperatives. She plunged the audience into a crisis that cannot be overcome by referring to conventional behavior patterns. The transformation of spectator into actor happened almost automatically as specified by the *mise en scène*. It was hardly the result of a conscious decision on the part of the concerned spectator. (2008, 15)

This is why we can think of hunger as a motor for behaviours that mobilise collective participation. The hypothesis would be that the genesis of participation is based on the coincidence of individual needs that lead to collective dynamics. Fischer-Lichte writes:

> Is it really legitimate to equate actors and spectators? Is not the contribution of the artists who prepare the production larger, given that they determine the course of the performance, while the audience at best reacts to it? How can the proclaimed dismissal of the artist as autonomous subject be reconciled with the common complaints about the despotism of theatre directors since the late 1960s who seem to consider themselves almighty? (Ibid., 163)

These needs can serve as organic impulses to transform the audience and actors of a political action into a performance.

The interminable crisis of revolutionary proposals and, above all, the crisis of paradigms of revolution and the political organisations that characterise contemporary times have opened up a space of insecurity and a lack of hope in the possibility for transformation. Yet they have also inaugurated creative possibilities in light of the void of normative models. Upon recognising this void, we are driven to find or invent alternative paths.

Many artists and theoreticians attribute to art the role that once belonged to political movements. The field of education has also considered itself as a territory of transformation. Thus, a combination has been fomented in academic spaces: To be an artist and to be a transformative individual, educating through art becomes a way to change the world by artistically intervening to question forms of power.

Even though modern art has always been related to a mandate for transformation, its relationship to political processes was one of criticism and transversal intervention. The dialogue with the political field took place through the recognition of their respective particularities, and this dialectic constituted its power as an autonomous instrument that could intervene with the anarchic liberty that the process of artistic creation supposes in modern life. Artistic individuals occupied places from which they became dissonant voices.

The arrogance that has characterised the world of art since the rupture caused by the Renaissance has driven artists to consider themselves as vectors of transformation. This explains their actions as interventions in the political field. However, the existence of militant organisations supported by mass movements could constitute the territory in which these relations are made concrete. This same arrogance, which always envisioned a dynamic role for artistic action, created a growing tension between the political and the artistic when the paradigms of political militancy entered crisis in postmodernity. Thus, when there were no parties or organisations capable of leading the struggle, artists were able to maintain the flame of resistance and confrontation against the order of capital and oppression.

It is important to note that there is an enormous difference between the role of the artist as an element of resistance—an element that is confronted with the organisation of power and uses its language to fight as an alternative voice—and that of artists who consider their actions to be a substitute for political actions that are made instrumental by people in the streets. When we see stencils and graffiti (or street art) that criticise the absurdity of occupation painted on a wall that is built by the Israeli state in the Occupied Territories, it is quite different from seeing young Palestinians throwing stones at Israeli tanks. It is difficult to encounter hierarchies of values in these two distinct elements because each fulfils a role within the political and cultural context. Nevertheless, it is possible to say that as creative and provocative an artistic action might be, it also might resonate among people as a discourse about something in the field of political action. This action could be an element that stimulates and mobilises—and could even be part of—a movement, but it will need people in action in order for it to have structural repercussions.

Even if artistic action cannot substitute, in an absolute manner, for the action of people, it is part of this process, and it makes the process more complex because it incorporates divergent readings into it. Art engages with individuals from their own space by constructing other possibilities for thinking through and understanding events.

In the same way that education can only transform the world in a radical manner when the world is in an acute process of transformation, art will fulfil a revolutionary role when it is joined with broader political processes that originate among the most thoughtful individuals who compose a given collectivity. This is related to the perspective that denies history the lulls that are inherent in cumulative and progressive processes because it understands that transformation is always a consequence that explodes from within an accumulated need.

The profound difference between the proposals of Meyerhold and Brecht reside precisely in the fact that while those of Meyerhold were generated in the cauldron of a revolution in progress (1905–1923), those of Brecht were the result of a period of conservative reaction (1928–1958). Meyerhold's work was the result of coexistence with a world in transformation, an invention of the future that experimented with various forms and discourses and that understood the chaotic and festive elements of the revolutionary process. Brecht reacted to the Nazi regime and dialogued with the Stalinist regime, adapting his work as a rationalisation of the normative historic processes. In Brecht's case we see that political action was thought of as participation from the premise of an understanding of processes. The call to participation became an ideological imperative and not the result of an organic need stemming from daily life and estimulated by a necessary future.

In theatrical performances it is common to discuss participation by considering the possibilities in spectators' shift from a "passive" situation to active participation. To break the dichotomous barrier between stage and audience was always the goal. For this reason directors experimented with different procedures. It is curious to observe that there are very few experiences in which we can see actions that are generated by spectator initiative. Who are the individuals who have a need to participate? How many people who walk on the street are able to participate in a performance without prejudice if the performance is by an artistic group that is not identified with popular culture?

Popular forms of theatre show us many modes of participation, but few of these modes, if any, are recognised by artists who work as part of militant theatre. In reality, the history of the dramatic arts is full of examples of participation that deserve greater attention from contemporary artists.

Although it is important to avoid falling into the simplification of using forgotten models to sharply criticise the spokespeople for participatory art, it is interesting to consider the idea of participation from a broader perspective. This is particularly necessary for understanding that participation cannot emerge only from the delineations created by the artists themselves. Participation must be faced as a concrete phenomenon that occurs when barriers are broken and a determined collective can perceive that the actions of each individual and of the collective have an effective result. Effectiveness is the element that allows one to identify with participation. This does not mean we should suppose there is an immediate effectiveness that transforms the world, but rather that there is an efficacy that can be identified collectively, even if not as a shared event.

Immersed in the world of artistic and critical discourse, we are moved in an inert manner, submitting ourselves to ideas and practices that absorb us. Are we aware that we can only repeat slogans without incorporating them in our practices until they take us to our own limits? What is our commitment to the permanent transformation that we make as creators?

Considering the perspective of Fredric Jameson, according to which in postmodernity we observe a complex fusion between the fields of culture and economic life, it is pertinent to question whether it is possible to continue to produce critical art without placing ourselves completely in crisis in relation to the meaning of our work. In fact, we are always facing the risk that our work can quickly become transformed into a type of merchandise and that any participation takes the form of simulation.

To recognise that only the perception of need mobilises us to act, and therefore to participate in a political action, is a form of breaking with this inertia and with the reiteration of the idealistic discourse that constructs artificial images of our spectators and ourselves. By proposing participation based on need, perhaps it would be possible to advance beyond participation as representation, opening new forms of participatory interaction with the citizens who pass through the streets. This is related to the need to construct alternatives for the creation of theatrical performances in cities that allow for integrating passers-by with parts of the dramatic text. By perceiving citizens as a dramatic element, it is possible to speak more directly with the needs that are identified through the social exchanges that are manifested in the political arena of the streets.

Risk as a Propulsive Element of Participation in Urban Space

Risk is a natural condition for performers because they are individuals who live in a universe of desired risks. In our daily reality we see the immanent risk in deciding to work in acting because, although we live in an era of simulation par excellence, the acting profession, as a rule, does not reap a level of financial reward that allows for a life of economic abundance. The only actors who receive high remuneration are those who are submerged in the economic structure of the "star system". Thus the social risk inherent in acting necessarily acquires greater dimensions when actors understand their art as a social practice based on a transformative function. In this case, the possibility for marginalisation and loneliness of those in theatre is evident.

The actor is an artist who is prepared to permanently confront dangerous conditions. By definition, the art of acting is a practice in which performers expose themselves and place themselves in unknown territory. They cross boundaries by exposing their bodies and minds to adverse conditions and, paradoxically, this is how they find pleasure. This is an age-old element of theatrical art: to expose oneself, thereby exposing the collective drive. If we think of this exposure as something that goes far beyond psychological exposure and a confrontation with the potential other (people/characters) that performers face, we can see other zones of risk that are part of their universe.

Even if we are confident in our political capacity and our critical perspective, can we effectively take part in a participatory experience without letting the representation of our place dominate the social interplay which joins us in artistic action that seeks participation? How can we mobilise energies of participation that generate processes of transformation based on art without assuming a position of control and direction that knows the final result? What type of transformation can be considered when we unleash artistic processes? Will there be consensus about the transformations and the need for them? These questions deal with the idea of risk in performances because the theatrical approach to the urban silhouette supposes a series of difficulties for a spectacle's development. Most of these difficulties are related to our notion of theatrical events that go into crisis mode when they accept the street's unspoken rules.

In *Phenomenology of Perception*, the philosopher Merleau-Ponty (1962) wrote that we are temporal beings endowed with a notion of time, affected by the very history we create. We are also spatial beings, cognisant of space in its different dimensions, living in a world composed of places. As spatial and temporal beings, our bodies are also sentient beings that are aware of themselves. In the streets we are dealing with space-changing references all the time, but our concrete relationships are determined by events between bodies in space, a space that is defined by the intense process of change. Our own perception of ourselves changes when we face a performance that works with risk because our perspective as spectators is broken, and we can experience the performance through our bodies.

During street performances, the audience soon realises that, in addition to the first level of receptivity, that is, the interaction between actors and spectators in their respective routines, there is a second level of interaction between the viewers and others who are there who see what happens as an unusual moment. That is why all street performances are part of an experience where we can observe how spectators perceive the reactions of the audience. As the actors move through their fictional spaces we are able to see, at the same time, the reality of spectators who are watching the performance. This can elicit surprise and exhilaration through a feeling of shared experience. Unlike in traditional theatre, in street theatre spectators are exposed to the gaze of other spectators. Their reactions to this exposure can change the conditions of receptivity, thereby creating a situation of risk where nobody knows or controls the complete process (Fig. 3).

Adversity in urban spaces means that a performance must coexist with permanent interference from a wide variety of noises and especially with

Fig. 3 *Pagina 469*—Grupo Engasga Gato. *Photo* Lev Rebostein

interference from the social life that incessantly flows through the streets while the theatre tries to occupy the same space.

This flowing life of the streets, which at times appears to be an obstacle we must overcome in order to achieve the highest possible level of interface with the theatrical phenomenon, can be considered the very essence of the scenic experience when an attempt is made to redefine the cityscape and the uses of public space. On a train, a street, or a bus, theatre must construct alternatives to gain meaning that goes beyond the characterisation of theatre as a simple spectacle that is proposed as a complement to the diversity of offers available to passers-by.

This experience certainly raises the possibility that spectators may question if the actors are truly acting or if they belong to a new reality. Why couldn't they be in spaces that are close by while also simulating distance? Is it important that they belong to an ordinary reality or the live in a new reality, a fantastical one? When the audience realises that a game exists that plays with the condition of being a spectator, it can create a feeling of risk. But at the same time, the audience can enjoy this situation as if it were a participatory game.

It is important to question whether this changes the artistic experience. Firstly, it is worth reiterating that the use of public space was born of the desire to conduct spectacles that play with the distance between the performer and the passer-by. Under these circumstances, making theatre requires the artist to seek a point of connection with the public, to operate by creating the possibility and convincing the audience to dedicate time and attention to the theatrical event. If the public is not convinced that they should offer their bodies and minds to the theatrical event, the attempt to create a performative ceremony will fail.

Performers who submits themselves to the exercise of risk will be required to take paths that are different from the traditional ones that are used to construct fiction and characterisation. Experimenting with techniques of risk supposes a series of situational experiences that range from an individual experience to that of the group. These require actors to focus on the perception of the function of the body–mind binomial in action. The radical and mandatory alteration of the quotidian physical state causes the body's functionality to be reconstructed by finding a new modulation for props, voices, and gestures. The balance between the dramatic performance and the experimentation of risk will shape the performer's essential place of work.

Techniques of risk use physical experiences to make performers directly face the universe of their fears. To overcome these fears supposes a work of self-knowledge and a re-elaboration of their attitudes in the face of theatrical productions and life itself. The process of confronting risk and the resulting attempts to develop techniques to decrease physical risk are essential components of the training process. Performers immersed in this class of experience are required to undergo a series of lessons that include the discovery of a point of equilibrium between the various components present in the process. It is the performer who must establish a harmonious relationship within the interplay between risk and the expressive potential that emerges from the learning process. It is also necessary to deepen the collective experience that is particular to manipulating the exercise of risk. The practices of these interdependent relationships that are based on reciprocal trust allow actors to assess up to what point they are, or are not, prepared to face a theatrical practice that advances them toward the development of a solid group creative process.

It is from this place that performers will see themselves committed to the task of exposing themselves to conditions that require multiple foci of attention and, minimally, a duplication of action. That is why performers must construct their fictional work at the same time as they are also obliged to undertake the procedures of risk proposed by the scenic actions. This duplicity, which is specific to the work of the performer, takes on particular characteristics, because it not only involves the dual existence of the real and the fictional, but also a radicalisation of the reality in a way that generates a particular fictional quality.

Street performances deal with a "surface of events" (Velloso 2011), which is represented by ideas formed via different conceptual and artistic flows that include the word, the body, and the image. The presence of risk introduces a special condition in this rhizomatic manner to create participation that becomes an aesthetic experience on the street.

On this "surface of events" the receptors and interpreters are agents that are always transmuting their states. This condition generates corporeal and mental forms that articulate ideas. This happens while producing the dramaturgy of the city, which is a text developed simultaneously with the participation of both artists and viewers in a drama that is not composed solely of words. Risk means, in this case, a kind of real-time composition. It could be an experience in which the performers and the audience collectively create an artistic practice.

What is sought through risk is a way of stretching reality, transforming it into a supra-reality because the "doers" are shifted out of their field of reality. Thus, we come to have three overlapping planes: the daily life of the actor; the daily life of both performers and passers-by, which is submitted to risk; and the generation of a fiction.

Working with real presence and risk as an element of the *mise en scène* means that we reveal the existing tensions between the performers and the audience. Therefore, to offer the audience as intense an experience as possible, we sought to maintain a close proximity between viewers and performers, and to escalate the sense of intimacy we decided to use on the streets as a way to offer a new perspective on street theatre. The feeling of being in the space of the Other—and, moreover, of having this Other so close—we hoped, would imbue the audience with a sense of being in contact with something real—or would, at least, create a need to question the reality of the material presented in the scene. The sense of reality stemmed mainly from the proximity of intimate spaces. This is a procedure that tries to put the spectator at risk, but at the same time, the performers are facing a risk that is extremely self-exposing. This could be seen in my performance titled "Agatha's Confession" when the actress, Lara Matos, asked a man in the audience to touch her breast while she told a story about love between her character (Agatha) and her character's brother. It creates tension for the actress, for the spectator, and for the rest of the audience, who experience a scene with an extreme element of sexual contact in the middle of a street.

Since the dramaturgical qualities of a theatrical text launched in the urban space are not sufficient for creating a space of profound relationship between "doers" and "observers", it is necessary to attempt to create a sphere of sensations. It was in this sense that we investigated the proposals of physical risk in a scene. By using this orientation for our work, we created an opportunity to develop a bond that was strong enough to create a theatrical ceremony.[1] The theatrical ceremony, in turn, catalysed the attention of the spectators and opened up space for the exchange of experience between the scene and the audience.

The imminence of disaster and physical misfortune throws the body into a dangerous adventure. This adventure allows the transmission of sensations based on the perception of the possible effects of the gestures and the movements of the performers when they project themselves in aerial space, revealing the possibility of falling. A performer who runs on stilts through tight spaces on a metro platform or who performs risky acrobatics inside a bus is proposing to the public a special physical state at the moment they present the experience. In the same way, performers experience particular physical sensations during their risky performances. The spectators cannot prevent themselves from reacting, stimulated by the perception of the performer's situation of risk. This type of event creates a thread of contact between the observer and the performer that is strengthened by their connection and by the unspoken convention that a disaster will not occur as everyone imagines. It is important to say that perhaps, in some hidden place, there is a timid desire that an actual disaster does take place. Wouldn't this secret be the same source of the sensations that promote a spectator's connection with the scene?

Unlike circus acts, where the imminence of the accident operates as the reference that allows for evaluating (and applauding) the quality of the performers' dexterity, in the theatrical phenomenon the physical risk is articulated by constructing a fictional structure. The risk is not a separate, particular, or exclusive element, but a component that constructs the possibilities of the fiction.

Conclusion

The training of actors based on risky conditions is related to the objective of placing performers at their limits so that they can have a profound experience at the moment in which they choose theatre as their field of artistic creation. The steering of the personal work of research and introspection that leads the performer to plunge into their own interior proves to be increasingly incapable of revealing the performer's possibilities. It is by exercising the function of representation that performers discover their possible paths. In this sense, work with physical risk seeks to incorporate in this experience difficulties that lead to a global reflection of the work of the theatrical performer. In conditions of risk, performers cannot fail to experience an encounter with their fears. When I refer to fear, I am thinking of all the dimensions of fear. In the act of representation it is necessary to expose to oneself and others (to oneself and to the public) to the practices that prepare the performance to test the depths of this relationship.

Combining fiction with the possibility of a real element is part of a game that seeks to seduce the spectator's gaze, to change or to break the dual position spectator-performer, as a strategy to create participation. The "theatre of invasion" tries to build a ludic space in which viewers experience intense sensations related not only to the development of the narrative, but also to the way performers interact in the street environment, taking into consideration themselves and the audience as part of this environment. In this regard, in this kind of theatre, viewers find themselves in an environment that bears no resemblance to the traditional arrangement of street theatre. Proximity is a key element in the construction of a scene that tries to produce risky situations, because risk is affectation and it generates a compromised body. Throughout my work I have insisted on intimacy, especially in the exposure of the actors' and actresses' bodies, in order to facilitate a tension with the audience.

The proposal of working with physical risk presents us with the problem of examining the repercussions of this work in the individual trajectories of the actors. One cannot forget that the questioning stimulated by the act of confronting risk supposes there is the possibility for an undefined series of consequences of a psychological order for the participants of the experience. One cannot believe that facing the risk functions only as a technical resource for achieving specific results. These practices are an integral part of a creative process that seeks to establish strongly organised nuclei for the work of theatrical investigation. This investigation signifies seeking to learn through both the realisation of a spectacle and through the process of constructing an articulated structure of solidarity.

If we think of creative work as existing at the limits of risk, it is possible to consider that theatrical performance in the city can be an instrument of participation. The theatrical approach to and appropriation of the urban silhouette, with the consequent transformation of the uses of space, can produce disturbances that we can exploit as possibility. This possibility can then generate genuine participation that results from a mutual understanding between performers and passers-by.

Nevertheless, it is impossible to face an urban space without confronting its ambivalence: a controlled space and a space for free expression is also a space for anonymity and a place to meet people. The street is a space characterised by porosity.

Even though we are able to say that contemporary cities are deterritorialised spaces and that we live in an era that emphasises the ability to produce virtual communications over interpersonal connections, it is still possible to propose that street performances provide a way to break down distances between people.

To be on the street can be a practice, a shared construction mediated by theatrical performance. Though this may reaffirm our sense of reality within the artistic experience, we can now be content to think of our world as something we construct and not as something given to us and external to our perceptions. As we cannot help questioning the veracity of things and information, given the suspicious times in which we live, it is natural that we question the ability of the real world to offer us a life filled with the relationships we crave. But a performance that creates and takes risks can create moments in which we can feel something very real and participate, even when it happens purely by chance.

Note

1. See the concept of "deferred social ceremony" by Jean Duvignaud in *Spectacle et Société*, Paris: Denoël, 1970.

References

Bishop, Claire. 2012. *Artificial Hells*. London/New York: Verso.

Bourriaud, Nicolas. 2002. *Relational Aesthetics*. Paris: Les presses du réel.

Cesaroli, Mario. 2014. Espacio público y calidad urbana. In *Identidad y Espacio Público*. México: Gedisa.

Debord, Guy. 1999. Teoría de la deriva. In *Internacional situacionista*, vol. 1. Madrid: Literatura Gris.

Deutsche, Rosalyn. 1996. *Evictions: Art and Spatial Politics*. Cambridge/ London: Graham/MIT.

Duvignaud, Jean. 1970. *Spectacle et Société*. Paris: Denoël.

———. 1980. *Le jeu du jeu*. Paris: Editions Balland.

Fischer-Lichte, Erika. 2008. *The Transformative Power of Performance: A New Aesthetics*. London: Routledge.

García Canclini, Nestor. 2005. *Imaginarios urbanos*. Buenos Aires: EUDEBA.

Lynch, Kevin. 1960. *The Image of the City*. Boston: MIT.

Merleau-Ponty, Maurice. 1962. *Phenomenology of Perception*. London: Routledge & Kegan Paul.

Neves, Victor. 2014. Los espacios públicos: vacíos con identidad. Lugares con poética. In *Identidad y espacio público: ampliando ámbitos y prácticas*. Barcelona: Gedisa.

Pedragosa, Pau. 2014. Identidad y diferencia en la ciudad genérica y en la ciudad histórica. Percepción y prácticas sociales. In *Identidad y espacio público: ampliando ámbitos y prácticas*. Barcelona: Gedisa.

Sánchez, José Antonio. 2014. *El Teatro en Campo Expandido*. Barcelona: Museu d'Art Contemporari de Barcelona.

Santos, Milton. 2004. *A Natureza do Espaço: técnica e tempo, razão e emoção*, 4th ed. São Paulo: Editora da Universidade de São Paulo.

Tytell, John. 1995. *The Living Theatre: Art, Exile and Outrage*. New York: Grove Press.

Velloso, Rubens. 2011. Cena Contemporânea e Tecnologia. *Moringa* 2 (1): 81–89.

Index

© The Editor(s) (if applicable) and The Author(s) 2017

A. O'Grady (ed.), *Risk, Participation, and Performance Practice*,
DOI 10.1007/978-3-319-63242-1

CPI Antony Rowe
Chippenham, UK
2017-11-30 12:22